ANCIENT EGYPT

THE BASICS

Ancient Egypt: The Basics offers an accessible and comprehensive introduction to the history, archaeology, and influence of this fascinating civilization. Covering key aspects of Egyptian daily life, this book also includes:

- A survey of Egyptian history from its earliest origins to the coming of Islam
- An overview of Egyptology, considering archaeological discoveries and important individuals
- Egypt's impact and reception through to the modern day

Lively and engaging, this is an indispensable resource for new students of Egyptian history, culture, and archaeology, and is a must-read for anyone who wants to learn more about Egypt's long and captivating past.

Donald P. Ryan is a Faculty Fellow in the Humanities at Pacific Lutheran University, Washington. His areas of interest include Egyptian archaeology and history of archaeology, and he is perhaps best known for his excavations in Egypt, including in the Valley of the Kings.

THE BASICS

ANCIENT EGYPT
THE BASICS

Donald P. Ryan

Routledge
Taylor & Francis Group

LONDON AND NEW YORK

First published 2016
by Routledge
2 Park Square, Milton Park, Abingdon, Oxon OX14 4RN

and by Routledge
711 Third Avenue, New York, NY 10017

Routledge is an imprint of the Taylor & Francis Group, an informa business

British Library Cataloguing-in-Publication Data
A catalogue record for this book is available from the British Library

Library of Congress Cataloging-in-Publication Data
A catalog record for this book has been requested

ISBN: 978-1-138-64150-1 (hbk)
ISBN: 978-1-138-64151-8 (pbk)
ISBN: 978-1-315-63044-1 (ebk)

Typeset in Bembo
by Book Now Ltd, London

This book is dedicated to the memory of Barbara Mertz, a friend and great Egyptologist, and with special appreciation to Sherry Ryan, Samuel Ryan, Maurice and Lois Schwartz, Dorothy Shelton, and Edmund Meltzer.

CONTENTS

ILLUSTRATIONS

FIGURES

TABLES

TO THE READER

Most people are fascinated with the past and without a doubt the most popular of all "lost civilizations" is Ancient Egypt. The remains of its culture possess something to captivate almost everyone. Apart from the many temples, tombs and other spectacular monuments, there are the hieroglyphs, along with mummies and other cultural aspects that never fail to surprise and delight modern people. Many are intrigued by the amazing ancient technological achievements that persist in perplexing modern engineers or marvel at the incredible archaeological discoveries that continue to be made on a regular basis. Still others are attracted by interesting and sometimes mysterious historical characters, esoteric metaphysics, or the Biblical connection with ancient Egypt.

Museum exhibitions featuring Egyptian artifacts will always draw huge crowds and millions of tourists from all over the world visit Egypt each year to take a look for themselves. Maybe you were one of those people or maybe you've seen something exciting about Egypt on television or read something in a book or newspaper. With me, it started as a small boy leafing through *National Geographic Magazine* to learn of great archaeological discoveries from Egypt's ancient sands.

In this book, we're going to do a little survey of the culture and history of ancient Egypt, in short, an introduction to Egyptology. I'll start by providing some basic information about the history of Egyptology, along with other topics, including some geography, archeology, and even hieroglyphs, to set you on your way. Next we'll examine the ways of life and death in ancient Egypt followed by a quick romp through history. Then we're going to look at several great discoveries along with some of the effects that ancient Egypt has had on subsequent cultures.

Obviously, it's a lot of ground to cover and this book can only provide you with a mere taste. But we'll be dipping into enough pies to give you a general feel for the subject in some of its many facets. If one aspect doesn't catch your interest, no doubt something else will; or if you're like me, you'll find it all quite interesting. Keep in mind that Egyptologists can be an argumentative bunch. Much of what is presented here can be argued in a variety of different ways and that's part of the scholarly process. In this book, though, you're going to get my basic version of the subject and later on, if you want to learn more, you can check into the ins and outs of whatever topic strikes your fancy. The final chapter of this book and the Appendix will aid you in further pursuing the subject.

ACKNOWLEDGMENTS

Appreciation is extended to Sherry Ryan and Samuel Ryan, Dorothy Shelton, Lois Schwartz; Pat Armstrong, Drs. Liisa and Richmond Prehn, Tom and Kelly Ott, Brian Holmes, John Adams, Dr. Steve Vinson and Dr. Sarah Ketchley for their support and encouragement. Special thanks are due to Dr. Edmund Meltzer, a superb scholar and a good friend, who provided some excellent suggestions.

ANCIENT EGYPT

THE LOSS AND RECOVERY
OF A CIVILIZATION

The ancient Egyptian civilization was certainly one of the most technologically and artistically sophisticated cultures that this world has ever seen. The Egyptians mastered the arts, accomplished magnificent building projects, and their mighty army engaged in adventures abroad. They were governed by grandiose rulers supported by a vast civil and religious bureaucracy in a society maintained by farmers and craftspeople.

This unique civilization persisted for more than 3,000 years, from about 3100 BC into the early centuries AD. Given the complexity and longevity of this magnificent culture, perhaps it is surprising that it is essentially extinct. Yes, bits and pieces do survive today, especially in certain agricultural and village practices, but the living grandeur of ancient Egypt is no more. Indeed, so much knowledge has been lost that a whole scholarly discipline appeared around 200 years ago with the aim of studying, reconstructing, and explaining ancient Egypt. It's called *Egyptology*, and its practitioners are *Egyptologists*. Even with the vast amount of information that has been recovered over the last couple of centuries, some might argue that we've still only scratched the surface, and a true vision of an amazing ancient reality has yet to be achieved.

WHY DID EGYPTIAN CULTURE DISAPPEAR?

So what happened to ancient Egyptian culture and, thus, the need to rediscover it? You may have heard of the notion of the "rise and fall" of civilizations. This idea is disliked by some scholars. By what standards can one measure such things, especially on a large scale? On the other hand, a focus on transformation and change emphasizes that in most cases these are processes rather than merely events. One might say that ancient Egypt never really vanished, but was transformed. In the chapters ahead, we will learn how the classical Egyptian culture flourished up until about 1000 BC, after which it had a hard time maintaining its grip in the face of outside invaders who brought political domination and foreign cultural practices. Especially after the time of what is called Egypt's New Kingdom (c. 1550–1069 BC), there were periods of civil disorganization during which rulers from such places as Nubia, Libya, and Persia held sway.

The Greeks, who would dominate Egypt, beginning in 332 BC with Alexander the Great's conquest, had the biggest impact on Egyptian civilization. The Greeks were not content merely to rule; instead, they actively engaged in spreading their own culture nearly everywhere their empire spread. Many Greeks immigrated to Egypt, and their language became the norm within the government and among literate people. In fact, the Egyptian city of Alexandria became the pre-eminent Greek cosmopolitan cultural center in the Mediterranean.

After about 300 years of Greek rule, the Romans incorporated Egypt into their own growing empire. Although they were not the cultural imperialists in the same manner as the Greeks, they nonetheless had an impact on Egyptian culture.

Of vital importance in terms of cultural transformation, was the introduction of major new religious philosophies that had a radical impact on the old Egyptian ways. Christianity appeared in neighboring Palestine during the first century AD and spread to Egypt relatively quickly, perhaps as early as 50 AD. This monotheistic religion shunned the ancient Egyptian gods, along with their priests, practices, and temples, and upset the foundation of the culture's traditional worldviews. A preference for the use of a modified Greek alphabet to write the ancient Egyptian language, especially for religious purposes, led to the eventual demise of the old and increasingly restricted system of hieroglyphs and the derived cursive hieratic and demotic scripts.

Perhaps the greatest transforming effect of all was the Arab invasion of 642 AD. Arming themselves with their new Islamic religion, the Arabs established themselves in Egypt during a remarkable sweep across North Africa and many other lands. The impact was lasting. The Arabic language is spoken today in the Arab Republic of Egypt, and although there is still a Christian minority, Islam is the official state religion.

The subsequent history of Egypt is complicated. After centuries of Islamic rulers, it was incorporated into the Ottoman Empire and both the French and British would become politically involved. It wasn't until 1952 that the Egyptians again were fully in control of their own country. No wonder we are left to pick up the scattered pieces of the ancient civilization!

Unfortunately, the destructive processes of nature, time, and humans have not been particularly kind to the remains of ancient Egypt. Certain things have survived quite well, while others have left little or no trace.

Climate and location also play a huge role in preservation. Few of the villages where millions of ordinary ancient Egyptians once lived have survived. Their homes were built of bricks of mud and organic materials, which have long since been broken down due to the annual flooding of the Nile, wind erosion, or other natural processes.

In the Nile Delta region in the north of Egypt, the climate is not well suited to preserving the past. The water table is high, the air can be humid, and even things made of stone can suffer considerable erosion. The drier climate in the south, though, has allowed for some remarkable preservation, especially for those things buried in the desert or hidden away in dry cliffs and valleys.

Some of the best preserved are those special things that were built to last for all eternity: temples and tombs of stone. Many of these have survived fairly well, some incredibly so. But just because the temples and tombs have survived while there are few traces of other structures, such as houses, we need to be wary of gaining the impression that religion and death were the primary focus of ancient Egyptian existence. Suppose that something terrible happened to wipe out our civilization, and archeologists of the future excavated only our churches and other religious structures and our cemeteries. What a curious impression of our culture they might gain!

We can't lay the blame solely on nature, though. Humans, too, have played an active role in the destruction of many of the ancient remains. Ancient sites have sometimes served as a source of raw material for new buildings. Many of the pyramids, for example, were quarried for their excellent stones, and the rotting debris of old town sites was sometimes mined for rich fertilizer. There are also many examples of the destruction of the ancient monuments by religious zealots and those seeking golden treasure. Old wooden funerary statues, coffin planks, and papyrus scrolls have served as firewood for the living while antiquities hunters and the sometimes crude methods of early archaeologists have all taken their toll.

Until relatively recently, people in Western cultures and others were aware of the existence of ancient Egypt, but only indirectly. Egypt was known primarily from two sources: the Holy Bible and ancient Greek and Roman writers. In the Bible, Egypt is mentioned numerous times. Notably, there is the dramatic and cherished story of Joseph with his coat of many colors which involves Egyptian palace intrigue. And the story of the Exodus, in which God delivers the Hebrew people from Egyptian enslavement, is a key story in the Jewish religion. Along with the accompanying spiritual and moral lessons, these biblical stories contained cultural and geographical data that shaped a vague notion of Egyptian society and places for readers of the Bible. Egypt in the Bible was portrayed as a powerful, industrious and polytheistic society ruled by a pharaoh and his coterie of priests, governors, and functionaries.

Apart from the Bible, literate individuals could derive information about ancient Egypt by reading the surviving documents of old Greek and Roman writers who had visited the land and wrote down their insights. One Greek author, Herodotus, is said to have visited Egypt around 450 BC. He has left us with a lengthy and patchy—yet, at times, detailed—description of the land and culture, albeit centuries after what some might consider to be its cultural zenith.

Herodotus (c. 484–420 BC) was a Greek historian from the city of Halicarnassus, located on the Ionian coast of what is today Turkey. His principal surviving work is known as *The Histories*. Along with a description of Egypt, it contains a vital record of the Persian Wars and other historical events around the time of what is called Greece's "Golden Age" in the fifth century BC. Because of his early attempts at recording events, Herodotus is sometimes called "the father of history."

Herodotus describes Egypt as a very odd place indeed, full of unusual customs and practices, and his report contains quite a bit of anecdotal material that might not be wholly accurate. Herodotus's lengthy description of the Egyptians is sometimes so at odds with what we now know about that ancient civilization that there are some scholars who doubt that he ever actually went there! Perhaps he collected his information from the cosmopolitan visitors and sailors coming through the port of his Greek home town, Halicarnassus.

Despite the suspicion, it's likely that Herodotus did indeed visit Egypt, but he was doing so at a time when the glory days of classical Egyptian civilization were long over. The pyramids were already ancient, the mighty empire-building pharaohs had long been mummified, and Egypt was under the domination of the Persians. Herodotus was probably collecting information from a lot of people who themselves did not understand the monuments and much of the old culture. It was ancient to them, too, and was dying out. Many scholars think that late foreign visitors to Egypt, such as Herodotus, might have been gullible enough to believe the fanciful stories told by creative guides or others who themselves were misinformed. (And modern tourists can enjoy the same experience from informal guides at various archaeological sites who will be pleased to show you many secret "wonders.")

We'll look at the development of Egyptology as a scholarly pursuit in Chapter 2, but, for now, let's take a look at the subject matter of that fascinating field of inquiry as it is practiced today. Egyptology is certainly one of the most interdisciplinary branches of learning to be found—that is, it incorporates insights, methods, and data from many numerous subject areas that are relevant to our search for the Egyptian past. It is a subject that one might classify within the humanities, yet it has aspects of both the social and natural sciences, and the fine arts as well.

Most scholarly and scientific disciplines have something to contribute to Egyptology. Biologists can help reconstruct the environment and assist in studying mummies and the remains of other once-living things. Geologists can help us determine the sources of stone and precious metals, and chemists can add insights into various materials as well. Anthropologists can draw on their comparative knowledge of cultural practices to contribute insights. Engineers can help us understand the techniques of the past and help us protect the monuments for the future. And such modern techniques as satellite imagery and radar are assisting in locating remains underground or otherwise unseen. The list goes on. The end result is a growing and gradually more complete view of the ancient Egyptian past. Let's take a look at some of the specific approaches.

STUDYING TEXTS

Fortunately, ancient Egypt was a literate society in the sense that there was a writing system, and there were people who could read and write (although probably less than 10 percent of the population.) Many texts have survived, especially on formal monuments such as temples and tombs, and some Egyptologists are genuine experts in ferreting out the subtleties of these written materials. A lot of Egyptology is text-oriented, and it is from inscriptions that we are best able to sort out many of the historical details that we now have, and gain insights into the ancient world's organization and perspectives.

Not surprisingly, many scholars continue to study and refine all that we can determine from what the Egyptians themselves wrote. Translating words can be difficult, but figuring out what they mean in the context of the ancient culture is vitally important. It's important, for example, to be able to tell the difference between a statement intended as political or religious propaganda and one meant as a sober public decree, or the difference between a historical account and a myth. These are things that must be carefully sorted out in our search for a reliable picture of the past.

One can argue that in terms of surviving writing, Egyptology is somewhat spoiled by its riches. In places such as nearby Israel, where ancient inscriptions are few, archaeologists have become experts in identifying pottery styles through time, often to within a few years of their manufacture. In Egypt, the date and owner of an object, tomb, or monument can be identified merely by reading an accompanying inscription. As a result, there are fewer real pottery experts in the Egyptological world than one can find elsewhere in the broader region.

Some Egyptologists specialize in art history which can open doors to insight in ways that other approaches cannot. Much can be learned by the study of artistic and architectural styles and techniques, as well as their changes through the years. Although it is tempting to believe the stereotypical notion that Egyptian art was essentially static through time, this is certainly not the case; "generally conservative" is perhaps a better term. Much of ancient Egyptian art is very symbolic, from the strong, idealized sculptures in stone representing the power and role of the ruler to the often subtle and esoteric meanings expressed on the walls of tombs and temples. And there are even experts on Egyptian art who can sometimes identify the handiwork of specific individual ancient artisans.

ARCHAEOLOGY

Of all the approaches within Egyptology, *archaeology* receives the most attention. Archaeology is the study of the physical remains of the human past and has developed many of its own methodologies, including techniques for excavation and artifact analysis. The public loves the glamour of discovery and Egyptian archaeology regularly delivers. There's something about searching for and finding things of the past that has widespread appeal. The discovery of King Tutankhamun's tomb in 1922, for example, accelerated an interest that has barely slowed down since. Today, even relatively minor discoveries in Egypt have received significant public attention.

The Indiana Jones movies certainly have added to the mystique of archaeology, even though he's definitely a fictional character and his approach to antiquities is less than scientific. (And if someone tells you that someone is or was the living inspiration for that character, don't believe it: I.J.'s creators made him up!) But to the public, Indiana Jones has become a frame of reference for action and adventure in archaeology. Believe me, there can be lots of excitement in archaeology, but rarely the exaggerated swashbuckling that Indiana Jones serves up.

Archaeology often involves some sort of careful digging. The level of difficulty of an archaeological project can vary, depending upon where or what one happens to be investigating. Consider, for example, the difference between excavating in a remote desert, where one must bring all supplies, including water, versus working in a highly populated region, where comfortable amenities are close at hand. No matter where the project is located, though, the work can be strenuous and expensive. And there is often a need for some of the specialists mentioned previously, along with a knowledge of history, hieroglyphs, and art.

Archaeologists from all over the world work in Egypt, including scholars from Britain, France, Germany, Australia, Poland, the Czech Republic, Japan, and the United States. That's the short list and several even have permanent research centers based in Cairo or elsewhere in the country. And, of course, the Egyptians themselves are busy at work conducting their own explorations. The country's Ministry of Antiquities has the tremendous responsibility for the remains of Egypt's past in general, and also supervises the scientific activities of foreigners.

While archaeologists often get the majority of attention in the Egyptological world, some of the most important work is done by *epigraphers*: specialists in recording the decoration and texts found on ancient monuments. In Egypt, where many human and natural forces continue to erode and destroy the ancient temples, tombs, and other antiquities, the epigraphers are racing against time to make permanent and accurate records of paintings and inscriptions that hopefully will survive even if the original monuments do not.

Chicago House, based in Luxor, Egypt, remains the most famous foreign mission involved in epigraphy. It is affiliated with the Oriental Institute of the University of Chicago and has been actively recording monuments in the Luxor area with photographs and line-drawings since it was founded in 1924. The work of the Chicago House epigraphers is extremely precise; they are not only actively involved in making records, but they also work on the study and conservation of the actual monuments. Their techniques have evolved through time. Once darkrooms and large photographic prints were the norm, but now modern digital techniques have greatly facilitated the epigraphic process.

So where are the remains of the ancient Egyptian culture to be found today? It's easy to look at Egypt today as one huge archaeological site and large quantities of its antiquities have made their way to distant lands. We'll go into more detail about how that happened in Chapter 2. Some of these exported antiquities ended up in private hands, while others are housed in many museums, where they can be enjoyed by the public. But much of what remains is still in Egypt—and perhaps the greatest treasures are yet to be discovered!

REDISCOVERING THE PAST

Let's look briefly at this recovery process, including some of the key events and players. It's a story full of adventure, speculation, and genuine scholarship. Apart from lists of kings and such, few records demonstrate that the ancient Egyptians themselves took much of an interest in exploring the remains of their own past. However, there are some rare examples: an Egyptian prince named Khaemwaset (c. 1250 BC), for example, restored some of the damaged pyramids at Sakkara belonging to earlier royal ancestors of the Old Kingdom, about a millennium before his time. Although this doesn't necessarily demonstrate a flair for archaeology, it does provide an ancient example of concern for the past.

As mentioned, the Greeks and Romans marveled at the remains of Egypt's past. Several travelers and writers have left us some intriguing accounts. Apart from Herodotus, Greek writers Diodorus Siculus (c. 59 BC) and Plutarch (c. 50–120 AD) provided some fascinating information, including insights into ancient mythology. Roman writer, Strabo (64 BC–22 AD) recorded a good deal of geographical information, as did Pliny the Elder (23–79 AD). The Romans, in particular, collected some antiquities and displayed them in Rome and Constantinople. They brought more than a dozen obelisks (stone shafts with pyramid-shaped tops) across the Mediterranean Sea from Egypt to Rome. Others would eventually end up in such places as Constantinople (now Istanbul), Paris, London, and New York.

Not too many works specifically address ancient Egyptian antiquities after the Arab invasion in 642 AD, but a few travelers' comments survive, as do some observations made by Arab writers. Egypt was becoming a real center of Arab and Islamic culture, so it is no surprise that there doesn't appear to be an overwhelming interest in the debris of the distant polytheistic past. During the European Middle Ages, though, travelers and religious pilgrims occasionally made their way to Egypt. Few ventured much farther south than the Cairo region, but a visit to the pyramids would not have been unusual.

The interpretations of these early travelers were no doubt greatly colored by the Classical Greek and Roman writers and the Bible. The pyramids, for example, might have been viewed as hollow granaries (they aren't), or perhaps as the handiwork of Hebrew slaves (wrong again), which relate to the Biblical stories of Joseph and the Exodus, respectively. Or, it might have been easy to envision that the Great Pyramid at Giza was built under the direction of the cruel pharaoh Cheops (Khufu), as Herodotus reported (there is no evidence that Cheops was a particularly cruel pharaoh).

Although these reports are interesting, what might be considered genuine exploration of Egyptian territory by Westerners didn't really begin until around the seventeenth and eighteenth centuries. During that period, some hardy European adventurers traveled south up the Nile, recording their observations and sometimes publishing them. The French Jesuit priest, Claude Sicard (1677–1726), for example, set out on a mission to convert Coptic Christians in Egypt to Roman Catholicism. Whether successful in that regard or not, he managed to travel extensively including farther south than previous explorers, all the while making maps, drawings, and written observations.

The Englishman, the Rev. Richard Pockoke (1704–1765) and the Danish naval officer, Frederik Norden (1708–1742) both explored Egypt around the same time, about 1737–1738. Trips up the Nile in those days could be somewhat tricky if not dangerous, and it's surprising how persistent some of these early visitors were. Upon returning home, their reports were published and translated into other European languages, and served to pique further interest in the mysterious land of Egypt.

Back in Europe, objects from ancient Egypt were not unknown. There were the objects that the Romans had collected, along with curiosities such as old amulets and other antiquities brought back by travelers and merchants, which no doubt invited plenty of speculation. Perhaps most strange was the trade in mummy products. A demand grew in Europe for ground-up Egyptian mummies because the resulting powder was believed to have medicinal benefits and also was a desired ingredient in some artists' paints.

Archaeological societies and museums were formed in England and elsewhere during the 1700s, providing forums for learned men to discuss such things as Greek and Roman antiquities, the origin of such ancient sites as Stonehenge, or the purposes of old stone tools found in the earth, and Egyptian antiquities as well. The British Museum in London, for example, was founded in 1753 and provided a home for a growing collection of antiquities from widely scattered locales. It received its first mummy in 1756.

Between the odd objects and the scattered reports of travelers, the notion of Egypt as a strange and mysterious home to a lost civilization was reinforced. As unlikely as it might seem, it was a dramatic military adventure that created a scholarly discipline out of the study of Egypt's past.

In 1798, a huge French land and naval force under the command of Napoleon Bonaparte arrived in Egypt. The French, in intense competition with the British, were hoping to secure trade routes to the riches of India and the Far East. This well-planned expedition not only was composed of military personnel, but it also included a diverse group of over 150 civilian scholars and special technicians whose job it was to observe and record the many facets of Egypt. There were natural scientists to study plants, animals, and other resources, along with surveyors, and mapmakers. Some noted the customs and practices of the native people, while others were artists and antiquarians with an interest in researching the remains of ancient Egypt.

These scholars accompanied the French army and conducted their work sometimes even in the heat of battle. Although it might all seem noble, and there is little doubt that these scholars were sincere, the information that they gathered could be used by the likes of Napoleon for the better control and exploitation of Egypt's people and resources. On the other hand, the French were quick to initiate a scholarly institution, the *Institut d'Égypte*, which they established in 1798.

The British quickly became alarmed with the French occupation of strategic Egyptian territory and brought their own fleet across the Mediterranean. A nasty battle at Aboukir, off the Egyptian coast, resulted in the destruction of the French naval force, effectively stranding Napoleon's army. His scholars continued their work, but the French eventually surrendered in 1801. The victorious English confiscated some of the choicer bits of antiquity collected by the French, including the famed Rosetta Stone, an unusual object which would facilitate the eventual decipherment of the hieroglyphs.

Although the French were defeated, the scholars of Napoleon's expedition had a lasting impact—to such an extent that they are often credited with founding the field of Egyptology. Returning home with their notes and drawings, they edited a monumental report of their findings published under the title *Description de l'Égypte*. The sumptuous volumes not only served as a magnificent research report, but they also stimulated an interest in Egypt within the literate communities in Europe. The *Description* is still considered a magnificent achievement today. Many of its drawings are superb. The artists accompanying Napoleon's expedition operated in the days before photography, yet many of their drawings exhibit an almost photographic quality.

Despite his shortcomings (no pun intended), Napoleon Bonaparte left a lasting positive mark by facilitating the group of scholars that accompanied his Egyptian expedition. In fact, in several cases, the *Description* is the only record of monuments, or portions thereof, that have since decayed or have been destroyed.

After the French were defeated by the British, Egypt fell back under the control of the Ottoman Turkish rulers. It was up to them, for the time, at least, to decide to what extent foreigners would be allowed to conduct business or other activities in that land. One such ruler, Mohammed Ali (ruled 1805–1848), was somewhat open-minded about European contributions to a developing Egypt and invited foreigners to present their ideas for modernizing the country. This set the stage for one of the most intriguing characters in all the history of archaeology: Giovanni Battista Belzoni.

Belzoni was born in 1778 in Padua, Italy. He was a very large man and eventually ended up in London, where he played giants in the theater and performed a strongman act in street carnivals. Hearing of Mohammed Ali's desire for Western technology, Belzoni traveled to Egypt with the idea for a revolutionary waterwheel to be used in irrigation. The design failed to impress, leaving Belzoni, his wife, and a servant essentially stranded in Egypt without many funds. At that time, a mad scramble for antiquities was about to begin, pitting rival nations against each other to compete for the best possible antiquities for their home countries and museums. Belzoni entered the fray when he accepted a commission from the British consul in Cairo to retrieve for the glory of Britain a large stone head from a temple about 400 miles upstream. This he was able to do, and thus began his career as an explorer, excavator, and collector. These are some of Belzoni's many accomplishments:

- He was the first man known to excavate in the royal cemetery known as the Valley of the Kings.
- He was the first known Westerner to enter the sand-engulfed temple of Rameses II at Abu Simbel.
- He studied the pyramids at Giza, which allowed him to discover the entrance to the pyramid of Khafra.
- He retrieved numerous objects of antiquity, both large and small, which made their way back to England and elsewhere.

The competition for antiquities was often ugly, and threats of violence eventually drove Belzoni back to England in 1819. His book describing his adventures became quite popular and he set up an Egyptian exhibition in London. Belzoni died in 1823 during a short-lived attempt to find the source of the Niger River.

Belzoni became something of a folk hero in his day. To more recent scholars, however, he is often the character cited to represent the worst of the early nineteenth-century exploitation of Egypt's antiquities. His book unabashedly describes crawling through mummy-choked tunnels, using a battering-ram as a tomb-opening device, and accidentally dropping an obelisk into the Nile. These kinds of antics, unfortunately, were far from unusual in his day. But what sets Belzoni apart from many of his peers is that he actually recorded and mapped many of his discoveries and then published much of that information. That's a far cry from the random snatch-and-grab tactics of the average collector in those times.

Many times I have heard museum visitors and others comment on all of the objects "stolen from Egypt." The truth is, sad or otherwise, that most of the antiquities found in foreign museums were legally acquired during times when the rules were very different than they are today. During the time of Belzoni, for example, one could take most anything with the permission of the pasha. As noted below, the regulations for exporting antiquities have evolved significantly over the last two centuries.

The activities of Napoleon's scholars, and even the work of the likes of Belzoni, brought Egypt increasingly to the attention of more scholars. With the help of the Rosetta Stone, the mystery of the hieroglyphs would be proclaimed solved in 1822. With new motivation, more scholars became interested in visiting Egypt to record and study its numerous monuments covered in inscriptions, or other items of artistic merit.

Several expeditions set out with such purposes in mind. The decipherer of the hieroglyphs, the Frenchman, Jean-François Champollion (1790–1832), along with the first Italian Egyptologist, Ippolito Rosellini (1800–1843), ventured out in 1828–1829 and returned to publish their findings. Even more ambitious was the Prussian expedition led by Karl Lepsius (1810–1884). Between 1842 and 1845, the well-organized and equipped expedition covered a tremendous amount of territory, all the while mapping, drawing, and collecting antiquities and making casts of others. They even ventured far south into the Sudan and east to Sinai and Palestine. The result of their achievement is a tremendous published report containing hundreds of accurate folio plates, entitled *Denkmäler aus Ägypten und Äthiopien*. Like the French *Description*, this work is still regularly consulted today.

Other important documenters of the remains of ancient Egypt from the first half of the nineteenth century include the Englishmen John Gardner Wilkinson (1797–1875), and David Roberts (1796–1864). Wilkinson's *Manners and Customs of the Ancient Egyptians*, published in 1837, provided an early comprehensive look at ancient Egyptian society based on a variety of archaeological and other sources. Roberts was a popular artist who visited Egypt and the Holy Land in 1838–1839. His beautiful colored drawings were published in folios and remain widely admired to this day.

With the increase in the number of scholars and others interested in Egypt, an unregulated antiquities market grew to meet the demand, and widespread informal digging and looting became increasingly common. Recognizing the potential catastrophic loss of knowledge as a result of such activities, Champollion and others formally expressed a desire for some sort of government control on the free-for-all antiquities grab in progress, even though they, too, were occasionally involved. In 1835, a government antiquities conservation ordinance was issued, although the effect was likely minimal.

Things finally began to change with the appearance in Egypt of a Frenchman by the name of Auguste Mariette (1821–1881) who went to Egypt to collect early Christian (Coptic) manuscripts, but ended up excavating pharaonic monuments instead. He became one of the most significant individuals in the history of Egyptology.

Mariette excavated numerous sites all over Egypt, amassing a collection which would serve as the basis for the first national museum in Egypt itself. He also became the first director of the Egyptian antiquities service in 1858, a government organization created to control activities involving the remains of Egypt's past, including issuing permits for excavation and attempting to rein in illicit digging and exportation of national treasures.

Mariette's successor, Gaston Maspero (1846–1916) was a true scholar and certainly one of the better directors of the antiquities service, serving during two periods: 1881–1886 and 1899–1914. Under Maspero's direction, the service matured into a professional organization, the supervision of archaeological activities increased, and the present Egyptian Museum in Cairo was opened. But even with government controls, many travelers from Egypt through the late nineteenth century and beyond returned home with all manner of interesting souvenirs. Antiquities dealers were more than happy to fulfill tourists' desires for artifacts, including mummies still in their coffins and even valuable papyrus documents.

EGYPTIAN ARCHAEOLOGY IS REVOLUTIONIZED

By the late 1800s, the recording of texts and paintings in Egypt had long been performed with relative competency for many years, but excavation techniques remained somewhat crude. Careful archaeological methods were barely known in the early nineteenth century, and there are many examples of dubious excavation methods that make archaeologists cringe today. In 1837, for example, a British military officer, Richard Vyse and an engineer named John Perring, used gunpowder to blast their way into the pyramid of Menkaura at Giza. Although a few people in Europe were precisely record-ing their excavations, what might be called modern archaeological technique was still in its very early stages. This changed, however, with the big advances in Egyptian archaeology (and archaeology in general) made via the contributions of a brilliant Englishman by the name of William Matthew Flinders Petrie (1853–1942).

Trained in surveying, Petrie came to Egypt in 1880 to measure the pyramids in order to test a theory that their dimensions embodied a mystical calendar. His findings showed otherwise, and thus began his long and stellar archaeological career, which lasted long enough to allow him to publish an autobiography entitled *Seventy Years in Archaeology*. Petrie's major contribution was to set high standards for archaeological excavation, a systematic approach that required the careful recording of objects as they were found, their conservation thereafter, and the formal publication of the findings.

Archaeology can often be a destructive process. When something is dug up, it is usually removed from its ancient context. Knowing exactly where something was found and with what other items is vital to understanding an object and its role in a culture. This con-textual information is extremely desirable but is generally unavailable from random digging or for objects purchased from antiquities deal-ers, as was so often the case in early Egyptology. Petrie recognized the importance of recording the details as a dig was taking place because it was the only chance to get much of the information. His 1904 book, *Methods and Aims in Archaeology*, was a practical textbook of sound archaeological technique for others to follow.

Unlike many of his early peers, Petrie did not focus only on col-lecting the larger or prettier objects; instead he was interested in retrieving the totality of information. He set an example by pub-lishing many volumes dedicated to smaller objects or those related to everyday life. Petrie also trained many of the better archaeolo-gists of his day. Despite the notoriously spartan living conditions in his field camps, an apprenticeship with Petrie was probably one of the best archaeological educations available. Petrie also made his mark in parts east, where he is often called "the father of Palestinian archaeology" for his pioneering work in the Holy Land. He died in Jerusalem at the age of 89.

EGYPTOLOGY BLOOMS

The late nineteenth century was a very active time for archaeological work. More scholarly institutions and support societies were formed, and Egyptologists were becoming well-established members of museums and universities. Notably, the London-based Egypt Exploration Fund was founded in 1882 with the aim of funding and facilitating the survey, exploration, excavation, and publication of Egyptian archaeological sites. Today it is known as the Egypt Exploration Society, and it remains very active in the sponsorship and publication of Egyptological activities.

In America, James Henry Breasted (1865–1935) became the first Professor of Egyptology in the United States. He was particularly interested in historical inscriptions, and he traveled extensively in Egypt to record as many as possible. He was the founder and director of the prestigious Oriental Institute at the University of Chicago, and he initiated the famous Epigraphic Survey that is still busy recording Egypt's monuments.

Egyptology was truly beginning to mature. Many museums sponsored excavations in exchange for a share of the artifacts. The antiquities service in Egypt supervised this "division," keeping the objects that it felt were best suited for the national collection. By the beginning of the twentieth century, Egyptology and archaeological excavation techniques had become quite sophisticated. Foreign scholarly institutions continued to establish permanent facilities in Egypt, and as is only right, more Egyptian scholars became involved in studying their past. Although initially directed by the French, the Egyptians took over responsibility for their own antiquities after their national revolution in 1952. Today, the Egyptian Ministry of Antiquities manages and regulates all aspects of Egyptian antiquities. The Ministry conducts many of its own excavations and conservation projects, maintains a number of museums within Egypt, and considers requests for foreign projects. And artifacts found in Egypt these days now stay in Egypt, although occasionally, magnificent traveling exhibitions of ancient objects will travel to cities abroad before returning to their original home.

Over the centuries, the study of ancient Egypt moved from the merely speculative interest of the Greeks, Romans, and Arabs to the destructive looting and antiquities dealing of the early Western explorer-adventurers, to the rigorous, regulated, and disciplined study of the past that it is today. And through it all, it's likely that Egyptologists have only scratched the surface of the past.

ANCIENT EGYPT IN SPACE AND TIME

Most people probably have a general impression of Egypt's location, that a large part of it is desert, and that the Nile River runs through it. But there are some other aspects to Egypt's geography that are important to understand in order to make sense of the country's ancient past. And it was the unique features of Egypt's geography that allowed the ancient civilization to flourish.

Egypt is situated in the northeast corner of the African continent. Scholars include it in a broader region given the name "the Near East" which was home to several early civilizations. If one looks at a modern map or globe, you'll see some straight lines on its south and west borders, and the Mediterranean and Red Seas on the north and east. These are *modern* political boundaries. Do not confuse them with the area of ancient Egypt—they aren't the same.

The civilization of ancient Egypt grew up around the Nile River. A lot of the area to the east and west on the modern map was desert then, just as it is today, and in ancient times, as in modern, the vast majority of the population lived along the banks of the Nile or in its triangular northern Delta. In concept, it's better to look at the land of Egypt in a way much different than the modern map. Think of it as resembling a beautiful lotus flower, with the Nile River forming its stem and the broad Delta as its bloom.

The Nile is the longest river in the world, stretching about 4,200 miles from its two major sources: the highlands of Ethiopia and lakes in central Africa. These two Niles, known as the Blue and White, respectively, converge near the city of Khartoum, in what is today the country of Sudan. From there, the river flows through a series of six cataracts, or stretches of rapids, until reaching the area of the modern city of Aswan. Flowing north for several hundred miles, the river today splits into two major branches just past modern Cairo before emptying into the Mediterranean Sea. During the time of the pharaohs, there were seven such branches.

Ancient Greek authors provided us with the following cliché: "Egypt is the gift of the Nile." This simple statement stands true as it was the Nile river and its natural cycles that allowed Egyptian civilization to develop and thrive. Every year, the river would go through a flood stage, leaving in its recession a nutrient-rich deposit of silt that would renew the agricultural farmland. This flooding process is known as the *inundation*. As one can imagine, the coming of the inundation was something of concern—too much water could cause some serious damage to human settlements, but, probably worse, too little could cause food shortages. A perfect inundation was obviously something desired by all, and, combined with intensive irrigation, Egypt could thrive as a fertile bread basket.

BLACK LAND/RED LAND/TWO LANDS

Because of the dark, fertile soil along the Nile, the ancient Egyptians called Egypt the Black Land, or *Kemet*. *Kemet* could also be contrasted with the Red Land, or *Deshret*, referring to adjacent desert regions. The land of ancient Egypt can be divided into two geographically distinct areas: the generally narrow Nile Valley in the south and the broad Nile Delta in the north. The Egyptians themselves were very aware of this distinction, which they constantly referred to as the Two Lands, and the unity of both territories of *Kemet* became a major concept in their notion of political unity and stability. One of the ancient capitals of Egypt, known by its Greek name, Memphis, was located near the junction of the two lands, as is the city of Cairo, the capital of modern Egypt. The territory of Upper and Lower Egypt was also politically divided into traditional provinces that are referred to by their Greek name, *nomes*. Twenty-two nomes could be found in Upper Egypt, and twenty in Lower Egypt.

Because the Nile River flows from south to north, we refer to the Nile Valley as Upper Egypt (upstream), and the Delta as Lower Egypt (downstream) (Figure 1.1). The unification of these areas was

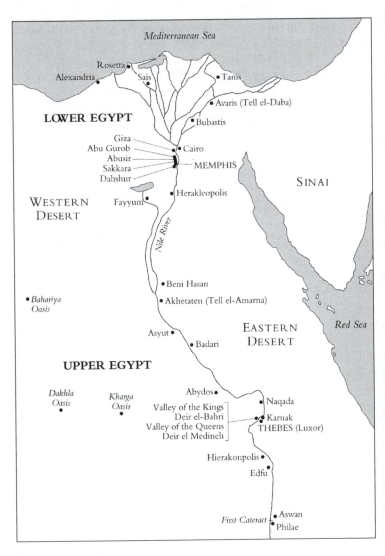

Figure 1.1 Map of Egypt

Source: Donald P. Ryan.

constantly reinforced in the titles and regalia of the ancient ruler. For example:

- The ruler was often referred to as Lord of the Two Lands.
- The ruler is frequently depicted wearing a double crown: a white crown representing Upper Egypt and a red crown representing Lower Egypt.
- One of the official names or titles of the ruler featured a sedge, a kind of aquatic plant (Upper Egypt) and a bee (Lower Egypt), and is translated as King of Upper and Lower Egypt.
- Another title of the ruler involves two goddesses: Nekhbet, in the form of a vulture (Upper Egypt), and Wadjet (Lower), in the form of a cobra.

As a geographical bonus, the ancient Egyptians were blessed not only with agricultural renewal, but also with a river that flowed north and prevailing winds that blew south. This, of course, allowed for travel up and down the Nile because travelers could use the current to propel them north, to Lower Egypt, and the wind to propel them south, to Upper Egypt. This facilitated the transport of goods, and political and military control.

The desert areas to the east and west of the Nile agricultural regions hemmed in the majority of the population, but several oases to the west were home to settlements from time to time. Southwest of modern Cairo is a region known as the Fayyum which was a Nile-fed lake. Today this lake, Birket Qarun, is brackish and greatly reduced in size, but the Fayyum still serves as a major agricultural region as it did in the past. The eastern desert features a chain of mountains running north/south and was regularly visited for quarrying and for the mining of precious materials such as gold. There were also routes from the Nile Valley to the east that provided access to the Red Sea, a launching point for expeditions to the south and elsewhere.

Egypt's position at the northeast edges of the African continent was convenient for interaction with the cultures of West Asia, including those in Palestine, Mesopotamia, and Persia. These interactions involved peaceful trade, foreign domination, and invasions coming from both sides. To the north, the Mediterranean Sea was a very active place in ancient times and provided access to and from the land of Egypt, as it continues to do today.

The geographical nature of the land also played a role in Egypt's belief system. To the west, where the sun set, lay the Netherworld, or the land of the dead. Consequently, many cemeteries were established on that side of the Nile. The cycles of the Nile as related to agriculture also inspired religious notions of fertility and rebirth.

FRAMEWORKS OF TIME

The ancient Egyptian civilization persisted for a little over 3,000 years, which is quite a sizeable time frame for any archaeologist or historian to work in. In an effort to organize where things fit chronologically, a system has been used to organize history into a series of time periods. Geologists have done a similar thing with their Mesozoic and Cenozoic eras, Jurassic and Pleistocene periods, and so on.

The traditional framework for organizing Egyptian history has its origins from an old source. An Egyptian historian and priest named Manetho (c. 305–285 BC) wrote down a list of kings organized into 30 dynasties. He probably had access to temple or other official records, and the list has proven to be relatively accurate. (An additional dynasty has been added to Manetho's list, bringing the number to 31.) The original text of Manetho's work on Egyptian chronology is not known, but fragments of his work have come down to us by way of other writers of the first millennium, who copied from him extensively.

With Manetho as a starting point, Egyptologists have further arranged these dynasties into a series of kingdoms and periods. Now, technically, a dynasty should represent a related set of rulers. From what we now know, this doesn't always hold true in Manetho's system. In fact, there are even some cases of overlapping dynasties.

Our knowledge of the order of rulers is also advanced by the existence of several ancient Egyptian lists of kings. One, for example, survives on a large stone fragment, three others were found in temples, and one was discovered on a sheet of papyrus. Unfortunately, most are incomplete, and occasionally they contradict each other. Some unpopular rulers were left off the lists or weren't included for other reasons. Nonetheless, these lists provide a lot of useful information.

Although this dynastic system is not perfect and could use some revision, it is firmly entrenched in the world of Egyptology; it serves its purpose well, and it is a tool that is universally used. Here is how it's arranged, beginning with a period around the start of Egypt's time of civilization. (Note that many of the earlier dates are approximate and have been subject to debate. And for those who are new to historical chronology, the abbreviation "*c.*" stands for "circa," meaning approximately or around that time.) Table 1.1 shows the chronology of the dynasties.

Although not within the traditional system, we can also add the Graeco-Roman Period (332 BC–395 AD) when the Greeks and Romans ruled Egypt and one can divide this into the Greek or *Ptolemaic* Period (332–30 BC) and the Roman Period (30 BC–395 AD) It should also be noted that some Egyptologists refer to a Dynasty 0 to designate a small number of rulers at the very beginning of the dynastic age.

The time leading up to the arrangement of the dynasties is usually referred to as the Predynastic period. This term is often vaguely used to describe the period of development leading to the classical time of Egyptian civilization. The term *prehistoric* also is sometimes used to describe anything preceding dynastic times, going as far back as the earliest humans to venture into the Nile Valley.

While Egyptologists might all use the system just described, they certainly don't all agree on exactly when everything happened. Dates for the lengths of reign for individual rulers are often disputed

Table 1.1 Chronology of Egyptian dynasties

Period	Dynasty	Date
Archaic/Early Dynastic Period	Dynasties 1–2	*c.* 3000–2686 BC
Old Kingdom	Dynasties 3–6	2686–2181 BC
First Intermediate Period	Dynasties 7–11	2181–2055 BC
Middle Kingdom	Dynasties 11–13	2055–1650 BC
Second Intermediate Period	Dynasties 14–17	1650–1550 BC
New Kingdom	Dynasties 18–20	1550–1069 BC
Third Intermediate Period	Dynasties 21–25	1069–644 BC
Late Period	Dynasties 26–31	664–332 BC

or revised as new information appears. There is also the problem of *coregencies*—a situation in which the reigns of two kings overlap in sort of a mentorship arrangement. This being so, you shouldn't be surprised upon opening two Egyptian history books to find different dates for the same time periods and events. Fortunately, the dates rarely vary by more than 50 years, although their certainty gets weaker the farther back you go in time. In this book, I prefer the chronological dates offered in *The Oxford History of Ancient Egypt*, edited by Ian Shaw (2004).

EGYPTIAN HISTORY IN A NUTSHELL

There's an easy way to help you remember how Egyptian history is organized. Think of the Archaic Period as the old and formative time in the development of Egyptian civilization. The three kingdoms (Old, Middle, and New) were times when Egypt was generally unified, strong, and prosperous. Each kingdom period was followed by an intermediate period, or a time when Egypt was economically depressed and/or politically disunited, and perhaps even vulnerable to foreign incursions. The Late Period is the prelude to the coming of the Greeks and Romans. With that in mind, we'll be filling in some of the exciting historical details in the chapters ahead.

EGYPTIAN TIME/EGYPTIAN NAMES

The Egyptians had their own sense of time and often recorded their dates, but not in the same way we do. Dates were usually noted in terms of the occurrence of a given event during the reign of the ruling king. For example, such and such happened during a specific year of the reign of a particular king during a specific month of an indicated season and a particular day of that month.

And since we're talking about reigns of kings, perhaps this is the time to mention a situation that might confuse some new to Egyptology. Some of the rulers in our chronology have been known by different names: a Greek version of a royal name derived from Manetho, Herodotus or other old sources, and/or an approximately reconstructed ancient Egyptian name. This is because the framework of Egyptian history from Greek sources was known well before the

Table 1.2 Greek names and their Egyptian equivalents

	Greek name	*Egyptian name(s)*
The builders of the three big Old Kingdom pyramids at Giza	Cheops Chephren Mycerinus	Khufu Khafra Menkaura
Name used by three Middle Kingdom rulers	Sesostris	Senusret Senusert Senwosret
Names used by New Kingdom rulers	Tuthmosis or Thothmes Amenophis Sethos	Djehutymose Amenhotep Seti

hieroglyphs were deciphered in 1822. So, the old Greek names have been around longer and are actually preferred by some, even in Egypt today. Table 1.2 shows some examples.

To make things even more complicated, many Egyptian cities and other sites have multiple names. In Upper Egypt, for example, Luxor (in Arabic) was known as Waset to the ancient Egyptians and later acquired a Greek name, Thebes, which has become standard in use. Same, too, with a major ancient Egyptian capital, Men-nefer, which is typically still referred to by Egyptologists by its Greek name, "Memphis." (The very name we use today, "Egypt," comes from the Greek, *Aigyptos*, which in turn was derived from the ancient Egyptian word, *Hut-ka Ptah* which was the name of a temple to the god Ptah in Memphis.) The fact is, there is still no universal and consistent use, and the budding Egyptologist will need to be familiar with a variety of names identifying the same people or places.

HOW OLD IS IT?

Determining age, or dating, is a crucial part of Egyptology, and there are a number of ways to go about it. We'll just take a quick look at three of the most important dating techniques that are used in Egyptology and archaeology in general.

Analyzing layers of dirt or debris, or strata, in an archaeological site is known as *stratigraphy*. By looking at how layers of dirt and debris are positioned in an archaeological site, it's usually possible to tell which layer with its accompanying objects is older than another. The older ones tend to be below the younger ones, but it's sometimes not so simple because things can get mixed up through a variety of processes. By the way, in Egypt, a mound representing the accumulated debris of past human settlement is often referred to as a *tell* or *kom*. Such mounds are often the obvious target of archaeological investigation.

Another very important way to date old objects is by their style. You can tell that a Model T automobile is older than a 1970s Camaro by the way it looks. Likewise, this is true of many other kinds of objects because styles tend to change through time. This concept theoretically allows an expert to pick up a piece of pottery and say whether it is a Predynastic storage pot or a much later Roman wine jar. There are also clever ways of ordering groups of objects based on their changing styles. This is called sequence dating or the *seriation* method, as it is more commonly known among archaeologists. The pioneering archaeologist, Flinders Petrie, is credited with developing this important technique, when he applied this method to pottery found in Egyptian Predynastic graves.

Some artifacts, including Greek coins and Egyptian beetle-shaped amulets called scarabs, are very portable. Finding one of these in your archaeological site doesn't guarantee that your site dates to the age of such objects by themselves. But it does mean that the layer in which they were found isn't older than such objects, unless it's been tampered with, which is possible by several different processes.

Radiocarbon dating, or carbon-14 dating, has received a lot of attention. It's not used as much for material dating to the time of Egyptian civilization, but for objects that existed during the time before writing in that land, it is a very useful technique indeed. Without going into tremendous detail, this dating method is based on the notion that all living creatures absorb a kind of radiation from the atmosphere. When they die, this radioactive material begins to decay at a known rate. The amount of radioactive material remaining in an archaeological sample can be measured; thus, it can be determined how many years it has been since the sample was in a living state.

Although this technique works very well, it is not perfect. It works accurately only with uncontaminated organic materials, and the older the sample is, the wider the spread of possible dates is. The technique also is good only for objects dating between about 400 and 50,000 years old, which isn't much of a problem for much of what is found of Egyptological interest. Very importantly, the dates are meaningful only in the sense that the sample is meaningful. For example, if I am trying to date an old building with a wooden beam, I might want to take into account the possibility that the wooden beam might be an old piece of wood reused from an earlier structure, so the radiocarbon date would be dating the wood, not necessarily the building in which it was found. You also need to keep in mind that radiocarbon dating cannot pinpoint a specific day or year, but gives a range of years in which the date will fall and this range gets wider the older the material!

Known astronomical phenomena have also played an important role in fixing calendar dates to the framework of ancient Egyptian history. When the Egyptians noted certain periodic star positions, for example, we can use our modern knowledge of astronomy to pinpoint the year in which it happened.

Fortunately, in Egypt, the plethora of inscriptions and our knowledge of art, history, and writing allow us to date things far more easily than in many other parts of the ancient world. Also quite helpful are dates that can be verified from written sources outside of Egypt's borders, including Mesopotamia, where precise dates can sometimes be more easily determined and then matched up with events taking place in Egypt. In short, the best approach to dating is determined based on the circumstance and, better yet, using a combination of methods.

WRITING AND TEXTS

Perhaps the greatest impediment to rediscovering the ancient Egyptian past was the mystery of the hieroglyphs, a puzzle that thwarted investigators for centuries. There seemed to be no end to these perplexing images that appeared in abundance on the walls of temples and tombs, coffins and stelae, and many other objects. What could these symbols possibly mean? Was it some form of mystical expression, or perhaps "picture writing," or was it an actual writing system conveying the sounds of a language?

The ultimate answer is that hieroglyphs are an actual form of writing, which we can define as language expressed in symbols. But the road to the discovery was long, and there was a lot of wild speculation before the issue was resolved. Let's look at some of the earlier ideas.

Take, for example, the hieroglyph that represents the *m* sound in the ancient Egyptian language. It is depicted by the picture of an owl. With the loss of knowledge of the hieroglyphs after the first few centuries AD, this owl became a mystery. Could it, for example, be some sort of philosophical statement in and of itself? Wisdom, perhaps? After all, the Bible refers to "the wisdom of Egypt," and in Western folklore, at least, owls are gifted with sagacity.

And if we maintain the opinion that the Egyptians were mystical, as evidenced by their numerous temples, along with ideas that ancient secret knowledge was passed down secretive groups such as the medieval masons, then *voilà*—we are left with an inscrutable mystery subject to our own speculative interpretations. In fact, it was not uncommon for would-be translators prior to the decipherment to propose lengthy, complex, and abstract interpretations of but a mere handful of hieroglyphic characters!

Another idea was that the hieroglyphs represented a form of picture writing, that is, the characters themselves represented what they depicted. Our owl hieroglyph, then, would represent that very thing, an owl. Now we look at what appears in front and what appears behind, and we have a story, so it seems. Let's say that we have three hieroglyphs: an owl, a man with a stick, and some legs facing the opposite direction. The imaginative translator might propose that what we have is the story of an owl who was whacked with a stick by a man who turned and left in the aftermath. This method, though, was obviously quite subjective and involved a great deal of imagination—and if we follow through with the owl example, we might be tempted to propose some sort of story to explain why the bird deserved such treatment.

The age of speculation eventually came to an end with the chance discovery of a chunk of stone by one of Napoleon's soldiers in 1799. While maintaining fortifications in the Delta town of Rosetta, a large irregularly-shaped fragment of black granite was discovered— 3 feet, 9 inches tall; 2 feet, 4 inches wide; and 11 inches thick, and weighing just less than 1,500 lb. In its complete form as a standing stone stela, or tablet, it probably stood between 5 and 6 feet tall.

One face of the stone was completely covered with three kinds of ancient writing displayed in three groups. The top portion contained an inscription in the mysterious hieroglyphs, the middle contained a cursive script known as Demotic, and at the bottom was Greek. The French recognized the potential importance of the stone and had it sent off to Cairo.

The Greek inscription on the stone could be read because the knowledge of that ancient language had never been lost; there were plenty of Western scholars capable of reading it. The Greek inscription indicated that the stone was a decree dating to 196 BC during the reign of Ptolemy V. The actual historical context of the inscription is not itself of profound importance. The key lay in the possibility that the Rosetta Stone might contain an identical inscription written in multiple languages and scripts, including the yet undeciphered Egyptian hieroglyphs! Copies of the stone were made and sent to scholars in Europe, who got busy comparing the Greek text to the scripts above it. Meanwhile, the Rosetta Stone was confiscated from the French by the British, who still retain it. It can be seen today in the British Museum in London, where it is a major attraction.

Like so many things in archaeology, the decipherment of the ancient Egyptian hieroglyphs was a process. A number of small steps made by different scholars contributed to a final conclusion, and at least one, an Englishman named Thomas Young (1733–1829), came very close. It had been proposed, for example, that a series of hieroglyphs specially enclosed in an oval symbol, or *cartouche*, were the names of the royalty mentioned in the Greek text (see Figure 1.2). This proved to be correct. Others made a surprising bit of progress with the cursive inscription. (And deciphering cartouches would eventually make it reasonably easy to date monuments and objects to the reign of a particular ruler or individual.)

After several years of study, a young French prodigy named Jean-François Champollion (1790–1832) proclaimed in 1822 that he had solved the puzzle: the hieroglyphs were basically phonetic in nature. By comparing the alphabetic Greek royal names on the lower part of the Stone with the individual hieroglyphs found in the cartouches, he was actually able to identify several phonetic signs. From there, rapid

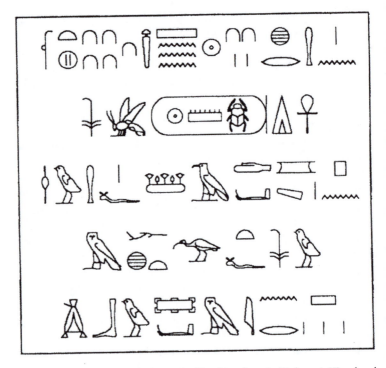

Figure 1.2 Egyptian hieroglyphic text telling how the ruler Tuthmosis III ordered
the dredging of a clogged canal. His name is found in the oval, or
cartouche.

Source: Donald P. Ryan.

progress was made in further decipherment, and Champollion himself went on to write, among other things, a grammar and dictionary
of ancient Egyptian.

Champollion was an interesting fellow. He was a master of many
languages—even as a child, he had studied Hebrew, Arabic, Coptic,
and Chinese. In 1826, he was made conservator general of the
Egyptian antiquities in the Musée du Louvre in Paris, and he led a
scholarly expedition to Egypt in 1827. Champollion accomplished
much in his relatively short life and is generally considered one of
the founding figures in Egyptology.

The decipherment of the hieroglyphs gradually revealed the ancient language behind the script. Today, linguists classify ancient Egyptian as a member of the Afro-Asiatic language family (formerly called "Hamito-Semitic"), a family that incorporates the Semitic languages such as Hebrew, Arabic, and Akkadian, and a number of African languages as well. (You might be interested to know that there are still some ancient scripts which lack credible decipherment. These include Linear A, found in the Mediterranean; the Indus Valley script found in Pakistan, and the curious symbols known as Rongo-rongo, found on remote Easter Island in the middle of the Pacific Ocean.)

Languages, of course, change through time. Word usage changes, new words are invented, pronunciations might differ with dialects, and even spelling might evolve. Compare, for example, the works of Chaucer, Shakespeare, the King James Bible, and so forth with contemporary English, and it's easy to see. In the case of Chaucer, it's often barely comprehensible to a modern audience in its original form. And as for Shakespeare, nobody today regularly communicates in such a florid manner unless a member of some sort of Medieval times re-enactment group. The dynamic of change applies to ancient Egyptian, and Egyptologists have identified five stages of the language through its 3,000-plus years of written history. Here are the five major stages of the Egyptian language:

- *Old Egyptian*: The language of the oldest-known texts, best represented from the monuments of the Old Kingdom, including the famous Pyramid Texts.
- *Middle Egyptian*: The classic form of the language, which was probably the spoken form from around the time of the Middle Kingdom, but persisted in written form into much later periods.
- *Late Egyptian*: The spoken and literary language common during the New Kingdom.
- *Demotic*: The stage of the language common during the Late Period.
- *Coptic*: The latest known stage. It still survives in the liturgy of the Coptic Christian Church.

Along with the different stages of the language, there were four primary scripts for writing Egyptian:

1 *Hieroglyphs*: A script that incorporated pictorial symbols and was used primarily in formal inscriptions.
2 *Hieratic*: A cursive form of hieroglyphs that was especially useful for writing on papyrus (paper) and other informal writing surfaces.
3 *Demotic*: An even more cursive form of writing that was used during the Demotic stage of the language.
4 *Coptic*: A script written with a modified Greek alphabet, including the vowels (which, as I'll mention later, were not directly incorporated in the other scripts.)

Let's return to the hieroglyphs. This is basically how the script works: first of all, vowels were not commonly represented in the phonetic script. Basically, the symbols represent words composed with consonants. How odd this seems to those familiar with European languages! Obviously you can't pronounce words without vowels. (If you don't believe me, try a few combinations with consonants such as $M + N$ and $B + V$, which will produce some interesting effects!) Ancient Egyptian is by no means alone in this writing phenomenon. Arabic and Hebrew are both commonly written without vowels, and anybody who knows these languages will tell you that they're not really necessary if you understand their very patterned grammar. Certain vowels are to be used in predictable places.

You should also know that the ancient Egyptian language contained some sounds that don't appear in English. A couple seem to be sounds made deep in the throat, while another seems to be a "kh" sound familiar in German and Hebrew. Hundreds of individual hieroglyphic signs exist, but only a couple dozen of the signs are alphabetical—that is, one sign signifies a single sound. Numerous other signs stand for combinations of two consonants, and yet others stand for three.

Hieroglyphs can be written from left to right, and also right to left, and also top to bottom. This isn't much of a problem if one knows the script and which direction a particular hieroglyph usually faces. This lack of consistency is actually an advantage as it allows hieroglyphs to be arranged artistically to fit required space or need on various objects or monuments.

Now perhaps you are wondering, how is it possible to tell the difference between words with the same combination of consonants but no vowels? Take the two letters representing the sounds "b" and "t." To use English, we could arrive at numerous words including *bait, bet, bit, boat, boot, bite, but, beat, bat* (and which one? the stick or the flying beast?), *beet*, and so on. The Egyptians had a nice way of dealing with this. They had hundreds of non-phonetic signs known as determinatives, which were usually found at the end of the word and indicated which of the possible choices was the intended one. After a man's name, for instance, often comes a hiero-glyph depicting a seated man, and a seated woman typically follows the name of a female. Verbs dealing with human motion might show some walking feet, and a word indicating a kind of cow might show just that: a cow. A cumbersome system, you say? Absolutely, but it worked, and the world would have to wait some time before a simple alphabet—in which a single symbol represented a single sound—would be invented and applied to various languages. And if you think that ancient Egyptian hieroglyphs are overwhelming, take a look at the classical Chinese script, in which there is a separate character for every word!

Most people are familiar with the idea of grandiose temples and other monuments covered with hieroglyphs carved in stone or painted on walls. Fortunately, stone wasn't the only material avail-able for writing. Much more portable and convenient was a kind of paper known as *papyrus* manufactured from an aquatic plant, *Cyperus papyrus*, which grew along the Nile. Although the exact method of manufacture cannot be definitively confirmed, the paper seems to have been made with overlapping strips of the inner pith of the plant. Under pressure, natural adhesives aid in binding the materials together, and individual sheets of paper and lengthy scrolls could be produced in such a manner. Scribes wrote on papyrus with a reed pen typically dipped in black or red ink. Do note that apart from referring to a specific plant, scholars refer to any document written on papyrus paper as a *papyrus*, plural: *papyri*.

A number of letters on papyrus survive, as do many complete scrolls bearing funerary texts such as the so-called Book of the Dead, as recovered from tombs. Keep in mind that papyrus is a very fragile commodity, and only a minute fraction of the documents that once existed has likely survived.

Other writing surfaces included convenient flat flakes of stone, typ-ically limestone, and broken pottery shards which Egyptologists refer to as "ostraca" (singular, "ostracon"). These were readily available for quick notes and short documents. Because of their durability, many of these documents have survived, some with quite interesting contents such as receipts from exchange of goods, or tallies of workmen, etc. And apart from what one might consider domestic or formal documents, hundreds of examples of ancient Egyptian graffiti have been found. Many of these are simply names of individuals scratched on rock, but others provide some real insights into history and even the nature of the environment during the times they were written.

The Egyptian uses of writing were much the same as they are today, including letters of communication between individuals, business transactions, construction plans, complaints, requests, receipts, and so forth. There are also plenty of writings relating to religious themes of the living and the deceased. Temples and tombs, especially in the dryer parts of the land, offer us a plethora of such inscriptions. Some fine examples of literature are known, sometimes in multiple copies, as recorded by students in scribal schools. Among the more interesting are traditional popular stories, and "instructions"—bits of sage advice to guide the student to a better life made with better choices.

What did ancient Egyptian sound like? No one knows, for sure. The situation with the lack of vowels certainly complicates things, but that hasn't discouraged some scholars from giving it a try. At least two approaches have been taken to reconstruct the spoken language. One is to look at ancient documents using Egyptian words but written in another script that indicates the vowels. Correspondence between foreign authorities and Egyptian royalty, for example, has been found with Egyptian names spelled out. This can really shed some light, but the words used tend to be limited. There is also the problem that the Egyptian names were written with a foreign script that might itself offer only an approximation.

Another technique is to study texts written in the Coptic script, which does indicate the vowels, and then try to work backward. Given the lengthy life span of the Egyptian language and its changes through time, this method cannot guarantee complete results, but it does provide some insights. As an interesting aside, some relatively recent attempts are worthy of notice. With Hollywood's desire for a certain sense of authenticity, an American Egyptologist, Stuart T. Smith, was hired to write Egyptian dialogue for several blockbuster films, including *Stargate* (1994), *The Mummy* (1999), and *The Mummy Returns* (2001). Although we aren't sure exactly how ancient Egyptian was pronounced, Smith produced some reasonable approximations that might be the closest thing that the public will likely hear of the old language. And it's a great way to employ an Egyptologist!

How, one might ask, are Egyptologists able to discuss these words among themselves if they can't even pronounce them? The answer is relatively simple. We usually insert a short vowel, typically *e*, between consonants. For example if we have glyphs representing the consonants *w*, *b*, and *n*, we would say "weben." And there are other informal rules that are used as well. Yes, it is a contrived system that all students learn, but the ultimate aim is that we are able to communicate with each other.

At first glance, hieroglyphs look intimidating in the extreme. One might surmise that it must take years and years for an Egyptologist to acquire a competent ability. Not necessarily so. With some good books or an introductory course, you will be amazed at how quickly you can actually read many inscriptions. It helps, too, that many surviving inscriptions are written in formulas that frequently repeat themselves. Many tourists have benefited from a study of cartouches, especially the more common ones, which allow them to delightfully identify royalty on monuments of different periods, with the side benefit of impressing their friends.

Those bold enough to want to really learn the grammar behind the script can anticipate some exciting challenges. The grammar of ancient Egyptian can be very unlike English. And when it comes to verbs, you're in for a *real treat*. The whole matter, again, is complicated by the lack of vowel structure, the vowels having the potential to more readily lead you, for example, to distinguish one verbal form from another. On the other hand, a knowledge of ancient Egyptian grammar will unlock the door to numerous intriguing texts and inscriptions.

One of the classic English-language texts on the subject was written by Sir Alan Henderson Gardiner. Gardiner (1879–1963) was one of the world's greatest Egyptologists and was the author of more than two dozen books and 200 scholarly articles. In particular, his book on ancient Egyptian language and writing, *Egyptian Grammar*, has influenced several generations of students. It is a big, heavy book that serves as an instructional grammar and even more important today, as a reference book. The book includes exercises requiring translation from Egyptian to English, and vice versa, and grammatical concepts and terminology that might make one's head spin. The satisfaction that comes as a result of learning Egyptian grammar, though, is well worth the effort.

Much progress in the study of Egyptian linguistics has been made since Gardiner's *Grammar* was last updated in 1957. However, the volume is still quite relevant and available, and many professors continue to use it in their teaching. Especially useful is the hieroglyphic sign list found in an appendix at the back of the book. It contains a list of the most common hieroglyphs, organized by category and accompanied by insightful explanations of their meanings.

A more updated approach to Egyptian grammar can be found in the new and highly regarded book by James Allen, *Middle Egyptian: An Introduction to the Language and Culture of Hieroglyphs* (2014). The book is loaded with interesting examples and exercises, and it takes care to explain the grammatical terminology in ways that are likely comprehensible to the average reader. For more gentle approaches, see some of the starter books recommended in this book's Appendix.

Where we have words, it's not surprising that we also have a dictionary—several, in fact. In the early twentieth century, a huge attempt was made to collect all know Egyptian words and organize them. The result was the impressive multivolume *Wörterbuch der Ägyptischen Sprache*—that's German for "Dictionary of the Egyptian Language." It's huge and it's expensive, and if you do find your Egyptian word of interest, you'll need some understanding of German if you wish to know the translation! Of more practical use to many beginners (and professionals, too) is Raymond Faulkner's *Concise Dictionary of Middle Egyptian* (1976). It's a single, relatively inexpensive volume, and it contains the majority of words that a student might encounter while studying Egyptian. Plus, the translations are in English. As scholars continue their work, new words continue to be collected and old meanings are refined. It's a continuous process that leads to further understanding.

And as a couple of final notes to this discussion of language, the reader should be aware that the proper term for the Egyptian writing system is *hieroglyphs*, not "hieroglyphics," as is so commonly but incorrectly used. The word *hieroglyphic* is an adjective that refers to a kind of pictorial script. We should also be cognizant of the fact that apart from its last vestiges found in the Coptic language, the ancient Egyptian language is essentially dead. The modern language of Egypt is Arabic and was introduced by the Arabs beginning around 642 AD.

2

LIFE AND DEATH IN ANCIENT EGYPT

Although it's easy to stand in awe of the ancient Egyptians and their many accomplishments, it's important to remember that they were people just like you and me, and they had the same needs as everyone else. In this chapter, we're going to look at ancient Egyptian daily life, including what they ate, what kind of jobs they had, and how their society was organized. We're also going to briefly explore their religion and worldview, and perspective on death and the afterlife.

Much of what survives from ancient Egypt comes from specialized sources—temples and tombs—that often were designed to last through time. Much of the ordinary, everyday stuff was perishable and simply didn't survive. But fortunately for us, the Egyptians loved life so much that they wanted it to continue in a similar way in the afterlife. Consequently, Egyptians included all kinds of objects from daily life in the tombs of their dead, and in some of the more expensive tombs they even painted scenes of daily life on the walls! Egyptologists have gleaned much of their information about Egyptian daily life from what they've found buried with the dead.

THE FAMILY

The typical family in ancient Egypt included a husband and wife and their children. Marriage was an arrangement between the couple or their families, and involved gift-giving, at least some of which was on the part of the groom. Egyptian girls were often married between ages 12 and 14. Marriages between half-siblings and cousins were possible.

There is no evidence of any special marriage rituals, although some might have thrown a party to celebrate the occasion. Typically, relationships were monogamous, with the exception of the ruler, who sometimes had several wives. It wasn't particularly difficult for couples to get divorced, and what divorces there were probably resulted mostly from incompatibility. When there was a divorce, a property settlement or division took place.

Lacking sophisticated medical knowledge, giving birth could sometimes be a dangerous thing, as could infancy and childhood. It was common for women to have several children in order to ensure the perpetuation of the family. Evidence suggests that the ancient Egyptians truly cherished their children, both boys and girls. The kids often assisted their parents in household or professional tasks and were expected to look after their parents in their old age.

Men and women had certain gender roles in Egyptian society. The women were usually household managers whose job it was to bear and raise children and maintain the home. They also ground grain and baked, and some engaged in textile production. In Egyptian texts, the wife is often referred to as "the mistress of the house." During the New Kingdom, the term "beloved sister" was sometimes used, referring to a special sort of closeness rather than a formal kinship relationship—unless you were the ruler.

The men were employed in any number of professions, from agriculture and crafts to government bureaucracy. Typically all government officials were males, although some women were priestesses or filled other religious roles. Even though they were rarely involved in government, women had equal status to men in many legal situations, and could own and manage land and engage in business dealings. In Egyptian art, men are typically depicted with reddish skin and women with yellowish skin. It has been suggested that this might be representative of their traditional roles: the men worked outdoors in the sun, and the women worked mostly inside the home. The average life expectancy of ancient Egyptians was between 30 and 36 years.

The family situation of the rulers was often altogether different. Polygamy was not unusual, and the king might have a chief wife plus a few minor ones, and perhaps maintain a concubine. It was not uncommon for the pharaoh to marry his sister or daughter. This served the purpose of keeping the ruling line close-knit, but it was generally not practiced outside of the royal family. Examples of royal intermarriage can also be found in Egyptian mythology, in which the both the gods Osiris and Seth married their sisters. It was possible for a pharaoh to take on foreign brides for diplomatic purposes as well.

WORK

As is typical of complex societies, the Egyptians lived in an occupationally diverse and socially stratified society. Egypt was a large agricultural society, and the majority of people were farmers or did farm-related work. Maintaining the crops and irrigation were certainly difficult work. There were also all manner of different craft specialists, such as pot-makers, butchers, and carpenters. Many of these skills were probably handed down from generation to generation, and it wouldn't have been unusual for a son to follow exactly in his father's professional footsteps. There were also slaves in Egypt, who were typically prisoners of war, but not enough of them that the Egyptian economy was dependent upon them.

The elite jobs, those of government officials and bureaucrats, were reserved for literate males, a requirement which kept most of the powerful jobs out of the hands of the commoners. Schooling in reading and writing wasn't available to everyone, but people who mastered those skills could be employed in thousands of elite positions. The overall literacy rate in Egypt seems to have been no more than 5 percent of the population at its greatest.

A fascinating and humorous text from the Middle Kingdom, known as the *Satire of the Trades*, offers insights into the nature of the working class. In the text, a student is lectured on how most everybody's job is miserable except that of the scribe. Here's a sample of some of the negative opinions offered:

- Carpentry will make your arms tired.
- Potters live a dirty and grubby existence.
- Clothes washers and fishermen face the danger of being eaten by crocodiles.

- Masons are dirty and wear loincloths made of twisted rope.
- Arrow makers get harassed all day long by mosquitoes and gnats in the marshy water.
- Farmers work harder than most and suffer horribly.

As a copying and writing exercise in a scribal school, advice such as this probably got the attention of the students! "Listen and learn" was the usual attitude at school, and mistakes could be rewarded with a beating from the instructor.

ROYAL ROLES

At the other end of the social spectrum from the lowly farmer was the king. The ruler of Egypt was considered to be the living embodiment of the god Horus, the son of the god Osiris. As such, he was thought to represent the people on Earth to those in the divine realm as the divine absolute ruler of Egypt for a life term.

The Egyptian word for the king was *nesu*. I personally prefer the term "ruler" over "king" because "king" has too many connotations based on European notions. As a living god on Earth, the Egyptian ruler *was not* equivalent to a medieval, or even modern, monarch. The word "king," however, is widely accepted, and we'll use it once in a while here. The term *pharaoh*, as a designation for the Egyptian ruler, actually wasn't used much until the New Kingdom. It is derived from the Egyptian words, *per-aa*, meaning, "The Great House" and refers to the palace, or the center of kingship (similar to the modern use of the terms "The White House" or "No. 10 Downing Street" to represent the American presidency or the office of the British Prime Minister, respectively).

The ruler had many responsibilities, including making major decisions, appointing officials, and handling the usual day-to-day activities of someone of such a high office. He also had divine responsibilities including serving as the supreme high priest, and most importantly, maintaining *maat*. *Maat* is the concept of truth, justice, and cosmic order and was represented by a goddess portrayed with a feather upon her head. *Maat* is the opposite of the undesirable state of chaos and could be upheld by striving to do that which is right and just. Keeping the forces of chaos at bay included fending off Egypt's enemies. As will be noted in later chapters, this was a large and necessary responsibility.

Fortunately, the ruler didn't have to thwart chaos by himself; he was served by a hierarchy of bureaucrats, whose jurisdictions covered Egypt and any outside lands under its control. The highest official below the ruler is referred to by Egyptologists as the *vizier*, who served as a prime minister of sorts. (The word is not Egyptian, but was derived from Turkish imperial terminology.) He was hand-picked, of course, and was often a member of the royal family or the son of a previous vizier. At times there could be two, one each for Upper and Lower Egypt.

Other very high and important offices included treasurers, high priests, and the Overseer of Works, who supervised the royal building projects. The next tier of workers included other overseers of all kinds. There were also military and priestly hierarchies. Special offices emerged from time to time, such as a Viceroy of Kush, who directed Egypt's domination over Nubia in the New Kingdom. And there were, in some periods, the governors of the various "nomes" or provinces, who maintained their own bureaucracies.

The Egyptian government extracted taxes from its people in the form of goods such as wheat, cattle, or other products. The supreme ruler also was able to draft people, so to speak, for a kind of national service. This might have involved serving in the army for a while or perhaps working on a pyramid or some other laborious project that required lots of manpower.

In short, Egypt was a highly stratified society, and although it was possible to move up through the ranks, most people probably stayed in the social and professional class they were born into. The elite ensured that their children would remain of similar status, too, by educating them.

HOUSE AND HOME

In the earliest times, the ancient Egyptians probably lived in a hut made of sticks plastered with mud and roofed with thatch. As villages became permanent features on the landscape, the average house was built of mud bricks with a flat roof. As a building material, mud brick is well-suited to Egypt's climate as it can provide a cooler environment during the heat of summer and insulation from the cold in winter. Most houses probably consisted of a living room along with storage and sleeping rooms, and a little back courtyard for cooking and other activities. A lot of the domestic activities were carried on outside of the house proper, so a great deal of interior space wasn't necessary. Woven mats provided a sleeping surface for the average worker while four-legged beds served the elite. Pillows were hard and made from something as simple as a block of wood with a notch for the head or fashioned for the king from ivory or other precious materials.

Houses could come in all sizes, of course, depending upon one's wealth, from the simplest crowded varieties just described to two-story villas with numerous rooms. Royal palaces, too, could be made of mud brick, with wooden ceilings supported by pillars. Few remains of royal palaces have survived, but from those that do, archaeologists can tell that some were quite elaborate and included painted walls and clever architecture.

Because they were built of mud brick and other perishable materials, not many Egyptian homes or settlements have survived. Archaeologists, however, have been able to excavate a few unusually well-preserved domestic sites including: the New Kingdom village of royal tomb-builders at Deir el-Medineh, the Middle Kingdom pyramid town of Kahun, and the short-lived Amarna Period city of Akhetaten. Each has given us special insights into daily life, but because each was a rare, somewhat specialized, settlement, we should be careful about generalizing from them. Still, people in pyramid towns needed homes and food like everyone else, and we are lucky that some of these sites have survived.

There probably weren't many of what we would call "cities" in ancient Egypt. Perhaps Memphis, Thebes and Akhetaten might fit the bill because they had relatively high populations. Smaller "towns" serving as administrative centers were likely the norm, with the majority of people living in what we might characterize as "villages."

The two big staples of the ancient Egyptian diet were bread and beer. The bread was made from flour ground from barley or emmer wheat and produced in flat, oval, triangular, and cone-shaped loaves. Beer was brewed from barley and could be sweetened with honey or dates. As something that could be consumed throughout the day, its alcohol content was likely quite low. Interestingly, archaeologists have found actual loaves of ancient bread in tombs, where they were left as offerings or food provisions for the deceased.

A variety of vegetables was available, including chickpeas, fava beans, lentils, lettuce, onions, and cucumbers. Meat was quite expensive, especially the larger animals such as cows. Wealthy folk went hunting for wild game, such as antelope and gazelles and marsh birds. Domesticated goats and sheep weren't quite as costly and were a source of milk products such as cheese, and there were also pigs. Lacking refrigeration, meat had to be consumed right away. The average Egyptian, however, probably enjoyed Nile fish and some tasty ducks. Ducks and geese were kept in pens, and the Egyptians ate their eggs. For a little variety, mice and hedgehogs were sometimes eaten as well.

Food could be spiced up with a little salt, parsley, coriander, cumin, and other enhancements. Available fruits included figs, dates, and grapes. The ancient Egyptians produced a lot of wine, including the traditional variety made from grapes, but also other types manufactured from pomegranates and dates. Wine imported from other lands, such as Canaan, was particularly prized. For sweetening up one's life, honey was a real favorite.

The Egyptian kitchen was generally an open-air affair. A large domed oven was typical, and ceramic pots were used for certain types of cooking. Kitchen utensils included long sticks for poking at things in the oven, copper knives, and wooden spoons and spatulas. Food could be grilled, boiled, fried, roasted, or baked.

Clothing in ancient Egypt ranged from the minimal—or nothing—to the expensively elaborate. Like many things in Egyptian society, clothing and status were often linked. For the male laborer, a simple loincloth might suffice, and children often ran around naked. For more general wear, a wrapped skirt or kilt reaching to at least the knees was common for both men and women. More elite women often wore a sheath dress, which was basically a cloth tube with shoulder straps. For party wear, the dresses were often much more elaborate, with shawls and cloaks serving as accessories for chilly evenings.

Generally, the cloth used in Egypt was linen manufactured from flax, and there were different grades of quality. White seems to have been the usual color, but some of the dresses had patterns, fringes, or beading. During some time periods, pleats, longer sleeves, and tunics were popular. And what about undergarments? Both men and women could wear a triangular loincloth beneath their other clothes.

It's likely that many Egyptians went barefoot, but sandals were also worn. Men's hair was generally short, and women wore theirs long and straight. Wealthier individuals of either sex might have worn wigs, some of which were made of human hair, while some priests shaved their heads, if not their whole bodies. Egyptian children, both boys and girls, typically had their head shaved except for a long lock of hair on one side, the "side lock" of youth.

It was quite common for Egyptians to use kohl to accentuate their eyes. They were noted for their personal cleanliness and bathed regularly. The Nile was always there for a bit of washing up (although beware the hippos and crocs!), and some of the nicer homes had a place to shower with water poured from a clay jar.

Like people everywhere, the ancient Egyptians liked to have a good time. They participated in sports such as running, jumping, wrestling, and stick fighting, as well as board games involving strategy and chance. The Egyptian game of *senet*, for example, was played on a game board marked out with squares. Players threw dice or sticks to move around the board in what was an ancestor to many similar games enjoyed today. Senet boards have been found in tombs, and replica versions can now be purchased and played in the twenty-first century.

Fishing and fowling were enjoyed along the banks of the Nile, with participants throwing sticks used to knock out the desired birds. The elite, including the ruler, could enjoy archery as well as hunting dangerous wild animals. And some things never change—kids back then enjoyed playing with toy animals and dolls as well. A favorite kind of doll might be considered a bit ugly by today's standards—a flat, painted paddle with some hair fixed to the top—but with a little imagination, they sure served their purpose well.

The Egyptians also loved a good party. The fancier ones included dancers, musicians, and singers. Musical instruments included the harp, lute, lyre, flutes, drums, rattles, and other noisemakers while lots of delicious food and wine were consumed.

Barter was the name of the game when it came to paying bills. There was no coinage, but there was a general sense of how much things were worth. Quantities of desirable and useful products could be compared and valued on a unit of exchange called a *deben* which was ultimately related to a certain weight of copper.

SCIENCE AND TECHNOLOGY

The Egyptians are well noted for their creative engineering and artistic abilities. They quarried and moved immense blocks of stone for hundreds of miles, built massive monuments, and fashioned complex, intricate jewelry. Although this ancient culture did not have the advanced knowledge of science and technology that we have today, their scientific and technical competence was impressive.

As we marvel at the ancient Egyptians' incredible architectural achievements—the pyramids, the Sphinx, obelisks, and temples— it's easy to jump to the conclusion that they were masters of arithmetic, geometry, trigonometry, and physics. That's not necessarily so. Although we don't have a lot of written information specifically addressing such matters, it seems that the Egyptian understanding of mathematics was somewhat rudimentary, which makes their architectural achievements even more remarkable.

In terms of arithmetic, the Egyptians worked in base 10, which is the same system we're generally accustomed to today. They had symbols representing 1s, 10s, 100s, 1000s, and so on, and numbers could be indicated by repetitions of these symbols. With these numbers they could easily add, subtract, multiply, and divide with whole numbers. They also were somewhat adept at fractions, although their methodology for computation would probably seem cumbersome to us. They did not use zero.

Despite their apparent limited knowledge of advanced mathematics, the Egyptians could readily calculate length, volume, area, and slope. This can be confirmed by looking at the proportions of finished monuments, which would have required at least some ability in these matters to be constructed. The most complete of the few surviving ancient Egyptian mathematical texts is known as the *Rhind Papyrus*. It was found in the mid-nineteenth century, and most of it resides in the British Museum. The papyrus is a kind of mathematical textbook with a wide number of problems and solutions.

Standards of measurements were of great importance in all ancient civilizations, especially in those such as Egypt where they didn't use what we'd call "money." Some sense of uniformity in size, weight, and volume was essential for such things as managing land, fair commerce, accounting, and construction. The standard Egyptian unit of measurement for length was the royal cubit, which was based on the length of the Pharaoh's forearm. A cubit was about 20.5 inches in length and was divided into seven palm-breadths composed of four finger-widths. Larger measurements such as the "rod," equaling 100 cubits, could be used for greater lengths. Standardized cubit sticks have been found that indicate a degree of uniformity.

For volume, the "hekat" or standard "wheat-measure" was used, not unlike the "bushel" is used today. It was probably equivalent to about a gallon. Additionally, there were smaller measures such as the "hin" or "jar," ten of which made a "hekat." For weight, including precious materials such as gold and silver, a unit known as a "deben" was used, weighing about 91 grams and composed of 10 "kites."

Like many ancient civilizations, the Egyptians produced a civil calendar to keep track of time and events. While some of the other nearby cultures based their calendars on the cycles of the moon, the Egyptian one was arranged around the sun. The Egyptian year consisted of 12 months of 30 days each. Five extra days were added to the end, for a grand total of 365 days a year. Each day was divided into 24 hours, 12 of day and 12 of night. The year was also divided into three seasons: inundation, winter, and summer. This calendric arrangement was adopted by the Romans and eventually became the basis for the system we still use today.

You might be aware that an actual year on Earth lasts 365.25 days. Given this fact, we need to correct our modern calendar periodically so that it keeps up with that of nature. That's why we have a "leap year" every four years, adding an extra day for adjustment. The Egyptians, unfortunately, didn't use such a correction, so consequently, the civil calendar was essentially six months off to the astronomical year after 730 years! Fortunately, nature is a reliable calendar, and such observable phenomenon as the rise of certain stars in certain places probably announced to the Egyptians the coming of seasons even if their civil calendar was off-track.

MEDICINE

Egyptologists have been able to learn about ancient Egyptian health problems and their medical treatments by examining mummies and skeletal remains. Furthermore, several medical papyri have been discovered, and they address a variety of ancient concerns, including study of the eye, gynecology, and internal problems. Given the nature of warfare in ancient times, it is not surprising that traumatic injuries and their treatments were described in the medical papyri as well. There were several kinds of physicians and medical specialists in ancient Egypt. A surgeon of sorts and experts in snake and scorpion bites might accompany desert workers or soldiers.

The ancient Egyptian understanding of the human body and how it works was quite different from ours. It was thought, for example, that the heart rather than the brain was the center of thought and emotion, and the Egyptian perception of the nature of circulation and bodily fluids was far from modern. They were, however, aware that the pulse can be detected in different parts of the body, and they were capable of impressive clinical observation, such as differentiating the symptoms of different skull fractures. Honey was applied to wounds as its infection-retardant properties were known. With their own view of how things work, the Egyptians were likely successful from time to time in treating a variety of ailments.

Egyptian medicine seems to have been a combination of practical or rational approaches mixed with the magical. A physical remedy such as a poultice or pharmaceutical recipe might be combined with an incantation, a magic spell, or the wearing of a magic amulet. There were also patron deities for such things as healing (Thoth), disease (Sekhmet), and scorpions and snakes (Selqet). Some of the remedies called for exotic products that likewise blurred the line between the physical and supernatural realms.

Dentistry was also practiced, but it's unclear to what extent. Because of their coarse diet, especially bread, which can contain a lot of grit from the threshing process, it is common to see a great deal of dental attrition in the remains of ancient Egyptians. They wore their teeth down, and gum disease and oral abscesses were not rare. There must have been at least a few dental specialists because a dental bridge has been found in the Old Kingdom, secured in place with gold wire. And apart from people, veterinary texts have also been found describing the treatment of various animal ailments.

SIMPLE CRAFTS

The remains of ancient pots are one of the most common and useful artifacts examined by archaeologists. Because these pots are made of baked clay, they tend to survive for long periods of time. And because they often break, they were continuously produced. The sizes and shapes of the pots give us an idea about their function, but, perhaps more importantly, their different styles through time serve as a very useful dating tool.

Most sources of clay contain slight chemical differences from each other. Some archaeological methods allow us to actually identify the very source location of the clay from which an individual pot was made. Egyptian and foreign styles of pottery can also give us great insights into trade and international commerce in ancient times. This is very useful, of course, in tracing trading practices, including imports and exports.

Pots could be made by hand or in a mold, but techniques involving spinning, such as using potter's wheels, were far more efficient. Decorative and functional features including handles could be shaped into the clay before firing. Pigments could also be added to provide a little color. A very special type of ceramic material often associated with ancient Egypt is called *faience*. It was typically shaped in molds for amulets, inlays, and small figurines, but it could also be used in plates and other vessels. Its usually glassy green or blue-glazed surface gives it its distinct character.

One benefit of living along a river such as the Nile was an endless supply of building material in the form of mud. Temporary "wattle and daub" shelters—that is, woven sticks covered with mud—seem to have been common in prehistoric days. Starting at least around the beginning of dynastic times, the use of brick in major construction became very common. The bricks consisted of mud and sometimes clay mixed with straw as a binder and pressed into rectangular wooden frames and then typically dried in the sun. Bricks of this sort are still manufactured and used in the villages of Egypt today. Structures of all sizes could be built of mud brick. Huge brick walls from ancient times can be found in Egypt—some are the remains of buildings, and others are enclosure walls. And, surprisingly, the constructions weren't necessarily ugly! Mud brick architecture could be spruced up by whitewashing, plastering, and painting.

Stone, of course, was an essential building material in ancient Egypt, and the three most common general types in use were granite, sandstone, and limestone. Sources of stone can be found far and wide, and the Egyptians were not averse to establishing quarries in distant places to obtain the best quality material for special projects. Some of the most desirable granite, for example, was found far south in Aswan, yet it was shipped hundreds of miles to the north for use in pyramid building and other projects (Figure 2.1).

The difficulty of quarrying and shaping stone varied, depending on the nature of the stone. Sandstone and limestone are relatively soft, and copper and stone chisels and hollow copper drills and saws were used to cut them. Granite is much harder and the Egyptians used hard stone pounding balls to free blocks of it from quarries, a task accomplished by hand that must have been utterly exhausting and mind-numbing. The remains of a huge obelisk sit in a granite quarry in Aswan. At 128 feet long, it would have been the largest piece of stone quarried in Egypt, had it not cracked in the process. Because the work was abandoned before completion, it has provided Egyptologists with wonderful insights into the quarrying process.

GOLD AND OTHER MALLEABLE METALS

Something about gold makes it universally appealing. It seems that most cultures throughout the world, ancient and modern, have valued this gleaming metal, which can be easily manipulated and transformed into treasures of all sizes. Egypt was no different. The ancient Egyptians considered gold to be the flesh of gods, most notably the sun god, Re. With the discovery of the tomb of Tutankhamun in 1922 and its enormous number of golden or gilded objects, the world evermore associated gold with the wealth of ancient Egypt. The main sources of gold in Egypt were from Nubia and the Eastern Desert. The oldest-known geological map in the world comes from ancient Egypt and shows gold mines in the Wadi Hammamat in the Eastern Desert. The map dates to the reign of Ramesses IV (c. 1150 BC) and

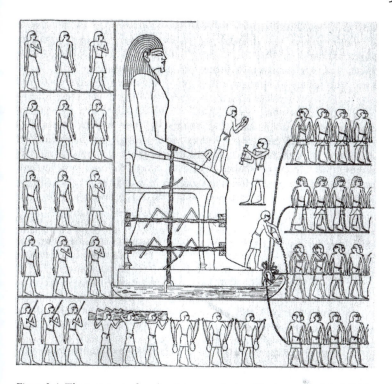

Figure 2.1 The transport of a colossal statue as depicted in the tomb of the Middle
Kingdom nomarch, Djehutyhotep, in the cemetery at El-Bershah

Source: Adolf Erman, *Life in Ancient Egypt*, London: Macmillan & Co., 1894.

resides in the Museo Egizio in Turin, Italy. Although silver was also
available, it was scarce and didn't seem to have the same sort of appeal
as gold during much of pharaonic times. At times, though, it was
portrayed as "the bones" of the gods.

Copper was especially desirable for tools and other utilitarian items.
Extensive remains of copper mining have been found in the Sinai, and
copper was in such heavy demand that it was also imported. Copper
smelting, which involves melting copper ore to refine it, began in
Egypt during Predynastic times. Bronze (copper plus an alloy, such as
tin) also was in use early on, but not extensively until much later days.

Gemstones were prized, and materials such as turquoise, carnelian, garnet, and jasper were mined or otherwise collected or imported and frequently were used in jewelry. One of the most exotic gems was lapis lazuli, a deep blue stone from Afghanistan. An extensive bit of trading and transport was required before this stone could make its way to Egypt.

WOOD

Another essential material that can be carved and shaped for any number of functions: wood. Egypt, with its desert climate, didn't have many stands of tall trees, but the larger ones included sycamore fig, tamarisk, and persea. Smaller trees such as acacia and sidder were sufficiently abundant and were used to make smaller items. For larger objects, including furniture, statues, and even coffins, several small pieces of wood were often skillfully shaped and joined together. If large planks were needed for boats or special projects, wood could be imported from Lebanon or Syria where massive cedar trees grew. Special wood, such as the exotic black ebony, could be obtained from Nubia through trade. The Egyptians employed a variety of woodworking tools, including chisels and mallets, adzes, drills, and saws. And the Egyptians occasionally manufactured things from ivory, which was obtained from hippo teeth or imported elephant tusks.

TRAVEL

Moving from one place to another doesn't seem to have been that difficult in ancient Egypt. Trails and roads connected villages and districts, and travel on foot would have been usual. Donkeys, though, were a common mode of transportation. As able beasts of burden, they could assist in many of the smaller domestic and economic chores and also could work in caravans.

Caravan routes traversed the Eastern Desert to quarry and mining sites, and to the Red Sea. Other trails led out to oases or other remote regions. A major thoroughfare known as "The Ways of Horus" led across the northern Delta into the Sinai and parts to the east. It is perhaps worth noting that although the camel is often identified with Egypt today, it didn't feature regularly as a beast of burden until relatively late, perhaps during the ninth century BC.

The Nile provided a veritable highway for the transport of people and goods. As noted in Chapter 1, the current of the river flows north, while the winds tend to blow south, allowing for travel in either direction. Dating back to Predynastic times, there are many depictions of boats on pottery vessels and in rock art although the details are often hard to sort out. Some of these early boats seem to be made of bundles of papyrus with upturned bows and sterns, a feature later imitated on wooden boats. During Dynastic times, boats came in all sizes, from little fishing skiffs made of papyrus to huge wooden barges capable of carrying many tons of material. Surviving examples of ancient Egyptian boats indicate that ships' planks could be joined together by wooden mortise and tenon techniques, and rope was also widely used to secure boards.

Despite their ability to construct sophisticated river craft, the Egyptians were not known for great seafaring prowess. Other peoples in the region of the Near East, such as the Phoenicians, were quite adept at sea travel, and many of them no doubt carried out extensive trade visits throughout Egyptian history. There is little evidence that the Egyptians themselves ventured regularly across the Mediterranean or had an interest in extended exploration by sea. There is at least one notable exception, though: expeditions down the Red Sea coast to the exotic Land of Punt, a source of exotic goods that was probably located in the region of Ethiopia or Somalia. (A voyage there is depicted in great detail in the memorial temple of Hatshepsut at Thebes.) Even then, the sailors probably hugged the coast. Another notable exception involves the Twenty-sixth Dynasty pharaoh, Necho II (c. 600 BC), who is said to have commissioned an expedition of Phoenician sailors to circumnavigate Africa. Leaving from the Red Sea and returning through Gibraltar, the trip took three years.

In the last few years, new insights have been gained regarding Egyptian seafaring. An exciting discovery was made on the Red Sea coast by a joint Italian/American expedition at the site called Wadi Gawasis. There, the remnants of what seems to be a small port was found including caves containing ships' timbers, and masses of rope that likely would have been used for rigging. It is likely that the ships embarking from Wadi Gawasis would have been constructed in the Nile Valley, disassembled, and then carried in pieces across the eastern desert to be reconstructed on the coast before journeys south to Punt or elsewhere.

A replica of an Eighteenth-Dynasty boat that was used for such travels was constructed by maritime archaeologist Cheryl Ward. In 2008, her 66 ft-long, 16 ft-wide boat, named *Min of the Desert*, sailed for 18 days down the Red Sea coast and the experiment demonstrated that not only was this sort of ship capable, it was fast too!

SOME SMALL TECHNOLOGIES

When one is in awe of huge and magnificent temples, tombs, and pyramids, it's easy to forget the small stuff. Some of these so-called "mundane" technologies such as rope and basketry played a vital role in both the everyday and the extraordinary doings of the Egyptians. How would it have been possible to drag massive blocks of stones or lower them onto a barge without rope? How will you tie up your donkey or hold your fishing raft together? Baskets can be put to use for any number of purposes, including transporting and storing food and objects and moving dirt in construction projects.

Yes, ropes and baskets served a myriad of important functions. They were made from natural fibers, including those derived from certain grass and palm species and papyrus. Ropes were made of all sizes—from string to cable—to serve different functions. Baskets were woven in several different styles and sometimes were attractively decorated. Some large diameter ropes made from papyrus were found in one of the quarries from which the stone for the Giza pyramids was hewn. A radiocarbon date demonstrated that they were much younger than the pyramids (from around the first century BC), but they still provide us with well-preserved examples of ancient rope and evidence of the long-term use of the quarry.

RELIGION: ORGANIZING THE WORLD

One of the most profound differences between ancient Egypt and our modern technological world is the way we perceive our universe and how its many parts work and interact. The development of "science" over the last few hundred years has provided us today with models to explain many things around us, from the components of life to distant galaxies. Religion continues to play an important societal role, but it occasionally conflicts with science. In the United States and elsewhere, the separation of church and state is seen as a major societal principle. In ancient Egypt, religion seems to have permeated most everything.

The reader is likely aware that the Egyptians recognized many gods—hundreds of them, in fact. There seems to have been a god linked to, or representative of, nearly everything in the world, from the physical facets of nature to abstract notions of the human condition. Great natural features, such as the sun and the moon and the Nile, were thought to be gods, but there were also certain gods that an Egyptian could appeal to if pregnant or bitten by a snake. There were plenty of gods to go around to suit any given occasion, and two or more gods could even be combined. The Greek historian Herodotus was aware of this and noted that the Egyptians were "religious to excess, far beyond any other race of men."

The Egyptians believed that the gods were the forces behind the phenomena that they observed or otherwise experienced. Today, for example, we explain weather by the complex interaction of various—and, ideally, predictable—physical factors. To the Egyptians, no such complexity was necessary. A god was behind the action, and that explained it. Egyptologists are not sure how or when some of the oldest Egyptian religious concepts came into being. The earliest written religious texts from ancient Egypt come from the time of the Old Kingdom. They were written on the walls of several pyramids and are known as the "Pyramid Texts." These difficult-to-comprehend writings provide some insights into the abstract thinking of the ancient Egyptians and continue to be studied.

Many Egyptian gods were associated with and depicted as animals, which is probably due to certain characteristics that the gods were thought to have. For example, Sakhmet, a fierce goddess, was depicted as a lioness, and the god Anubis, the protector of the cemeteries, was a jackal, a kind of wild dog that roams the hills by night. Many gods were portrayed as *anthropomorphic*—that is, in human form; at other times, these same entities might be portrayed with human bodies and the heads of the animals they were associated with. (Some Egyptologists believe that this stems from the practice of priests sometimes wearing animal masks.) The Egyptians seemed satisfied with either depiction; whatever way the gods were depicted, they were considered to be the personification of reality and/or concepts. Very few people probably claimed to actually see these gods in the form that they were depicted in art, yet they felt the gods' presence and believed that they could be appeased and appealed to.

A VIEW OF THE WORLD

To understand the Egyptian worldview, it's useful to see how the people viewed the structure of the universe. Looking around them, the ancient Egyptians saw the same things that we do: the sky above, with the sun, moon, and stars, and the Earth below. Whereas we believe that there is a vast expanse of space filled with stars, planets, and constellations, the Egyptians had other ideas. They believed that their world was basically surrounded by water. The sky was thought to be the edge of the eternal waters, as represented by the goddess, Nut. The Earth, represented by the god, Geb, was separated from Nut by the air god Shu. On the opposite of the Earth and below was a parallel land of sorts, a netherworld known as the Duat, which was home not only to the blessed dead, but was full of devious creatures, demons, and damned souls as well.

How might they have formed such beliefs? The Egyptians did not know that the Earth travels around the sun in a regular orbit. Instead, they believed that the cycles of night and day were created by the sun god making a westward journey across the sky. After traveling beneath the Earth into the land of darkness, the sun god was triumphantly reborn each day in the east.

With this sort of thinking, the daily travels of the sun became a repetitive cosmic drama. The movement of the sun could be seen as a great divine boat traversing the waters of the sky, or perhaps it was propelled by great celestial wings, like a slowly flying falcon. Or, the circular sun might have been pushed across the sky by a great cosmic dung beetle, a conceptualization of the real-life insect that lays its eggs in dung and then pushes it along the ground, forming a round ball. In some examples of religious art, the goddess Nun is seen spread out across the universe, swallowing the sun, which travels through her body during the twelve hours of night to be reborn in the usual way the next day. Ancient Egyptians could believe all of these things to be true at the same time without contradiction—each way of representing something was simply a different facet of the same phenomenon.

Whereas the Egyptian deities rarely, if ever, showed their actual faces to the average Egyptian, the gods were believed to be able to communicate their will through dreams. The tricky part was in the interpretation! And occasionally, the gods served as oracles when their cult statues were paraded through town during festivals. A voice from the vicinity of the statue borne by priests or a slight tip of its carrying bier might provide an answer to a commoner's question.

IN THE BEGINNING

Most humans are curious about their ultimate origins. So, too, were the Egyptians. There were several versions of the creation story of which the following scenario is representative: Before creation, eight gods existed in the eternal waters of Nun in a time of infinite darkness and nothingness. The eight pre-creation gods represented various abstract concepts of this boundless watery void. Out of this void appeared a primeval mound, from which emerged a creator god by the name of Atum. Atum then proceeded to create a male and female pair of gods who started the process of the formation of the known universe. The first couple—Shu, representing air, and Tefnut, representing moisture—became the parents of Geb, the Earth, and Nut, the sky. Artistic depictions survive showing Shu (the air) separating Geb (the Earth) from Nut (the sky). Geb and Nut, in turn, produced two more pairs of important gods, Osiris and Isis, along with Seth and Nephthys. This first and vital group of nine early gods is referred to by Egyptologists as the *Ennead*.

Another later version of the creation scenario involves Ptah, a god associated with crafts. As he conceived the ideas of things, Ptah spoke their name, and they were converted into reality. And where did people come from? The ram-headed god Khnum created them on a potter's wheel, both their physical reality and a kind of spirit life-force double known as the *ka*.

Different gods could be associated with different cities, towns, or places. Ptah, for example, was the favored god of Memphis, while Amun became closely associated with Thebes. Gods often appeared in triads of a paired male and female deities plus their offspring. At Memphis, Ptah and Sekhmet were at home with their son, Nefertum, and at Thebes, Amun and his wife, Mut, could be found with their son, Khonsu. During most of Egyptian history, there seems to have been no real national requirement to worship any one god, and the Egyptians were apparently able to pick and choose whichever ones appealed to them or might be helpful to them in any given situation.

The gods were also sometimes mixed and matched. Ptah, for example, was occasionally combined with another favorite god of Memphis, Sokar, who was associated with the dead (as was Osiris); thus, Ptah-Sokar-Osiris was worshiped as a composite entity. The sun god, Ra, was joined with other gods, including Amun, Horus, Atum and Monthu, to be envisioned as Amun-Ra, Ra-Horakhty, Ra-Atum and Monthu-Ra. The modern Western mind rebels at such concepts, but the Egyptians didn't see these seemingly contradictory propositions as an intellectual fallacy. To them, these various divine incarnations and permutations not only explained the workings of the world, but again, also provided viewpoints that acknowledged different perspectives of what we might consider to be one phenomenon.

EGYPTIAN GODS: THE SHORT LIST

Here's a very short list of some of the principal gods:

- Amun: The great god of Thebes.
- Anubis: The jackal-god patron of embalmers and guardian of cemeteries.
- Aten: The sun disk.
- Atum: The creator god.
- Bastet: The cat goddess.
- Bes: A curious dwarf-like fellow who was a domestic protector.
- Geb: The Earth god.
- Hapi: The god of the Nile flood.

- Hathor: A sky goddess who sometimes appears as a cow, associated with fertility, love and pleasure.
- Horus: A falcon god and the son of Osiris. Identified with the living king.
- Isis: Wife of Osiris and mother of Horus.
- Khnum: Ram-headed god who created people on a potter's wheel.
- Khons: The moon god.
- Maat: Goddess of truth, justice, and order.
- Monthu: Theban god of war.
- Mut: The wife of Amun.
- Nekhbet: Vulture goddess representing Upper Egypt.
- Nephthys: Wife of Seth and sister of Isis.
- Nut: The sky goddess.
- Osiris: Husband of Isis and father of Horus, god of the netherworld depicted as a mummified king.
- Ptah: Patron of crafts.
- Ra: The sun god.
- Sakhmet: The fierce lioness wife of Ptah.
- Seth: The god of chaos, violence, and storms.
- Shu: The air god.
- Taweret: A goddess in the shape of a hippopotamus, and a patron to women in childbirth.
- Tefnut: The goddess of moisture.
- Thoth: The divine scribe and the inventor of writing, associated with the ibis bird and sometimes an ape.
- Wadjet: A cobra goddess representing Lower Egypt.

Although there is no doubt that the Egyptians were *polytheists*—that is, they worshiped many gods, some scholars suggest that there are inklings of the belief in a supreme god to be found among the numerous theological concepts. One of the more interesting religious phenomena in Egypt was the emergence of the god Amun, whose cult was centered at Thebes, especially during the New Kingdom when huge temples were built for him. Amun was considered a great, infinite, and unknowable divine presence, and he came to be perceived as almost a universal god incorporating all of the other gods. This might be as close to monotheism as the Egyptians ever got, although during the curious Amarna period, the worship of the sun-disk Aten was promoted as superior to all other gods.

Many stories about the different gods tied a lot of diverse ideas together. Some of these myths played a significant role in under-standing life and death, and one of the most powerful was that of Osiris and Seth. Osiris was killed by his brother, Seth, the god who personified evil and chaos. After Osiris's body was wrapped as a mummy, he was "resurrected" and served as the king of the Afterlife. Osiris plays an important role in the Egyptians' notions of a life after death, which was very real to them. He was believed to have been buried at Abydos, which was a cult center for his worship.

After killing Osiris, Seth continued his mischief and battled it out with Horus, the son of Osiris. At one point, Seth wounded one of Horus's eyes, but it was restored by the god Thoth. The phases of the moon were thought to replay this drama regularly, with the waning of the moon representing Horus's damaged eye and the waxing moon representing its restoration.

Horus eventually triumphed over Seth, which was a worthy role for the ruling pharaoh, who was thought to be the living incarnation of Horus. After all, it was the ruling pharaoh's job to triumph over chaos, violence, and confusion, and to maintain *maat*. The pharaoh's father then, the previous ruler, was thought to be Osiris.

By the way, when depicted in animal form, the god Seth is a very odd creature, with a long snout, short ears, and a pointy, upright tail. There have many attempts to try to identify this creature with a known animal. The possibility remains that it is purely a mytho-logical creature. To Egyptologists, it is known as "the Seth-animal."

MANSIONS FOR THE GODS

Ancient Egyptians built temples to the various gods all over Egypt, including at the gods' cult centers. A temple was a specific area or building established as a holy space separated from the profane world. There was no single plan for all temples, but many featured courtyards and a series of rooms, with entrance to the smallest restricted to a small number of qualified priests. Inside the restricted area was a shrine, which contained a stone, bronze, gold, or gilded wood image of the god to whom the temple was dedicated. The statue was considered to be a resting place for the god, who could visit or inhabit the image if it so chose and consume the offerings presented to it.

As noted, the pharaoh served as the supreme high priest and intermediary between humans and gods. Making sure that all was in order with the universe was one of the king's primary concerns, and service to the gods was a big part of this responsibility. Among other things, it was thought that attending to the gods was required to ensure that the sun was reborn again each morning and to keep chaos at bay. The pharaoh himself, in theory at least, was supposed to conduct the daily temple rituals. Of course, this was a physical impossibility because there were temples throughout Egypt, so it was necessary to have priests associated with every temple to do the necessary deeds. However, the pharaoh was often symbolically present by means of his statues or by his images on temple walls. He probably did actually participate in some of the more important events or festivals.

There was a hierarchy of priests, and, until the New Kingdom, most seemed to have been part-timers recruited from the upper classes. With the building of huge temple complexes in the New Kingdom, a large number of priests became necessary to attend to everything from cleaning the sacred buildings to making accounts of the temple estates, income, and expenditures.

The priests at the top of the hierarchy performed the necessary rituals three times a day. In the morning, a qualified priest approached the inner sanctum of a given temple and opened the shrine. The priest bathed, clothed, and otherwise prepared and renewed the image of the god and performed rituals to ensure a hospitable home for the god. Finally, the priest was left with a tasty meal.

Is should be noted that Egyptian priests cannot be equated with Christian pastors or Jewish rabbis. They didn't conduct rituals before a body of parishioners, nor did they offer personal counseling. Some types of priests were apparently knowledgeable in healing and magic, however, and were thus able to occasionally assist the needs and desires of individuals.

Two of the biggest and best-preserved temples in ancient Egypt are in modern Luxor, the site of ancient Thebes. Beginning in the Twelfth Dynasty of the Middle Kingdom, religious structures were established at a site known as Karnak. With subsequent rulers repeatedly adding onto the site, especially from the New Kingdom onward, this is now a sprawling complex of structures encompassing over 247 acres and is principally dedicated to the god Amun. The site is an extremely complex mix of pylons, columns, walls with carved reliefs, obelisks, statuary, and even a sacred lake. Apart from Amun, major temples can be found at the site for his wife and son, Mut and Khonsu. The spectacular Luxor Temple is located on the southern end of Thebes and was built primarily by the New Kingdom ruler Amenhotep III and, like Karnak, was augmented by later additions. These two temples were connected by a processional road about 1.5 miles long

Many of the temples in Egypt were probably painted in gleaming white and bright colors, and by modern standards, must have appeared quite gaudy. Most of the coloring has long ago worn away, and the monuments tend to appear a uniform light brown. Traces of paint can still be found on less exposed surfaces, giving us an idea of their once splendorous condition. Some of the temple doors were once sheathed with sheets of copper or gold, and some of the painted decorations were also encrusted with semiprecious stones. Needless to say, those particular features are long gone.

Apart from the temples dedicated to the gods, mortuary temples (also called by Egyptologists " memorial" or "funerary" temples) were dedicated to the memory of the formerly living gods on Earth, the pharaohs. The pharaohs built these monuments in honor of themselves during their lifetimes, and some of these buildings are the most impressive surviving stone structures in Egypt. While relatively small mortuary temples or chapels were built as part of pyramid funerary complexes during the Old and Middle Kingdom, huge and grandiose independent buildings were constructed at Thebes during the New Kingdom to serve the dead rulers who were buried a distance away in a mountain valley. These temples, too, required priests and rituals to maintain the cult of the dead pharaoh centuries after a ruler's death.

There are also instances of temples and religious cults dedicated to the divine ruler even before he died! Rameses II was especially notable in this regard and had numerous giant statues and other monuments to himself created throughout the land. Although such state temples were restricted to the priests, religious rituals could be carried out by ordinary people at the funerary chapels of private individuals.

If average Egyptians were ever able to visit a temple, they probably weren't allowed to see much. The only time that someone might see the image of the god (that was usually hidden away in the innermost restricted part of the temple) was during special festivals but even then, the image was probably concealed in a shrine. There was an annual festival calendar for various gods in various places. Two of the biggest events took place at Thebes. During the Opet festival, the image of the god Amun was carried by priests during a procession between the Karnak and Luxor temples. During the annual Valley Festival, the images of Amun, his wife, Mut, and their son, Khnonsu, were carried to the western side of the Nile river to visit special cult sites, such as the royal mortuary temples.

One of the most unusual festivals was known as the *Heb-sed*, a ritual meant to demonstrate the vitality of the living god-king. Special festival facilities were set up, and, among other activities, the king had to ritually renew his power and demonstrate his physical fitness by sprinting around a track. Traditionally, it is said that the *Heb-sed* occurred during the thirtieth year of a ruler's reign and then perhaps every few years thereafter. A few rulers seemed to have bucked the trend, though, and celebrated theirs on earlier occasions.

As noted, the Egyptians also believed that some animals were associated with, if not actual incarnations of, certain gods. At Memphis, the sacred Apis bull was considered to be a living incarnation of the god Ptah in animal form. The beast bore special markings and was treated quite well. When it died, it was buried in royal splendor, and a search was begun for its divine successor.

Other species of animals were held as sacred, not as gods themselves, but as living representatives of a particular god. Ibises could represent the god Thoth, falcons could symbolize Horus, and so forth, with crocodiles, cats, rams, and other animals filling the bill for other gods. At some cult centers for various gods, a person could essentially sponsor the burial of a representative animal as a kind of votive offering, in hopes of receiving divine goodwill. At Sakkara, extensive subterranean cemeteries have been discovered in the form of catacombs containing literally millions of mummified animals including ibis birds, dogs, and baboons. Most impressive of all are the burials of the Apis bulls in huge underground chambers with each mummified animal interred in a massive stone sarcophagus.

The average Egyptian didn't participate in the big temple rites, but worship could be conducted at small shrines which were sometimes included in homes for private worship. Scarab amulets are one of the most commonly found Egyptian artifacts. The Egyptian name for the beetle and the word for "existence" are very similar, so the two concepts became linked. The scarab beetle lays its egg in dung, which it rolls in a ball from which little beetles eventually emerge into existence.

DEATH IN ANCIENT EGYPT

Mummies and tombs have long been popularly linked to the modern public's conception of ancient Egypt. This isn't surprising, given the technical achievements of burial monuments such as the pyramids or the discovery of remarkable tombs full of exotic objects. And as the remains of ancient people, mummies have a certain kind of macabre appeal.

But before we unravel the mysteries of the mummy, it's necessary to point out again that Egyptians were *not* obsessed with death. They were, instead, obsessed with life and wanted it to continue after the physical death of their mortal body. Furthermore, just because the vast majority of artifacts that we have from this ancient civilization are related to death and religion—temples, mummies, tombs, and so on—this doesn't mean that death and religion were the primary obsessions of the ancient Egyptians. These simply were the things that were built to last, often in stone, or that were situated in dry locations.

The Egyptians believed that the human body was made up of both physical and spiritual components, as follows:

- the physical body itself, with the heart as the center of intellect and emotion;
- the *ka*, or life force;
- the *ba*, very roughly translated as one's soul, often depicted as a bird with a human head;

- the *akh*, roughly translated as the spirit, through which the person could act "effectively" and transform him or herself;
- the shadow;
- the name.

The body was considered to be the earthly home of all these entities. Upon death, preserving the body was a means of providing a home for the spiritual elements, such as the *ka* and the *ba*, which Egyptians believed continued to exist after the body ceased to function. It was important to perpetuate a person's name, too, because it was thought to be the embodiment of the complete person.

The perpetuation of the name of an individual was considered vital to their survival in the afterlife. The Egyptians wanted their names to live, and writing them down in their tomb inscriptions was one way to maintain their survival. Consequently, erasing or destroying a deceased individual's written name was one way of attacking and possibly eradicating that individual.

Let's pretend that you are an ancient Egyptian who has just died. It's time for your spirit to take a trip through the netherworld. It's a bizarre voyage full of intimidating creatures bent on tricking you into making fatal mistakes. Fortunately, there's a handy guidebook available to help you navigate such perils. In the Old Kingdom, magical funerary texts were available in some of the pyramids for the deceased ruler's use. Egyptologists refer to these conceptually difficult inscriptions as, not surprisingly, "Pyramid Texts." In the Middle Kingdom, these kinds of texts became more accessible to the population at large and were sometimes written on wooden coffins ("Coffin Texts"). From the New Kingdom onward, scrolls popularly referred to today as the "Book of the Dead" served as a guide to the navigating the netherworld.

Many copies of the Book of the Dead have survived. Ancient Egyptians could buy or commission these expensive scrolls and even have them personalized with the name or picture of the deceased. Although they address the afterlife, these books were not referred to as Books of the Dead by the ancient Egyptians, but were known as the Book of Coming Forth by Day.

Your soul, having successfully traversed the terrifying obstacles of the netherworld, reaches the judgment hall, where your fate will be determined. The trial to determine your ultimate destiny takes place in front of the god Osiris, who is rightfully seated on a throne. Forty-two judges, or assessors, are in attendance to quiz you on the goodness of your life. You are asked several questions, and you give the so-called Negative Confession, in which you deny having committed wrong, including having murdered, stolen, cheated, caused pain and suffering, and other offenses. A Book of the Dead will prepare you for the ordeal.

After your proclamation of innocence, you come to the moment of truth. The god Anubis places your heart on one pan of a giant scale, and on the other pan Anubis places *maat*, the concept of justice and right behavior, which is represented by a feather. The ibis-headed god Thoth stands by and takes notes.

Your heart and the feather of truth had better balance, or you are doomed! An odd and frightening creature named "Ammut," with the head of a crocodile, the forefront of a lion, and the hindquarters of a hippo, waits to devour you if your heart is heavier than the feather, at which point you would become a nonentity for eternity. If your innocence is confirmed, then you become an *akh*, an "effective spirit," and you will live for eternity.

MAKING MUMMIES

For the *ka* and *ba* to continue after an individual's death, ancient Egyptians needed to preserve the body in a recognizable form in order to sustain a home for its surviving spiritual elements. (The *ba* could leave the body, visit places, and return; the *ka* rarely left the tomb.) There was good reason, then, to keep the body intact.

How did the ancient Egyptians figure out that mummification would preserve their dead? Egyptologists aren't certain, but perhaps it began with the realization that bodies interred in simple graves in the dry, hot desert had a tendency to remain more or less intact, albeit dried out. Attempts to keep the bodies intact by wrapping them and burying them in simple coffins are known from predynastic times. From the later Old Kingdom onward, ancient Egyptians manipulated the body in order to preserve a living semblance so that its spirits might recognize it and find it hospitable. In addition, the mummification process and ritual had the goal of transforming the perishable dead person into a divine being: an "Osiris."

The word *mummy* is derived from the Persian word *mummia*, which refers to bitumen or tar. The use of resins during mummification could give a tar-like appearance to some of the ancient preserved bodies. By the way, the ancient Egyptians weren't the only ones who practiced intentional mummification. It was also performed in some way or another by other ancient cultures on every continent except Antarctica. (The practice continues today, albeit in a temporary way, in the American funeral industry.)

There are no surviving Egyptian texts which explicitly explain the mummification process; the Greek historian Herodotus, however, describes the procedures as it might have been performed in his day. The process, he says, took seventy days. Professional embalmers made a small slit in the abdomen of the deceased, through which they removed all of the internal organs except for the heart. The liver, stomach, intestines, and lungs were retained and were mummified separately. Embalmers also removed the brain by inserting a hook through the nose to mash up the brain before pulling out or draining the residue.

A naturally occurring chemical drying agent, known as *natron*, was used to desiccate the body. Its main components include salt and sodium bicarbonate. An area known as the Wadi Natroun in Egypt's Western Desert is a plentiful source for this substance. The natron was placed in small bags within the body cavity, and then the entire body was covered with natron or perhaps even soaked in a solution of the substance. Afterward, the body was washed out, perhaps with palm wine; aromatic, and perhaps preservative, oils and resins were then applied. The abdominal cavity was packed with different substances, including straw, sawdust, or wads of linen.

The body was then typically wrapped in bandages or swaths of linen. Protective and magical amulets were sometimes mixed in the wrappings. A special scarab-shaped amulet bearing a chapter from the Book of the Dead was occasionally placed over the area of the heart. These heart-scarabs could serve as a substitute in case anything happened to the original, and help to ensure the favorable testimony of the heart at the judgment. Flimsy jewelry suitable for burial purposes has been found on many mummies, although precious ornaments were often buried on the bodies of elite persons. The intact mummy of the New Kingdom ruler Tutankhamun, for example, contained more than 140 amulets in its wrappings, as well as real daggers and incredible pieces of ornate jewelry. The face or whole head of some bodies were covered with a funerary mask that would show the deceased looking good even if his mummified face wasn't.

Specific internal organs that were kept after evisceration were also mummified and routinely placed in four vessels, usually made of stone, known to Egyptologists as *canopic jars*. The lids of the jars usually depicted the heads of the four protective sons of Horus in either their animal or their human forms and held the mummified liver, stomach, intestines, and lungs of the deceased. The canopic jars and their contents—along with the mummy in its coffin—were an important component of the physical burial of the deceased.

The actual procedures of mummification varied through time. There were also different qualities of mummification available depending upon how much one might care to spend. The same was true of coffins, which show a great variety of style and quality. Relatively simple decorated rectangular coffins were common in the Middle Kingdom, and the classic "mummy case" appeared not long afterward, with its shape in the form of a human body complete with painted face and hands. Elite individuals sometimes had multiple coffins, perhaps even gilded, or made almost entirely of gold in the case of some royal burials. Large stone sarcophagi with heavy lids could secure the coffins of the most prestigious of burials.

Some of the most intriguing recent examples of what might be called experimental archaeology have involved mummification research conducted on modern cadavers. In 1994, a team led by American Egyptologist Bob Brier and anatomist Ronald Wade, used ancient tools and procedures to mummify a 76-year-old human male. Most of the entrails were taken out through a small incision in the abdomen, and the brain was removed through the nose. The body was then covered with natron imported from Egypt. The experiment was a great learning exercise and Brier and Wade were successful in producing a modern Egyptian-like mummy. A similar experiment was conducted in the UK in 2011. Alan Billis, a 61-year-old cab driver dying of cancer, generously donated his body, and again, the lessons learned were insightful. Both of these modern mummies likely will survive indefinitely.

TOMBS

The quality of burials also varied considerably through time. The poorest of laborers might be placed in a hole with a few items such as a pot, a knife and other tools, and maybe a comb or other personal items. At the other extreme, the pyramids and other royal burial structures took years to build and involved a tremendous number of resources. In between the two extremes are simple one-room tombs carved into rock, just big enough to hold a coffin or two and a few items. High-ranking officials had more elaborate settings with chapels bearing decorated walls.

Most sophisticated tombs consisted of two parts: the actual subterranean burial site and a place above the burial site where offerings could be placed to sustain the *ka* of the deceased. In its simple versions, a wooden or stone tablet (a *stela*), might note the location of the burial, where plates of food could be left during festivals, or whenever desired. More deluxe were superstructures with small chapels and, if affordable, a professional priest who could regularly make the offerings. On the largest of all scales were the New Kingdom royal mortuary temples, built apart from the actual secluded burials and requiring a permanent staff dedicated to the cult of the deceased ruler.

The burials included items, many of them symbolic, that were intended to help the *ka* pursue a happy afterlife. Funerary texts on tablets or decorated on the walls of expensive tombs represented offerings to the deceased. A typical text described the presentation to the deceased of large quantities of bread and beer, meat, fowl, linen, alabaster, and other items. Painted scenes of daily life and work, nice meals, and good times were not unusual.

As a life force, it was thought that the *ka* required at least some sort of food, so, apart from offerings in writing or decoration, actual quantities of food were often placed in the tombs. A number of examples have survived, including prime cuts of preserved beef, and birds such as ducks, which were themselves mummified and wrapped. Wine, oils, linen, clothing, and sometimes furniture have been found in some of the more expensive burials. When it came to royal burials, it wasn't unusual to include chariots, gilded furniture, and chests full of expensive clothing.

To assist the deceased in the afterlife, many burials included artificial servants, typically miniature figures of workers or offering bearers, or even little dioramas of workers doing their jobs at work. The most popular version of this idea was the *shabti* (also referred to as "ushabti" or "shawabti".) *Shabtis* were little images usually made of wood, stone, or faience that were placed in the tomb to do the bidding of the deceased and to report for duty when the deceased was called to do work in the afterlife. Some tombs included a *shabti* for every day of the year or more and some of them were little specialists who were experts in different tasks.

Egyptian funerals were loaded with rituals. A procession including a priest, family members, and other mourners carried the coffined mummy to the tomb, where the coffin was stood on end. Some of these mourners may have been professional wailers who could guarantee ample grief for the occasion. Very esoteric ceremonies then took place, including the "Opening of the Mouth" ritual, which was intended to animate the mummy of the deceased. Offerings were given, and a banquet was held. The mummy was then placed into its appropriately provisioned tomb and the door closed (hopefully, but rarely, for good).

The practice of burying the dead with the things of this life proved to be quite a temptation for those who had little respect for the deceased. Of the innumerable ancient tombs in Egypt, relatively few have survived intact. In the case of the richly furnished royal tombs in the Valley of the Kings, none completely escaped the attention of tomb robbers, even that of Tutankhamun, as we shall see.

Sadly, in places where small tombs were located quite close to each other, the robbers' work could sometimes be made easier by busting through the wall of one tomb into the one next door. Some archaeologists have been surprised to find that what appeared to be intact doorways leading to unviolated tombs had been robbed through adjacent chambers.

The tomb robbers were particularly interested in finding materials that could either be sold or used without their original source being known, or materials that could be recycled and thus made anonymous. In the first case, materials such as linen, oils, and perfume were actively sought by thieves. For recycling, gold or other precious metals could be melted down, and expensive woods and ivory could be recarved. To the tomb robber, few things were sacred. In most cases, they seemed to have no qualms about tearing through a wrapped royal mummy to remove jewelry or other valuable items.

Tomb robbery was definitely a problem in ancient Egypt, and, amazingly, a few old records have survived to prove it. The Leopold II–Amherst Papyrus, dating to the late New Kingdom, contains the transcripts of interrogations and even confessions of ancient tomb robbers. Some of the accused were beaten, and those found guilty no doubt suffered an unpleasant death, sometimes apparently by impalement. Interestingly, ancient graffiti has been found near the tombs, written by officials inspecting their security. Obviously it was not enough.

WHERE DID THEY ALL GO?

Considering that intentional mummification was practiced in Egypt for more than 2,000 years, it's possible that over that time, hundreds of thousands, if not millions, of human mummies were created and buried. They are still plentiful in Egypt today, but their numbers have decreased considerably.

In approximately the twelfth century AD, ground ancient mummies became a hot commodity in Europe, where the substance was used as medicine to treat a variety of conditions. Many pharmacies carried "mummy" as a regular product, and the demand was filled in Egypt by pulling ancient bodies out of their graves. Apparently the demand was so great that some unscrupulous individuals even engaged in making their own mummies from recently dead individuals and pawning them off as the ancient real thing. Mummies have been exported for other purposes, too. A nineteenth-century American paper manufacturer attempted to make paper out of old linen mummy wrappings, and a huge quantity of cat mummies was shipped to Britain for use as fertilizer.

Many mummies were collected as souvenirs, especially in the nineteenth century, and they ended up in Europe and North America. Some of the stinkier ones were thrown away, but lots survive in museums around the world. As entertainment for the curious—but often called educational exercises—mummies were sometimes unwrapped in public. Although some of this was cheap showmanship, much was learned, and several scholars looked upon the study of mummies as serious research.

Modern research has shown that we can learn much about the ancient Egyptians from their mummies. More sophisticated techniques, such as x-rays and CAT scans, are far less intrusive then the old methods of dissection. These images can help reveal such things as the age, health and cause of death of a particular individual. A number of DNA studies have been conducted, most notably with royal mummies from the New Kingdom, especially with hopes of finding family ties. Skeptics, however, will argue that it is very difficult to extract viable samples from such old and processed specimens, although improving analytical techniques will now likely improve that situation.

The ancient Egyptians would no doubt be appalled if they knew that they were being pulled out of their tombs and poked, prodded, and put on display. But if modern science, through its research, has taught us the importance of preserving the receptacles of those ancient spirits and, especially, perpetuating their names, then the Egyptian deceased should be confident of their ultimate survival.

3

ANCIENT EGYPT

THE EARLIER YEARS

For eons, humans lived a relatively simple lifestyle, gathering the available resources of the land and hunting and fishing. And then, around 10,000 years ago, something extraordinary happened. In several places around the world, some of these groups of people began to settle down, live in villages, and tend crops and animals. This idea caught on and spread far and wide. Then, in a just a few places, beginning around 5,000 years ago or so, some societies that were significantly more culturally complex began to emerge from this agricultural foundation. Egypt was one of them, and the explanations for these changes continue to challenge archaeologists.

PREHISTORIC HISTORY

Archaeologists and Egyptologists have specific uses for the words *prehistory* and *history*. *Prehistory* generally refers to the time before written records, and *historical* times are those when such records are available. In Egypt, for example, writing appears around 3100 BC, and the time before that is considered prehistory in Egypt. Archaeologists who deal in such preliterate time periods are often called *prehistorians*.

Without the luxury of texts, prehistorians must scrutinize a wide spectrum of physical evidence. Their techniques are often meticulous in their attempt to squeeze the most data out of whatever they might uncover. Prehistorians tend to be multidisciplinary and are interested not only in stone tools and other surviving artifacts, but also in reconstructing the total physical and cultural environment in which ancient humans lived, to the extent that it is possible. Ask them to read some hieroglyphs, and many wouldn't know where to start. But give them a trowel and turn them loose, and they'll come up with information that won't appear in any ancient inscription. Although perhaps their areas of interest don't have the glamorous appeal of pyramids and golden mummies, their work is essential for understanding the thousands of years that led to the development of the classic Egyptian civilization. In other words, pyramids didn't just appear overnight.

PALEOLITHIC

The current scientific consensus is that humans originated in Africa and spread out from there. The remains of *Homo erectus* have been found in East Africa and Israel, suggesting that these early humans migrated from Africa, through Egypt, and into Europe and Asia perhaps 1.8 million years ago. Although skeletal remains of this human ancestor haven't been found in Egypt, numerous examples of very ancient stone tools have been found there, suggesting that parts of Egypt were inhabited by people perhaps 300,000–400,000 years ago and probably much earlier. Thus far, the oldest human skeleton discovered in ancient Egypt is a 55,000-year-old child, found in a burial at Dendera in Upper Egypt.

Archaeologists refer to these early days of humanity as the *Paleolithic*, or "the Old Stone Age," a time period characterized by the use of stone tool technology and a lifestyle based on hunting, gathering, and sometimes fishing. Don't let the name of the time period confuse you—people during that time probably had a variety of different products made from different materials, not just stone. The stone items, though, are what typically survive from such a distant past and thus must serve as the basis for a good deal of archaeological research and interpretation.

One way to examine the social structures of the past is to compare them to those of similar peoples today. The few surviving hunter-gatherer groups observed in recent times tend to be organized into small groups, and they more or less live within the natural carrying capacity of the land. They seem to be generally egalitarian, sharing their resources among their group. Hunter-gatherers tend to move around a lot, taking advantage of food and other resources during different seasons of the year. As a result, they tend not to have permanent buildings or large possessions that they would have to lug around with them. Some of the exceptions include caves which have provided shelter for eons as well as a wealth of data for the archaeologists who excavate them.

A popular image of Paleolithic times is that of a harsh existence with people regularly on the edge of starvation and a high mortality rate. Studies of recent hunters and gatherers, however, suggest that these people had a relatively content existence, with lots of leisure time. On the other hand, studies of the remains of early people suggest that they didn't live very long. Hunting wild animals can be dangerous and injuries which today would be considered unproblematic could result in infection and death.

Do keep this in mind: the environment in Egypt has experienced substantial climatic changes. In much of prehistoric times, wide portions of the Western Desert, for example, were very habitable. There were savanna-like grasslands and lakes of various sizes. Animals more reminiscent of modern southeast Africa roamed the region where today there is little more than sand. Ancient rock art found in now-arid locations can attest to this.

Just a thought, but maybe at our core we are still hunters and gatherers, and these primal instincts manifest themselves in modern society by a fascination with the unknown and the seeking of lost information—archaeologists and Egyptologists, for instance.

NEOLITHIC

As noted, humans hunted and gathered on Earth from their earliest days, until something dramatic and still somewhat unexplained occurred about 10,000 years ago. At that time, a major shift in lifestyle occurred. In just a few places at first, people started settling down, raising crops, keeping animals, and constructing permanent buildings and villages. One thing led to another. People needed to harvest, store and process grain so different kinds of tools and pottery were developed. The food surplus created by domestication and agriculture meant that more people could live together in much larger groups. This revolutionary new way of living is often referred to as the *Neolithic*, or New Stone Age, and is sometimes called the "Neolithic Revolution." This change in lifestyle had profound effects.

The earliest-known evidence for this Neolithic phenomenon comes from the Near East, in the area around modern Iraq. From there the notion of agriculture apparently gradually spread to neighboring areas. In Egypt, it appears around 8,000 years ago, and emmer wheat and barley were the crops of choice.

Plants are considered to be domesticated when they are altered in some way that makes them more useful to humans. It can involve something as simple as pulling weeds from a favorite stand of wild wheat or as complicated as organized agriculture involving the selective breeding of crops. Many domesticated plants are distinguished from their wild brethren by attributes that, while making them useful to a hungry human, make it difficult for them to survive on their own in the wild. For example, humans prefer that the seeds of wheat stay on the plant, where they can be removed at will, rather than having them disperse with the wind as nature would require in the wild. Through domestication, some plants became completely dependent upon humans for their existence, and vice versa.

A number of animals were also domesticated during the Neolithic. For example, the wild equivalent of that modern, peaceful, slow-moving, domesticated cow in the field can be very aggressive and dangerous. To make cattle more useful to humans, a process took place that probably involved the capture and breeding of the slow, fat ones to the point where a cow gives milk, provides meat, and is well behaved, if not trustworthy. This process took place in the Near East with goats, sheep, dogs, pigs, and several other popular beasts. (As for domestic cats, it still remains a mystery who controls whom.) Although we tend to look at an animals or plants as being domesticated or undomesticated, it's not that black or white. Domestication is not a single event, but a process that takes place over time.

One might be tempted to conclude that the farming life sounds quite good compared to a hunting and gathering lifestyle, but some theorists consider the Neolithic to be the downfall of the human species. Archaeologists have found ample evidence that disputes and fighting become commonplace with growing populations living closely together in permanent settlements and accumulating private possessions and differing levels of power and wealth. The assumed egalitarian existence of hunters and gatherers is transformed as chiefs or leaders with more power and/or wealth than others emerge. Furthermore, we find that humans begin to alter and transform the natural environment in radical ways that are not necessarily "as nature intended."

A number of ideas exist about why the Neolithic revolution occurred, but there is not yet any firm consensus. Could it have been an intentional invention encouraged by the radically changing environments after the Ice Age about 12,000 years ago? Some prehistorians suggest that it could be the result of pressures from expanding populations. A rather fun (and sometimes seriously presented) theory is that the desire to produce beer was the incentive. For whatever reason, the "revolution" happened, and from that Neolithic foundation, great ancient civilizations arose in several places in the world, beginning around 5,000 years ago.

After the end of the Ice Age, deserts began replacing grassland in Egypt, perhaps leading to the concentration of people in the Nile Valley and Delta regions. And then, perhaps around 6000 BC, domesticated wheat and barley, along with goats and sheep, were likely introduced into Egypt from the area of Syria-Palestine to the northeast, where they had already been in use about 2,000 years previously. Cattle, however, seem to have been a mainstay of a prehistoric culture in the Western Desert and were likely domesticated in Egypt or elsewhere in Africa earlier on to become a particularly valuable resource.

Some of the earliest evidence of Egyptian agriculture has been found in the Fayyum region, which had a far more lush environment in the past than it does today. There, stone sickle blades and grinding stones along with silos and other agricultural artifacts suggest that people in that area led a farming lifestyle but also hunted and fished. Archaeologists working there have not only found the scattered remains of stone tools, but also the bones of ancient creatures, including fish, lying out in the middle of the desert. Environmental changes over the millennia have left them "stranded" in now inhospitable surroundings.

PREDYNASTIC TIMES

In Egypt, the Neolithic time period leading up to the time of civilization or cultural complexity is generally referred to as the Predynastic period, beginning about 6,500 years ago. As I've already mentioned, the lack of written documents tends to make the study of this period quite different from what one finds later during literate dynastic times. Prehistorians have been busy at work on the subject for perhaps a hundred years now. Many sites have been examined, and a cultural chronology of sorts has been devised, based on artifacts found in graves and ancient settlements. Actually, it's more like two parallel chronologies, one for Upper Egypt and one for Lower Egypt. Because we don't have texts from this time and don't know what the earlier people in Egypt called themselves, prehistorians have named the various cultures that they encounter after the sites where they are first or best represented.

In Upper Egypt, these Predynastic cultural phases are organized as follows:

- Badarian (*c.* 4400–4000 BCBC);
- Naqada I (*c.* 4000–3500 BC);
- Naqada II (*c.* 3500–3200 BC);
- Naqada III, which is also known as the Protohistoric Period or "Dynasty 0" (*c.* 3200–3000 BC).

Most of the Predynastic period in the Delta is perhaps best represented by what's called the Maadi Cultural Complex (*c.* 4000–3200 BC).

Given the difference in archaeological preservation and degree of exploration, the sequences from Upper Egypt have been based more on cemetery sites than on the settlement sites in the Delta. But even in the cemeteries of Lower Egypt, a difference between the two lands can readily be seen. In both Upper and Lower Egypt, we find that technology became more sophisticated over time. Trade may have played a role in the development of the two lands, and the delta region was well situated for the import of foreign goods and culture, especially from the east. The Upper Egyptian Naqada II culture is especially noteworthy, with major sites in the Nile valley at Naqada, Hierakonpolis, and Abydos. Their pots were sometimes painted with geometrical and representational designs and often depict boats, the latter leading some prehistorians to conclude that travel and commerce were important, certainly along the Nile, if not beyond. The components of Naqada II culture began making their way into the delta, and, by the time of Naqada III, the Upper Egyptian culture had spread over all of Egypt.

The prehistorians who work on these earliest periods are some of the unsung heroes in the exploration of ancient Egypt. Gertrude Caton-Thompson (1888–1985), for example, was a British archaeologist and explorer who spent many years working in Egypt. Her special area of interest was prehistoric times, conducting notable work in such places as the Fayyum and the Kharga oasis. And during the 1960s, when the lake created behind the new Aswan Dam in southern Egypt was rising, archaeologists raced to save not only pharaonic temples, but also the prehistoric remains from Egypt's earliest human past.

"CIVILIZATION"

Before turning to the specifics of Egypt, it's time once again to address another vital notion: What is a civilization? The word has its origins in the Latin word *civitas*, which means "city" and implies a densely populated and organized living center. What we mean by a "civilization," however, requires much more than an extra-large village or a city. Many scholars today prefer the term *complex society* to *civilization*—even then, it is much easier to describe than it is to define.

A complex society tends to have a tiered social, political, and religious system, that is, kings, bureaucrats, priests, merchants, slaves, peasants, generals, soldiers, and so forth. Plus, it has a lot of artisans and occupational specialists. Contrast that to the hunters and gatherers and perhaps even many of the early agricultural societies, in which people could probably do each other's jobs without much training.

Complex societies tend to build large religious or political structures, such as temples and palaces, and most have some sort of writing system. All of these signs of a complex society are evidenced in the things that archaeologists dig up. In an ancient city, one can expect to find the sophisticated homes of the wealthy and the decrepit little shacks of the poor. Burials, likewise, tend to show a difference in wealth, and you might find many kinds of workshops belonging to a variety of crafts specialists. The grave goods of various Naqada II burials, for example, vary in terms of quantity, variety, and quality, thus demonstrating an increase in craft diversity and the power and status of individuals.

Temples, elaborate tombs, and palaces speak for themselves, especially if there is writing on the walls, and this is exactly what is found in Egypt. Just as the change to agriculture is of great interest to archaeologists, the origins of civilization, or complex societies, pose another huge problem for scholars to solve.

Complex societies didn't develop everywhere, and the timing of those that did is interesting. Besides Egypt, other early complex societies emerged in Mesopotamia, the Indus Valley, China, Mesoamerica, and Peru.

A number of theories attempt to explain it. One of the most prominent ideas is that the practice of organized irrigation might stimulate the creation of cultural complexity by the need for decision-makers and a variety of different jobs. Writing might develop for record-keeping and communication, and differences in wealth might arise as some irrigated lands flourished more than others.

Others have suggested that population growth inspired cultural complexity because of the need to deal with the requirements of organizing more people. But could not the contrary be argued as well, that complex cultures might provide conditions conducive to population growth? Another interesting theory involves warfare and population. As populations increase and resources become limited, a group might choose to conquer its neighbor. In doing so, status and wealth differences are created between the two, and the characteristics of complex societies develop as a result. Still other ideas suggest climate change as playing a significant role.

In short, we don't really know how the ancient civilizations came about. In some cases, they seem to appear almost instantaneously, a phenomenon that has given rise to all manner of exotic explanations. One scholar, G. Elliot Smith, was impressed by similarities in ancient civilizations in diverse corners of the world and advocated a single origin for all civilizations: Egypt. And from there it all spread, far and wide. Others have even called upon visitors from outer space. We'll deal with some of that silliness in a later chapter.

It is possible, too, that certain elements of early Egyptian civilization might have been introduced from elsewhere. For example, certain things characteristic of Mesopotamian culture, including architectural features and some artistic motifs, are present in Egypt during the crucial time period. Some have even suggested specifically that the Sumerians, an early Mesopotamian civilization, might have been involved, perhaps even inspiring the hieroglyphic writing system. If it's not direct evidence of cultural influence, it's probably at least evidence of trade.

There are many unresolved problems. Although in some instances it looks as if civilizations instantly appear, we shouldn't forget that one inch of dirt separating a buried Neolithic village from a city built on top might represent a couple hundred years of change and development. We should likewise remember that certain important things, such as the unwritten exchange of ideas between people, do not leave direct traces for the archaeologist to examine.

UNIFYING THE TWO LANDS

Both the ancient Egyptian lists of kings and Manetho, the Egyptian historian previously mentioned, attribute the origins of ancient Egyptian civilization to the unification of Upper and Lower Egypt. The first king of the First Dynasty, and presumably the unifier, is noted as Meni or Menes. What sort of evidence is there of this being truly the case? We've already seen that this notion of the Two Lands played a very symbolic role in kingship and culture, and, given the eventual dominance of the Predynastic Naqada II culture, the suggestions seem to be that the south overwhelmed the north culturally, if not militarily. This is a tempting conclusion, but the fact remains that it is very difficult to come to definitive conclusions for the very beginning of Egyptian "history."

Whatever the ephemeral details of the actual unification of Upper and Lower Egypt might be, the result of the process would have amazing cultural consequences over the next 3,000 years. The combination of a ruler with command over Egypt's many resources, along with an industrious and talented people, produced a civilization like no other. Within a few hundred years of unification, the Egyptians would go from building structures of mud brick to constructing massive stone pyramids that to this day astound and impress.

It is quite likely that this fellow named Menes, who is said to have unified the Two Lands, and established the capital of Memphis at their junction, was not the first to rule Egypt. There is evidence of rulers that might predate the unification, including one known as Scorpion. Egyptologists have placed these kings in a protodynastic period that is often referred to as Dynasty O.

At the Upper Egyptian site of Hierakonpolis, a cache of objects bearing their names was excavated in the late nineteenth century. One of these artifacts is a ceremonial stone mace head depicting an individual wearing the crown of Upper Egypt, holding a large hoe, and perhaps carrying out some sort of agricultural ceremony. A glyph of a scorpion near his head seems to indicate his name, Scorpion. Behind him are poles with dead lapwing birds hanging from them, which some interpret as representing conquered peoples. Some scholars think that this might depict a conquering Upper Egyptian ruler just before the unification of the Two Lands.

One of the most intriguing artifacts from ancient Egypt is also from Hierakonpolis and likewise relates to this controversial time period. It is a decorated commemorative stone made of green slate and is called the Narmer Palette (Figure 3.1). On one side, an individual named Narmer is depicted wearing the white crown of Upper Egypt and smiting an enemy. On the other side, he is shown wearing the red crown of Lower Egypt. There is a lot of violent imagery suggesting that Narmer is victorious and rules both lands. Many Egyptologists have argued that the Narmer Palette commemorates the actual event of the unification. Narmer, then, might be the legendary Menes. Lacking an ancient written explanation, however, the palette has been subject to other interpretations including the possibility that the vanquished are foreign enemies. The interpretation of art, of course, can be a tricky thing. It's important to try to understand the intent of a given object as manufactured by its maker and also attempt to suspend personal biases. In many cases, the best that can be done is a well-argued guess.

It's important to note that in Dynasty 0, the names of rulers begin to appear drawn or carved in what is called a *serekh*, which resembles a rectangular palace façade. This sort of frame was

Figure 3.1 One side of the Narmer Palette depicting Narmer wearing the red crown of Lower Egypt

typically surmounted by a falcon, probably representing the god Horus with whom Egyptian rulers would be divinely identified. This trend continued, with few exceptions, well into Dynasty 3. Whatever role Scorpion and Narmer might have played, the unification of Upper and Lower Egypt seems to be confirmed under an early king of Dynasty 1, a fellow with the royal name of Hor-Aha. Hor-Aha can be translated as Fighting Hawk, and, interestingly, his second royal name was Men, thus dragging him into the Menes debate.

Except for funerary monuments, there aren't a great deal of sites that have been explored for Dynasties 0 through 2. Some of the earliest remains of these crucial time periods are buried deep below the debris of later settlements, have long been destroyed by the deteriorating effects of Nile flooding, or are otherwise inaccessible or poorly preserved. However, the royal grave sites and a few impressive burials of important officials can provide us with some insights.

The typically rectangular brick tombs of the early dynasties are usually referred to as *mastabas*, the Arabic word for "bench," referring to their rectangular shape. Later in the Old Kingdom, such mastabas were built of stone and served primarily as burials for royal family members and important officials. Large numbers of these sorts of tombs can be found in the vicinity of such royal cemeteries as those at Sakkara and Giza.

The royal cemetery for the earliest dynasties was at the sacred site of Abydos in Upper Egypt. These burials typically consist of brick-lined chambers, and some seemed to have been quite well equipped with food and other supplies for the afterlife. When excavating these graves, archaeologists were surprised to find dozens and occasionally hundreds of related subsidiary burials. Most of the remains therein were found to be that of young men. It is possible that these were human sacrifices, perhaps servants or retainers who were killed to accompany the ruler in the afterlife. Fortunately, this practice seems to have been exclusive to the First Dynasty.

German archaeologists working at Abydos have excavated an interesting tomb to which they have given the name U-j. It dates to around the time of Dynasty 0, and although it was well robbed in antiquity, surviving labels from some of the burial goods give us some of the earliest examples of what might be considered writing from ancient Egypt. The grave also contained a large number of ceramic jars imported from Palestine.

Throughout the Early Dynastic Period (Dynasties 1 and 2), the development of a distinct, centralized Egyptian society and state continued. If the data about the First Dynasty is fairly elusive, that about the Second Dynasty is even more so. We know the names of several kings, each following the practice of presenting their names in a serekh. But near the end of the dynasty, we have a bizarre permutation of that tradition: a ruler by the name of Peribsen displayed his name not with Horus, but with the Seth-animal. Seth, you might recall, was the devious twin brother, or uncle in some versions, of Horus. Egyptologists have speculated that there was likely some sort of political upset at this time. Whatever it might have been, it seems to have been resolved by his successor, Khasekhemwy, whose serekh is surmounted by both Seth and Horus. These kinds of situations beg for interpretation, but the evidence is limited. And we don't see Seth alone on a serekh again.

Like most of his predecessors, Khasekhemwy was buried at Abydos. His tomb featured a huge number of storerooms full of grave goods. More importantly, it is perhaps the earliest large-scale construction utilizing stone, a trend that was taken to extreme proportions in the years that followed. It should also be noted that some of the most important royal officials and family members (most of whom were no doubt one and the same) had truly impressive tombs at Sakkara, the necropolis adjacent to the capital at Memphis. This gives some serious hints of a growing bureaucracy and the nature of the distribution of power.

THE OLD KINGDOM

With the Third Dynasty, we have the onset of what is called the Old Kingdom. As mentioned in Chapter 2, this somewhat artificial chronological structure portrays periods classified as kingdoms to be times of political unity, economic wealth, and cultural sophistication. This seems to be a very appropriate description for most of the Old Kingdom (c. 2686–2125 BC) comprising Dynasties 3 through 6. In this arrangement of time, we cannot necessarily argue for a clear break between the earliest dynasties and those of the Old Kingdom, with the latter being a development of the former. Some real architectural changes, however, can be seen in the Third Dynasty.

Not much is known about the first ruler of the Third Dynasty, Sanakhte, but his successor is one of the most famous and impressive individuals in Egyptian history. His name is Netjerikhet, also known as Djoser. It is during the reign of Djoser that we see some major indications of the growing power and elaboration of Egyptian society. Djoser built for himself an incredible funerary complex at Sakkara on an architectural and artistic scale hitherto unknown. Rather than constructing a mud-brick mastaba as had been previously common, Djoser built his tomb out of stone—stone bricks and blocks.

This massive tomb experienced design changes in the process of its construction and the end result was essentially six mastabas stacked one atop the other, forming a step-pyramid 197 ft tall over subterranean burial passages. The interior of the pyramid itself is an incredibly confusing mix of tunnels and chambers. The associated funerary complex is perhaps even more impressive and uses stone to imitate palatial architectural elements of wood and other perishable materials, preserving them in perpetuity like an eternal Memphis. The complex also contains an artificial Heb-Sed court along with shrines and other dummy features in stone. The surrounding enclosure walls measure about 850 by 1700 feet.

Credit for these provocative innovations is given to Djoser's architect, Imhotep, who was also a high-ranking official and a priest of Heliopolis, a religious center for the worship of the sun not far north of Memphis. Such was his reputation that he was deified in later ages and was revered as a great sage and physician. He likely has a tomb at Sakkara but despite attempts to locate it, it has yet to be discovered. Very little was known of Djoser's successor, Sekhemkhet, until the discovery of his unfinished pyramid (you can see more specifics of this intriguing find in Chapter 6).

During the Egyptian Fourth Dynasty, there was an intense spurt of monumental building in Egypt, unsurpassed anywhere else in the world at that time. The new dynasty was led by a ruler named Snefru. He was quite active and an early king-list brags about an expedition to Nubia which returned with 7,000 captives and 200,000 head of cattle during his reign. Other ventures engaged in peaceful trade to retrieve wood and other commodities from Syria-Palestine. Building on the experience of the possibly failed Meydum project described below, Snefru created the first true pyramid, setting a vigorous trend for others to follow. He built two large pyramids in an area south of Memphis called Dahshur.

The ultimate immense power, organization, and control of the Old Kingdom state are represented in Snefru's son and successor, Khufu (Cheops in Greek), who built what is known to the world as the Great Pyramid at the site of Giza, a limestone plateau just north of Memphis. Herodotus describes Cheops as a mean and ruthless ruler, although Egyptologists have found little evidence substantiating such a claim. Perhaps he was under the impression that the only way such a massive structure as the Great Pyramid could have been built would have been under intense duress. Despite the lasting fame of Khufu, the only known sculpture of this great ruler is a small ivory carving less than 3 inches tall that bears his name. It was found by Petrie at Abydos in 1903 and is exhibited in the Egyptian Museum in Cairo.

Khufu's son, Djedefra, had a short reign of about eight years. He started to build a pyramid at a site named Abu Rawash, but the monument was never finished. Interestingly, Djedefra was the first since the Second Dynasty (which included a king Nebra or Raneb) to incorporate the name of the sun god, Ra, into his name. He was also the first to use the title Son of the Sun, which became a regular component of Egyptian royal titles.

Another son of Khufu, Khafra (Chephren in Greek), exercised his might by building a pyramid at Giza nearly as large as that of his father. Along with this was an impressive funerary complex that included the famous mammoth sculpture known as the Great Sphinx, with the body of a lion and the head of a pharaoh. After Khafra, the pyramids began to decline in size. His successor, Menkaura (Mycerinus in Greek), built a much smaller pyramid on the Giza plateau. The ruler that followed, Shepsekaf, chose to be buried in a mastaba.

PYRAMIDS

While on the topic of pyramids, an elaboration on the subject is justified here, especially given that for many modern people, the pyramids of Egypt are perhaps the most readily identifiable symbols of that ancient civilization. They have been looked upon with awe for thousands of years, and they continue to command a good deal of attention even now.

Overall, there are more than 100 known pyramid structures—of various sizes and designs—from ancient Egypt. Let's take a closer look at the pyramid phenomenon during the Old Kingdom, including the building of the Great Pyramid, the Sphinx, and some other less famous but equally-as-interesting monuments to the dead. We'll also begin to consider just how the ancient Egyptians actually managed to build these massive structures. (I'll be considering, here, only the explanations accepted by Egyptologists; alternative viewpoints regarding the pyramids will be noted in Chapter 6.)

As already noted, the pyramids of Egypt were built to hold the remains of the rulers of Egypt, who were considered to be living gods on Earth. The pyramidal shape itself is quite important. Some scholars argue that it represents, in stone, a version of the primeval mound or hill found in the old Egyptian creation stories. Perhaps it was inspired by the natural cycle of the Nile; as the Nile receded every year after the inundation, mounds of fertile earth would appear. As such, it represents regeneration and resurrection. The pyramids also rise to a point aiming at the heavens, where the ruler's soul will take its place among the immortal stars. Pyramids were given names. Those at Giza were "Horizon of Khufu," "Khafra is Great," and "Menkaura is Divine." The Greek name for Egypt's Old Kingdom capital, Memphis, is derived from the name of the pyramid of Pepi I (Men-nefer), which means "the beautiful establishment."

As previously mentioned, many of the early dynastic graves were rectangular mastabas made primarily of brick. During the Third Dynasty, the innovations of Djoser and his architect Imhotep resulted in the amazing step-pyramid at Sakkara. The Fourth Dynasty ruler Snefru is given the credit for building the first true pyramid with a square base and four triangular sides, but dating just before this is a very odd pyramid at the site of Meydum near the Fayyum. Many Egyptologists think that it was built by Snefru's predecessor, Huni, and was probably finished by Snefru. It is quite an extraordinary sight today. Its sloping sides have disappeared revealing a blocky inner core. Many Egyptologists believe that the pyramid's faces experienced a catastrophic collapse due to a weak foundation. Others argue that the sides were massively quarried for use in other building projects.

We do know that Snefru built two pyramids of his own at Dahshur, south of Memphis. His so-called Bent Pyramid takes on a less steep angle of ascent about two-thirds of the way up. Not surprisingly, there are various explanations for the change in shape, including an engineering miscalculation or modifications made in the aftermath of the disaster at the Meydum pyramid. Whatever the reason for the bend in the Bent Pyramid, Snefru got things right with his other Dahshur construction, the Red Pyramid.

A standard plan for pyramids developed that included several components. An orientation toward the cardinal directions was typical and would allow the eastern side to face the rising sun. On the inside of the pyramid was a burial chamber, of course, and on the outside were two temples. A "mortuary temple" stood next to the pyramid itself, and a "valley temple" was located some distance away. The mortuary and valley temples were connected by a causeway which would have facilitated burial ceremonies. The mortuary temple would serve as a venue for offerings in perpetuity. The pyramid itself was often surrounded by a walled enclosure.

THE GREAT PYRAMID

The Great Pyramid of Khufu at Giza is rightly celebrated for its sheer size and architectural sophistication. Some are surprised that such a monument appears so early on in the 3,000-year course of Egyptian civilization: a singular monumental construction never to be surpassed in subsequent generations. It is a product of a well-organized and resource-rich Old Kingdom under a ruler with sufficient power and status to pull off such an incredible accomplishment. Let's take a look at some of the specifications:

- *Base dimensions*: Originally 754 feet on each side, now 745 feet due to quarrying of outer facing stones. Approximately 13 square acres and oriented to the four cardinal directions.
- *Height*: Originally 481 feet tall, now 449 feet due to quarrying of summit blocks.

- *Angle*: A little over 51 degrees.
- *Amount of stone*: Perhaps more than 2.3 million blocks of stone, mostly limestone but also some immense granite blocks used in such interior features as the burial chamber.
- *Estimated time needed for construction*: There are many estimates but perhaps between 20 and 25 years.

Associated with the Great Pyramid are three subsidiary "queens' pyramids" located on its east side, and numerous mastabas and shaft tombs belonging to relatives and officials.

The size of the Great Pyramid is indeed imposing, but don't forget that there are very impressive structures within (Figure 3.2).

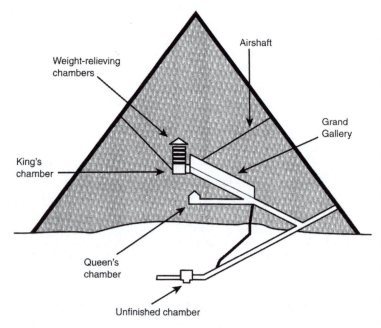

Figure 3.2 A cross-section of the Great Pyramid of Khufu at Giza showing its inner chambers

Source: After I.E.S. Edwards, *The Pyramids of Egypt*, London: Penguin, 1986.

An entrance on the north side leads to what is called the Ascending Passage, which is a tall vaulted corridor that ultimately leads up to the so-called King's Chamber containing a granite sarcophagus. The King's Chamber is walled and roofed with immense granite slabs, and a series of relieving chambers were constructed above the chamber to take some of the weight off the room below. Lower down is a smaller chamber referred to as the Queen's Chamber. And elsewhere, a small, steep passageway leads to a large unfinished room carved into the very bedrock. Overall, it's a sophisticated design, and the exact functions of its various features are still debated among Egyptologists.

There are some people who have questioned the identity of the builder of the Great Pyramid because Khufu's name does not appear formally carved anywhere within the huge structure. Ancient workmen's graffiti on some stone blocks such as those in the pyramid's relieving chambers, however, clearly indicate that they were working for their boss, Khufu, and his name appears on blocks from the causeway belonging to his complex.

Looking at the neighboring pyramid of Khafra, it almost appears bigger than that of Khufu and, in size, comes pretty close. Khafra, however, built his pyramid on slightly higher ground than his father, thus giving the impression of greater height. The internal structure of Khafra's pyramid is not nearly as elaborate, but it was accompanied by a truly magnificent valley temple, which apparently held many fine sculptures of the ruler. Khafra's pyramid is especially interesting today because it still retains a good bit of its original limestone casing near its top. When intact, the white limestone exterior of this and many other pyramids must have been gleaming and spectacular.

The Italian explorer, Giovanni Belzoni, was the first to enter Khafra's pyramid in recent times (1818). In doing so, he wanted to be sure that he would be the one to receive the credit for this achievement, so he painted his name and the date in large black letters on the wall of its burial chamber, where they can be seen today. As usual, he found the sarcophagus empty of its intended occupant. Curiously, he did find some bones of a bull in the sarcophagus, likely from its reuse by an animal cult long after the pyramid had been breached and robbed.

Some skeptics like to point out that an intact pyramid burial has never been uncovered. Empty pyramids and sarcophagi, they insist, suggest that maybe the pyramids had some function other than that of royal interment. Keep in mind that few intact royal burials have been found from anytime in Egyptian history, but there's plenty of evidence of robbery. The practice of burying royalty with grandiose grave goods was an alluring attraction to thieves at all times of Egyptian history.

Egypt's pyramids still might hold some secrets, perhaps even additional chambers as yet unknown. In recent years, robots with cameras have been sent into the Great Pyramid's so-called airshafts: small rectangular tunnels that run diagonally up from both the King's and Queen's chambers. Obstacles within the shafts have prevented their complete exploration. In 2015, several prominent pyramids were scanned using infrared thermography and other sophisticated technologies. The results show anomalies that will require further investigation.

THE GREAT SPHINX

Next to Khafra's valley temple is another readily recognized symbol of ancient Egypt: the Great Sphinx. The Sphinx is a gigantic sculpture—240 feet in length and about 60 feet in height to the top of its head—with the body of a crouching lion and presumably the head of Khafra. It was carved out of a natural limestone outcrop with the rear of the body excavated into the surface bedrock. At one time it was colorfully painted and sported a beard. This magnificent sculpture has suffered much through the years; its nose has been smashed, and its beard has fallen off. Fragments of the latter can be found in museums in Cairo and London. The whole monument has been subject to intensive attempts at preservation, and its conservation continues.

Menkaura's pyramid, the third giant structure at Giza, is significantly smaller than those of Khufu and Khafra. It measures only 355 feet across each side, with an original height of 215 feet (now 203 feet). Its lower portion was faced in red granite from Aswan. Despite the fact that its limestone casing blocks have been quarried and its north face is marred by the gashes of treasure hunters, it is still a beautiful little pyramid.

When Richard Vyse and John Perring entered Menkaura's pyramid in 1837, they found a badly damaged wooden coffin bearing the ruler's name along with a stone sarcophagus. The style of the coffin indicates that it was a replacement item from a much later age (Dynasty 26), as if Menkaura's burial was being restored. Both items were forwarded to London for the British Museum, but the ship bearing the sarcophagus sank at sea, where it remains. The coffin is on display.

THE LATER PYRAMIDS

After the Fourth Dynasty, the Old Kingdom pyramids became smaller and simpler. What they lacked in size might be made up for with the Pyramid Texts which, as noted, first appear at the end of the Fifth Dynasty. Pyramid-building seems to have slowed down dramatically during the tumultuous First Intermediate Period which followed the Old Kingdom with only a handful of small examples known. Monumental building, however, was resumed during the Middle Kingdom. The first ruler of that new era, Mentuhotep II, built a large tomb complex at Deir el-Bahri on the west bank of Thebes in Upper Egypt. It has been argued that it was crowned with a small pyramid.

The Twelfth Dynasty ruler Amenemhet I built a pyramid at Lisht near the Fayyum, liberally borrowing small blocks of limestone from some of his Old Kingdom predecessors. His was the last to be built with a core of stone blocks. Those who followed used stone rubble or mud brick for their fill. As a result, most of these pyramids haven't survived very well after their casing stones were removed.

It's possible that pyramid-like features were included on some of the tombs of the late Seventeenth Dynasty Theban rulers, but the evidence isn't extensive. During most of the New Kingdom, royal tombs were carved in a special place, the Valley of the Kings, which was situated below a huge pyramid-shape peak which might have served the same symbolic role as those artificially constructed. During the same period, several private individuals in the Theban area incorporated a small, steep-sided pyramid feature into the design of their tombs.

After a hiatus of hundreds of years, the practice of building royal stone pyramids was taken up by Nubian rulers beginning in the Twenty-fifth Dynasty (c. 750 BC). These relatively small and steep-sided Egyptian-inspired structures were constructed at such sites as Nuri and Meroe in what is today the country of Sudan.

CONSTRUCTION AND CONTROVERSY

The pyramids still hold several puzzles for Egyptologists and archaeologists, but one of the biggest is their very construction. Particularly for the great pyramids of the Fourth Dynasty, we are still trying to figure out how, without modern machinery, it was possible to quarry, transport, and install such an enormous number of large blocks of stone while maintaining a high degree of geometric perfection. Such a task would be quite difficult to accomplish even today, and the costs would be astronomical. Most of the discussion on this subject revolves around the Great Pyramid itself, the biggest and most architecturally impressive of the lot.

The Egyptians were adept at quarrying stones, and limestone is one of the easiest stones to cut. Most of the blocks for the Giza pyramids seem to have been quarried near the building site, and a limestone quarry at Tura, on the east bank of the Nile, was a favorite spot for obtaining brilliantly white casing stones. Boats, rafts, or barges would have been needed for transport from quarries across the river, as well as for bringing down exceedingly heavy pieces of granite from such places as Aswan, several hundred miles upstream.

We are also not completely certain how they managed to get the massive stones to the building site. The annual flooding of the Nile during the inundation could greatly facilitate the bringing of materials closer to the construction zone. Ropes were no doubt used, but to what extent rollers and sledges were put to work isn't known. The Egyptians probably didn't have a lot of wood to build the huge quantities of these sorts of tools that would be needed. Enough men using brute strength to pull stone blocks along a lubricated runway or ramp might very well have been sufficient to do the job.

There are two general theories explaining how the large stones were lifted and placed on the growing structure: ramps and levers. One version of the former involves a huge ramp running up the side of the pyramid or a series of ramps positioned at the corners. Such ramps, though, would be amazing constructions in and of themselves and would involve a tremendous volume of material. And they would need to grow with the pyramid to maintain a reasonable angle for transporting blocks. Another version calls for a spiraling ramp winding its way around as the pyramid is built. Some experts question the stability of such a structure, but it would involve far less material than the first idea. But what happened to all of the materials from the ramps? Surely it would be noted by archaeologists?

Herodotus was the first to suggest the second theory for the construction of the pyramids. He wrote that the Great Pyramid was built using levers to lift the blocks from layer to layer. This, too, is controversial in terms of the amount of energy needed to transport blocks to higher levels in this manner and also because of the wood scarcity issue. It's also possible that a combination of both ramp and levering methods was used very efficiently to produce the stunning final result. Among other engineering ideas that have been presented over the years include a theory that the blocks of the Great Pyramid were created by a kind of poured cement or that an "interior ramp" was involved. Neither of these ideas have wide support.

Recent experiments in quarrying and moving stone blocks have demonstrated that many of the seemingly arduous tasks of building a large pyramid could be readily accomplished with surprisingly few people. One study indicated that the Great Pyramid could be built in 20–40 years with a regular crew of about 5,000!

Because it is so utterly impressive, many of those interested in the pyramids tend to focus on the engineering and symbolic nature of the monuments. We must never forget, however, that these structures were built by people, and these people had their needs. A work crew of perhaps 20,000–35,000 or more people needed to be fed, housed, and provided with various other amenities to keep them healthy and hopefully content. How and where the work crews were housed was somewhat of a mystery at Giza until excavations on the plateau beginning in the 1980s revealed what appear to be some of the workmen's facilities, including a large bakery, barracks and cemeteries.

Perhaps the most reasonable of the many "building the pyramids" schemes is that they were organized as great public works projects. A permanent crew of specialized workmen year round was augmented by state-recruited labor, which was especially abundant during the time of the annual flooding of the Nile. In return, the workers were employed and did their national duty, plus reaped whatever extended spiritual value there was for participating in perpetuating the afterlife of a god-king. And there is no evidence that any significant numbers of slaves were used in building the pyramids, and certainly not Hebrew slaves who apparently worked on other projects more than a thousand years later.

OLD KINGDOM TIMES

The Old Kingdom was indeed a time of great wealth and creativity. There were few threats from abroad, and the Egyptians engaged in vigorous trade and occasionally raids to secure whatever resources they might desire. Sculptures in both wood and stone demonstrate extraordinary artistry, whether carved in relief or three dimensions.

Very telling are the huge number and variety of titles of officials involved in the Egyptian royal government during this time. Here is just a sample:

- royal scribes, secretaries, and seal-bearers;
- overseers for dozens of things, including ships, household goods, linen, all the trees of Memphis, beef fat, boat nets, the duck pond, granaries, and ladies of the harem;
- directors of wheat measurers, brewers, hairdressers, interpreters, scribes, singers, and gold smelters;
- inspectors of dancers, manicurists, prophets, priests, and sculptors;
- eye physician of the palace;
- bookkeeper of the royal documents;
- carpenter of the Great Dockyard;
- royal Sandal-Bearer;
- sole companion (of the ruler); perhaps a funny title to us because it could be held by several individuals at the same time.

Egyptologists tend to have their favorite time period and some will argue that the Old Kingdom—and the Fourth Dynasty, in particular—was the apogee of ancient Egyptian civilization. In terms of such things as art, relative political stability, and monumental architecture, it's the opinion of many that the following 2,000 years just can't compete!

During the Old Kingdom, the system of hieroglyphs became ever more developed, to the point that it was fully expressive in communicating the Egyptian language. Although there are fewer known texts from the Old Kingdom as compared to later historical periods, much of what has survived is very insightful. The oldest ancient Egyptian religious documents, for example, are the Pyramid Texts, carved on the inner walls of Old Kingdom pyramids beginning with the last king of the Fifth Dynasty.

Autobiographical statements found in the tombs of bureaucrats who proudly served their rulers also provide us with valuable insights. One of the most famous such inscriptions from the Old Kingdom comes from the tomb of Weni at Abydos. Weni served under three rulers of the Sixth Dynasty: Teti, Pepi I, and Merenra. During his long career, his jobs included confidante to the king, judge, and governor and he led some notable military expeditions described with some detail, although boastful as one might expect. An ancient document known today as the Papyrus Westcar tells stories set in the time of the Old Kingdom, although the papyrus itself dates to hundreds of years later. These interesting tales include an attempt to cheer up Snefru with a boatload of scantily clad rowing girls (and a subsequent miracle), a magic show for King Khufu, and a story of the divine births of three Fifth Dynasty kings.

During the Fifth Dynasty, there was a spurt of activity in further developing the sun cult. Its first ruler, Userkaf, built a temple to Re at Abusir, a practice that was followed by some of his dynastic successors. Userkaf's sun temple included a large, stubby obelisk atop an elevated platform surrounded by a walled ceremonial complex.

There was also an increasing trend of smaller, cheaper, and more simply constructed pyramids. The Fifth Dynasty pyramid of Unas, for example, is tiny in comparison to the giants of the Fourth, but contains the first example of Pyramid Texts, a trend that continued into the Sixth Dynasty. In the Pyramid Texts, it's possible to see that the sun cult that was dominant in these days was being joined in popularity with that of Osiris, the god of the dead.

The smaller pyramids and other declining building projects during the Sixth Dynasty suggest that the glory days of the Old Kingdom were near their end. Beginning at least during the reign of the last three rulers, Pepi I, Merenra, and Pepi II, there is evidence that regional governors ("nomarchs") were gaining more wealth and power. The central authority of the ruler of Upper and Lower Egypt was weakening. Egypt was about to become immersed in civil conflict.

CHAOS AND STABILITY

With its centralized authority under a divine ruler, the period called the Old Kingdom flourished for about 500 years (*c.* 2686–2160 BC). After the Fourth Dynasty, though, there was an increasing trend in which provincial leaders exercised more power, and this ultimately had severe consequences for a unified Egypt.

As we've already learned, the largest and most expensive pyramids ever constructed in Egypt were built during the Fourth Dynasty of the Old Kingdom. With such projects as a measure of wealth and control, the rulers of that era were indeed powerful. When we start heading into the Fifth and Sixth Dynasties, however, the building continues but the monuments get smaller. Some Egyptologists suggest that this is an indication of more austere, if not less motivated, times.

After the extremely long reign of the Sixth Dynasty ruler Pepi II, signs of instability become evident. A few provincial rulers, or nomarchs, began to flex their muscles, and Egypt was soon thrown into civil disarray. Why did this happen? The subject is controversial and Egyptologists don't know for sure, but one idea is that the disorder was exasperated due to the exceedingly lengthy reign of Pepi II, the penultimate ruler of the Old Kingdom. In power for perhaps as long as 94 years, Pepi II might have eventually become unable to keep a tight grasp on national affairs, leaving an opening for some of the wealthy and ambitious nomarchs to step in. By this time, many of the nomarchs were already building their own provincial bureaucracies and lavish tombs.

It is also a possibility that famine or other environmental factors significantly contributed to the civil disarray. Scientists have discovered that around this time, there was a severe drop in rainfall, so that low Nile inundations and resulting famines may also have been a factor.

During the Seventh and into the Eleventh Dynasties, there were power struggles between competing Egyptian rulers. According to Manetho, the Seventh Dynasty was composed of seventy different kings. This is highly unlikely and probably a kind of metaphor for some serious administrative chaos at Memphis. The Eighth Dynasty is nearly as obscure as the Seventh, but we know that in the Ninth and Tenth Dynasties, rulers were based out of the city of Herakleopolis, which is about 45 miles south of Memphis. These rulers challenged the authority of a now politically weak Memphis and proclaimed themselves the rulers of Egypt.

In reality, these new rulers controlled only a portion of Egypt because the powerful southern district of Thebes wanted no part of it, and their own Eleventh Dynasty line of rulers likewise competed for power. One of these early Theban rulers, Intef II, was so cocky that he self-assuredly called himself the King of Upper and Lower Egypt, although he, too, controlled but a fraction of the Two Lands. At one point, yet another entity, the nomarch of Hierakonpolis, entered the fray from south of Thebes, only to be defeated.

With the central authority of a unified Egypt utterly compromised, some scholars look upon this somewhat confusing so-called First Intermediate Period as a veritable Dark Age. A number of nomes and their nomarchs no doubt thrived during this period, but the Old Kingdom's foreign policy and trade, along with national building projects, could not continue as before. Overall, the details of much of this historical interlude are rather meager. And as a personal subjective aside, I find that even the art of this period appears habitually shabby!

The Tenth Dynasty of Herakleopolitan rulers began fighting in earnest with those in Thebes. The Theban Eleventh Dynasty line of rulers eventually prevailed under their leader, Mentuhotep II, and Egypt was once again united. With central authority restored, the chronological period known as the Middle Kingdom (c. 2055–1650 BC) began, and, as in those other periods called "Kingdoms" by Egyptologists, Egypt exercised the benefits of its centralized authority. Great building projects resumed, and the arts once again flourished. Most of the Middle Kingdom rulers held the names Mentuhotep, Amenemhet, and Senusret. The name Mentuhotep means, "[the Theban war-god] Monthu is satisfied." Amenemhet means "[the god] Amun is foremost" and Senusret means "man of the goddess Usret, i.e. the mighty one."

With Mentuhotep's victory, Thebes became a prominent place and remained that way for many centuries. The Theban god Amun became popular at the national level, and what would become the massive temple complex of Karnak was regularly augmented. Mentuhotep built a massive funerary complex on the west bank of Thebes, and the role of the mighty ruler was re-established.

The Eleventh Dynasty rulers following Mentuhotep II continued the consolidation process, and a new dynastic line of rulers was begun with Amenemhet I. Dynasty 12 is often seen as a kind of golden age in Egyptian history. Egypt really thrived politically, economically, and culturally during this time, and its rulers were strong and active. The style of art and writing from this period would be regarded as "classical" and emulated throughout the remainder of Egyptian history. And one of Amenemhet I's many accomplishments was to establish a new administrative capital away from Thebes and closer to the juncture of the Two Lands at a place called *Itj Tawy*, probably about 20 miles south of Memphis. It was a pleasant location, strategically located so that Amenemhet could keep a close eye on activities to the north and the south. The actual site of this capital had been long lost to archaeologists, but recent attempts to locate the buried city could potentially result in its rediscovery.

Amenemhet resumed the pyramid-building practice of his Old Kingdom predecessors and built a large one at the site of Lisht, not far from the new capital. He also initiated the practice of *coregency*, in which a royal successor is chosen and rules alongside the reigning king with the idea of ensuring a smooth and competent succession after the death of his mentor. (Occasionally it can cause chronological headaches for Egyptologists when they discover that certain reigns did or did not overlap as previously thought.)

Amenemhet was apparently assassinated, but his son and coregent, Senusret I, ruled ably as a political stabilizer and great builder. A text from the Twelfth Dynasty is known as the *Instruction of Amenemhet* and is addressed to Senusret I as if written by his deceased father. It offers advice to Senusret, including the warning not to trust anyone. Their successors, Amenemhet II and Senusret II, were also exceedingly capable. The latter is especially known for transforming the Fayyum region near the new capital into a greatly productive agricultural region.

The Twelfth Dynasty was also a time of great trade. Egypt occupied its southern neighbor, Nubia, and maintained forts there, and also a maintained a presence in Palestine. Items from as far away as the Mediterranean island of Crete have been found in Egypt at this time, and a few Egyptian items have been found in Crete as well. The expeditions to quarries and gold mines continued, and each ruler continued to build structures for himself, the gods, and the people of Egypt.

In 1936, French archaeologists excavating at a Middle Kingdom temple dedicated to Montu at the site of Tod, south of Luxor, found a bronze box bearing the name of Senusret II. Inside were precious silver cups (perhaps from Crete), some gold ingots, a lion made of silver, and some lapis lazuli cylinder seals from Mesopotamia. Apart from its artistic value, this find, known as the "the Tod Treasure" indicates widespread relations between Egypt and other lands.

Senusret III was a great warrior pharaoh, engaging in military campaigns in Nubia and Palestine. He also restructured the Egyptian government to curtail any ambitions for power that the provincial nomarchs might entertain. His successor, Amenemhet III, is considered to be the last great ruler of the Middle Kingdom. Very little is known about Amenemhet III's son and successor, Amenemhet IV, but when he died, his sister, Sobeknefru, took over in a rare example of female-as-ruler in ancient Egypt.

Before continuing with history, let's take a brief look at a couple of the cultural aspects of the Middle Kingdom—namely, religion and literature. With a single divine ruler no longer in control during the First Intermediate Period, some interesting cultural changes took place. As noted, when the nomarchs grew in power, they began building larger tombs for themselves, and this trend continued even after control was consolidated in the Middle Kingdom. Cemeteries of rock-cut tombs, such as that at Beni Hasan in Middle Egypt, feature beautifully decorated walls. Unlike the sculpted and painted walls typical of the Old Kingdom mastabas, the walls of these rock-cut tombs were usually covered with plaster and then painted. Wooden funerary figures of servants and little daily-life dioramas were quite popular. These models are quite delightful to examine today in that they also give us a miniature three-dimensional perspective of homes and other buildings, activities, and even plants and animals of the time.

Interestingly, the funerary practices that were previously reserved for the divine ruler seem to have become democratized and available to the masses during the Middle Kingdom. Variations of the esoteric texts that were once found written solely on Old Kingdom funerary monuments, the "Pyramid Texts," began to appear on the coffins of ordinary mortals. (Mortals who could afford the more expensive coffins, that is.) Many of these "Coffin Texts" survive on the typical rectangular painted wooden coffins of the First Intermediate Period and the Middle Kingdom. In an even more radical change, it became common for the deceased to be identified with Osiris, the god of the dead, just as the divine ruler was. So now, even the lowliest peasant could become an Osiris when it was all over! The god Osiris really rose to prominence in this period and his city of Abydos became a center of pilgrimage.

The Middle Kingdom is well known for its literature. Many copies of the more popular texts survive, as they were used as teaching exercises in scribal schools for many years to come. Those stories that involved advice, or morality stories, served the double purpose of teaching good behavior while helping students master the art of writing. Here are a few of the favorite tales from this time:

- *The Story of Sinuhe*—An official in the court of the Twelfth Dynasty ruler Amenemhet I flees when he hears of the king's death. He is adopted by Bedouins and creates a good life for himself in West Asia, yet he dearly longs for Egypt. Eventually he is invited back to his beloved homeland, where he receives a hearty welcome.
- *The Tale of the Shipwrecked Sailor*—A man becomes a castaway on an exotic magic island which is home to a giant talking snake.
- *The Story of the Eloquent Peasant*—A peasant is abused by a higher-ranking man who confiscates his property. The peasant pleads his case, and his petitions are so articulate that he is invited back to repeat the performance more than once. Eventually justice prevails.

These are wonderful stories, but when you read them in direct translation, don't expect the same style and flow as if they were originally written in English. Egyptian literature requires a little getting used to, but you'll eventually find that not only are the stories good, but there are loads of interesting cultural insights to be gained!

Although the Thirteenth Dynasty is considered part of the Middle Kingdom, it increasingly bore little resemblance to the political strength of the Twelfth Dynasty. The Thirteenth Dynasty consisted of numerous rulers, mostly obscure individuals with short reigns. Egypt's political stability was seriously in question and would in fact be rudely taken advantage of. Even during the Middle Kingdom, groups of traders and herders from the area of Palestine, perhaps fleeing famine, had settled in the eastern Delta and elsewhere in Egypt. They must not have been considered much of a threat because there seems to have been a sizeable population of these foreigners at the time. Sometime around the time of the Thirteenth Dynasty, the settlers got organized and established their own dynasty in the Delta and claimed rule over all of Egypt. They were known as the Hyksos, and it was the first time that Egypt was dominated by outsiders (it wouldn't be the last).

Egyptologists aren't certain who, exactly, the Hyksos were. The name actually comes from the Greek spelling used by Manetho, who probably derived it from the Egyptian word *hekau-khasut*, meaning "rulers of foreign lands." They appear to be of West Semitic origin, meaning probably from the Palestine region. They established a capital called Avaris in the eastern Delta, and a series of six Hyksos rulers reigned during the Fifteenth Dynasty. This period of Hyksos domination is known as the Second Intermediate Period (*c.* 1650–1550 BC). As with the First Intermediate Period, Egypt was no longer strong and unified. The site of Avaris is known today as Tell el-Dab'a and has been explored for many years by an Austrian expedition. Their many interesting discoveries include donkey burials, pottery imported from the island of Cyprus, and what appear to be Minoan frescoes which indicate at least a small contingent from Crete.

You might be wondering what happened to the Fourteenth Dynasty. There is very little to say about this utterly little-known dynasty (1773–1650 BC) other than that it might have been a short-lived phenomenon in the eastern Delta, if it existed at all, and overlapped with Dynasty 13. And don't expect much information on the Sixteenth Dynasty (*c.* 1650–1580 BC), either. Egyptologists know very little about it except that it seems to represent some minor rulers contemporaneous with (and probably under the authority of) the Fifteenth Dynasty Hyksos (1650–1550 BC). The Hyksos actually sacked Memphis, and, needless to say, the Egyptians weren't pleased. A rival group of Egyptian rulers based in Thebes emerged, the Seventeenth Dynasty, and they at first at least pretended to try to get along with the ruling foreigners.

The Hyksos weren't necessarily all bad for Egypt. In their own way, they made concessions to the culture of Egypt, incorporating the cult of the god Seth into their religious practices. They brought some new things to Egypt such as horses and chariot technology, something the Egyptians would use to great effect. Their cultural ties with Western Asia would benefit Egypt in later years. Domination of Egypt by foreigners, though, would not be tolerated for long and the Hyksos would eventually be run right out of Kemet!

4

THE AGE OF EMPIRE AND BEYOND

Before considering Egypt's age of empire, it's necessary to understand a little about the greater region in which it became increasingly involved. A few of the neighbors have already been mentioned, including Nubia. Interactions of these lands with Egypt became increasingly complex through time, especially from the New Kingdom onward.

Archaeologists and Egyptologists are very cautious when discussing commerce and foreign interactions. For example, a scientist could find foreign objects in Egyptian tombs and jump to the conclusion that some sort of contact had been made between Egypt and a distant land. The object, though, doesn't necessarily define the relationship in terms of how it was obtained. It could have been purchased, traded, given as a gift, stolen, or captured as war booty. It also may have passed through many hands before reaching its final destination. In short, it can often be difficult to determine the nature of such connections based on a limited number of artifacts and texts. Furthermore, relationships between foreign lands can change dramatically over time.

A VIEW TO THE EAST

The desert to the east of the Nile Valley was regularly exploited for mining and quarrying operations, but paths also provided access to the Red Sea. As noted, Egyptian expeditions to the Land of Punt were launched somewhere from there, and if visitors from the Persian Gulf region came by sea, this is where they'd end up. Just across the way is the Sinai peninsula, another area that provided excellent mining opportunities.

The northeastern Delta region provided land access both into and out of Egypt, and it was used in times of peace and war. The region along the coast of the southeastern Mediterranean, referred to geographically as Palestine or Syro-Palestine, was home to diverse groups of people and has its own very complex history. As the cross-roads between Egypt and West Asia, Palestine was the scene of great triumphs and tragedies through time, and the area remains so today.

The people to the east were often referred to by the Egyptians as "Asiatics" and were typically depicted as having beards, light skin, and foreign costumes. A group generally known as the Canaanites lived in Palestine during much of Egyptian history (through the New Kingdom) and were later joined by the Philistines who appear to have migrated from the northern Mediterranean, and then by Hebrew tribes who left Egypt, according to the Bible, and others. Many fortified cities existed in the region, which indicates its volatile nature. Nearly every major Near Eastern civilization pounced on Palestine at one time or another, and the people who lived there didn't necessarily always get along with each other either. There was interaction between Egypt and Palestine as early as the late Predynastic era, and items from each source have been found in both places.

Figure 4.1 shows some of Egypt's neighbors. To the north of Palestine is the Lebanon region, which was a great source of exceptional wood for the ancient Egyptians from early on. The port of Byblos was an especially notable center of commerce. A great trading and seafaring civilization known as the Phoenicians were especially dominant there, beginning around the time of the New Kingdom.

THE LAND BETWEEN THE RIVERS

Even farther to the east was the homeland of one of the other great civilizations of the ancient world: Mesopotamia. Mesopotamia has often been called "the cradle of civilization," and its status as a

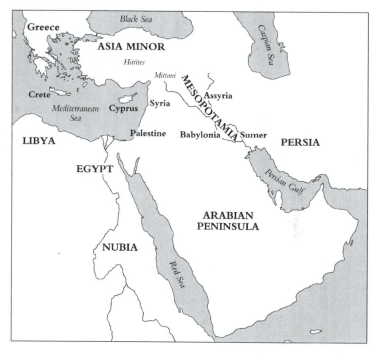

Figure 4.1 Ancient Near East Map, showing some of Egypt's neighbors

Source: Donald P. Ryan.

complex society seems to slightly predate that of ancient Egypt. In this area, which encompasses much of modern Iraq and stretches to the Persian Gulf, we have some of the earliest evidence of the domestication of plants and animals and the development of large towns and then cities. The word *Mesopotamia* means "the land between the rivers," these rivers being the Tigris and Euphrates, which flow south to drain into the Persian Gulf. Irrigation and the rich soil of the rivers' flood plains provided the basis for agriculture and population growth.

The histories and cultures of Mesopotamia and Egypt were quite different. Whereas Egypt maintained relatively civil stability for a good portion of its 3,000-year existence, the dominant cultural group in Mesopotamia changed a number of times. (At this point, it should be mentioned that the study of ancient Mesopotamia is called *Assyriology* as practiced by scholars known as *Assyriologists*.) Like Egyptologists, they are interested in all aspects of the civilization of the region and are usually trained in reading its ancient scripts.

By 3500 BC, there were large towns in much of Mesopotamia. Not long after that time, we find evidence of the Sumerian culture, which was the first major civilization in the area. The origins of these people remain a puzzle and their language is not related to any known, ancient or modern.

It's possible that the Sumerians might have had some sort of role in the development of Egypt's complex culture. This is a very controversial subject. Some Egyptologists argue that their beloved Egyptians by no means required any outside stimulation to develop as they did. Others, including myself, have no problem with the idea that Sumerians or others might have been in some way involved. The evidence is quite provocative and there is, arguably, artistic, architectural, and artifactual evidence of contact between Egypt and Mesopotamia in the late Predynastic and Early Dynastic periods. Archaeologists have found small, tubular, engraved stone cylinder seals (rolled across clay as official seals) and these objects are very characteristic of Mesopotamia. Furthermore, Mesopotamia didn't have very much stone, so its people developed interesting ways of building with mud brick, including the uses of niched façades, which are used in early Egypt as well. At the important early site of Buto in the Delta, for example, walls have been found which are decorated with clay cones that are similar to those found in early Mesopotamia. Could this be evidence of a foreign colony in Egypt during its formative years?

Mesopotamian-like motifs have been found on the famous Narmer Palette, which many believe celebrates and depicts the unification of Upper and Lower Egypt which traditionally heralded the birth of Egyptian civilization. The Palette depicts two very un-Egyptian mythological beasts with intertwined necks along with a niched fort or palace façade. And the Narmer Palette is not the only item from this era with unusual motifs.

Questions also arise about the origins of Egyptian writing. Some Egyptologists have suggested that perhaps the very idea of Egyptian hieroglyphs was imported. Writing appeared in Mesopotamia before it did in Egypt, and in its earliest form it was pictographic in nature. Whether or not there was some sort of foreign influence on Egypt, the writing systems in both areas developed in dramatically different ways. In Egypt, picture-like symbols remained, whereas in Mesopotamia, the *cuneiform* script developed. The script's wedge-shaped symbols were typically impressed into clay tablets and it was in wide use in Mesopotamia and other ancient cultures in the surrounding region.

Contact with Mesopotamia might have been indirect, but some Egyptologists have pointed out that artistic depictions of possible foreign boats with high prows might indicate more direct interaction. Egypt certainly had direct contact with Mesopotamia in later times.

The history of Mesopotamia is often defined by one dominant group after another exercising control over all or part of the land. The Sumerians were followed by the Akkadians, a Sumerian comeback, the Old Babylonians, the Kassites, the Assyrians, the Neo-Babylonians, the Persians, the Greeks, the Romans and we'll leave it at that.

The New Kingdom pharaoh Tuthmosis III, for example, took his army to the edge of the Euphrates River. Of more serious consequence were Assyrian (one of the groups that dominated Mesopotamia for a time) attacks on Egypt during the late Twenty-fifth Dynasty. And the Twenty-sixth Dynasty was even established with Assyrian-approved Egyptian rulers.

Another great empire appeared to the east of Mesopotamia: Persia. The Persians, who were centered in what is today Iran, tussled with the Greeks and anyone in their way and eventually conquered the Land between the Two Rivers. The Persians made their way south and west, passing through Syria and Palestine and right into Egypt during the time of the last dynasties. The Persians were eventually kicked out of Egypt by the Macedonian Greeks under Alexander the Great.

Another competitor in the region was the Hittites, who lived in the central region of modern Turkey, and became one of the great powers to emerge in the Ancient Near East. The Egyptians were in contact with them beginning approximately 1700 BC, and over the years the relationship between the two fluctuated wildly, the

Hittites playing a significant role in Egyptian affairs during the New Kingdom. Actual written correspondence exists between Hittite and Egyptian rulers, giving us an idea of attitudes toward one another and important events.

During the early New Kingdom, Egyptian warrior pharaohs had established dominance in several areas of Palestine and in Syria, which the Hittites wanted to include in their own sphere of control. As the competition escalated, the great Nineteenth Dynasty pharaoh Rameses II fought the Hittites at Kadesh in northern Syria, and eventually the two rival powers agreed to a peace treaty, often said to be the first known of its kind. As a measure of reconciliation, the Hittite ruler sent two princesses to join Rameses II in Egypt. The Hittite empire was destroyed not long afterward, apparently by a group of wandering marauders and colonists from the northeast Mediterranean known as the Sea Peoples. These people also gave Egypt a good bit of trouble.

Another group Egypt had to contend with was the kingdom of Mitanni in northern Mesopotamia. Most of our knowledge of these people comes from their neighbors, who had quite a bit to say about them. The Mitannis competed with the Hittites for foreign territory, invaded Syria and Palestine, and battled it out with some of the Eighteenth Dynasty pharaohs. This scrappy little entity was eventually absorbed by the neighboring Mesopotamian empire builders. Several Eighteenth Dynasty pharaohs, including Tuthmosis IV and Amenhotep III, married princesses from Mitanni. These sorts of marriages were one way of securing a truce or alliance between the two competing powers.

To the north, the Egyptians referred to the Mediterranean as "the Great Green," and although they don't have a reputation as being great roving seafarers, they certainly were able to import and export items to and from Egypt by sea. Egyptian items have been found on the islands of Crete and Cyprus in the Mediterranean, and items from those islands have been found in Egypt. Boats could easily move items from here to there, especially when they're manned by Phoenicians. Crete is especially noteworthy as home to a very unique and sophisticated sea-oriented civilization known as the Minoans. During the New Kingdom, visits by foreign emissaries, including those from Crete, are sometimes depicted on wall paintings.

Archaeologically, one of the greatest shipwreck discoveries from ancient times was found at Ulu Burun in Turkey. The ship, which sank around 1306 BC, contained many tons of diverse cargo, including ingots of copper (probably from Cyprus), tin and glass, and jars containing items such as olive oil. Hundreds of other items, such as ebony, elephant and hippo ivory, and precious objects from Egypt (including a golden scarab bearing the name of Queen Nefertiti), Palestine, and elsewhere indicate that this ship (whose home port is unknown) was really making the rounds in the Mediterranean!

The deserts to the west of the Nile Valley and Delta weren't of much interest to the Egyptians. If the agricultural areas in the Delta and Nile Valley themselves didn't form a kind of western border, certainly the north-to-south chain of oases to the west served as the outermost extremes. The oases were connected to the Nile Valley by overland routes.

The Egyptians referred to different ethnic groups living to their west as Libyans (with various tribal names), and these people seem to have been nomads and herders. They weren't a particularly literate people and they didn't leave any texts, so we don't know very much about them. They did, however, occasionally make the Egyptian enemies list. They became a bit threatening in the New Kingdom, and some forts were built in the western Delta to keep them away. And joining a coalition with the Sea Peoples to attack Egypt didn't enhance their popularity. Some of these people settled in Egypt and some of their descendants actually ruled parts of the land during the Third Intermediate Period.

The northern border of the land of Nubia, Egypt's southern neighbor, begins at the Nile's first cataract, near the modern Egyptian city of Aswan, and extends north of modern Khartoum in Sudan. Nubia played host to major civilizations and it figures prominently in much of Egyptian history. Nubia connected Egypt to much of Africa's many riches, and all kinds of desirable and exotic goods made their way north to Egyptian territory from, and through, Nubia. Such products included gold, ivory, ebony, ostrich feathers, leopard and panther skins, exotic oils and resins, and even monkeys.

Nubia can be divided into two geographical territories: Lower Nubia between the first and second cataracts of the Nile, and Upper Nubia to the south. Lower Nubia enjoyed a situation similar to that of the Nile Valley, in which agriculture was sustained along the great river's banks. The Upper Nubian climate was somewhat more harsh, yet ancient people nonetheless were able to thrive there.

Like the Egyptians to the north, the people of Nubia participated in the development of agriculture and the various accompanying Neolithic phenomena, including the establishment of permanent settlements. These settlements were in full swing during Egypt's late Predynastic times. As in the case with Predynastic Egypt, archaeologists obtained most of their knowledge about these early Nubian cultures by excavating their graves.

Trade between the Egyptians and Nubians is mentioned many times in Old Kingdom texts. During the Middle Kingdom, the Egyptians built forts near the second cataract of the Nile. During Dynasty 13, Egypt lost control of this territory, and the Nubians occupied the Egyptian forts. And toward the end of Dynasty 17, the rulers of Nubia and the Hyksos rulers were treating one another as equals. This situation would change when the Hyksos were expelled from Egypt.

The Egyptians referred to Upper Nubia as Kush (and often, "vile Kush"). The Kerma people there developed into a powerful entity with rulers whose burials were accompanied by the deaths of a large number of sacrificed humans. The Kerma people began working their way north into Lower Nubia during some of the weaker moments in Egyptian history, but when power was consolidated again, the Egyptians worked hard to control both Upper and Lower Nubia. It took a lot of effort and fierce fighting, but during the New Kingdom, Nubia was incorporated as a territory of Egypt and was ruled by a special viceroy.

With Nubia under Egyptian control, it seems that many Nubians had been absorbed into Egyptian culture. The Egyptians spread their culture south, and a number of impressive temples were constructed south of the first cataract. They would certainly convince anyone from Nubia or elsewhere that Egypt, its rulers, and gods were powerful and intimidating. The largest temple was carved into a mountainside at Abu Simbel by the Nineteenth Dynasty pharaoh Rameses II. Egyptian influence in Nubian culture is notable in the adoption of Egyptian writing, art styles, and religious practices, including a special preference for the worship of the god Amun.

Egypt would once again lose its own grip during the Third Intermediate Period, and when Egypt was weak, those under its dominance grew strong. This is certainly the case in Nubia, where the Kingdom of Kush grew into a substantial power. During the Twenty-fifth Dynasty, the kings of Kush actually were the rulers of Egypt. The culture that they maintained is a very interesting coalescence of both Nubian and Egyptian characteristics.

The history of the civilization of Kush is divided into two periods, named after the capital city at each time: the Napatan Period (c. 900–295 BC), after the city of Napata, and the Meroitic Period (c. 295 BC–AD 320), after Meroe. Napata is located near the fourth cataract of the Nile, and the city of Meroe is found south of the fifth. One of the most interesting characteristics of both periods is the building of little stone pyramid superstructures for their royal tombs. Fields of these steep-side structures can be found at such sites as Nuri, Kurru, Gebel Barkal, and Meroe.

During the Meroitic Period, symbols ultimately derived from Egyptian script were used to write the language of the dominant Kushite group. Although inscriptions survive, we're really not quite sure what that ancient language is, or what all of the grammatical details are. So, in a sense, it remains only partially deciphered.

Nubia was home to a truly great ancient African civilization. It's a fascinating subject all its own even as it played a great role, indeed, in the history and economy of its northern neighbor, Egypt.

THE NEW KINGDOM

The time period known as the New Kingdom (c. 1550–1069 BC) is certainly one of the most interesting to Egyptologists. It was an age of great wealth, political and military zeal, unusual and powerful rulers, and religious fervor. While some might argue that the Old Kingdom, with its pyramids and other monumental and artistic wonders, epitomizes the best of ancient Egypt, others see the New Kingdom as the pinnacle of Egyptian civilization. It is comprised of the Eighteenth, Nineteenth, and Twentieth Dynasties.

As stated earlier, the term "kingdom," as applied to Egyptian history, refers to a time when Egypt was unified and strong. When we last left off with our historical summary, it was the Second

Intermediate Period, and the Hyksos controlled Lower Egypt and ruled from their capital of Avaris. In the south, Theban rulers held on to power, and resentment toward the northern occupiers grew. For Egypt to be once again united, the Hyksos certainly would have to go! During the latter part of the Theban Seventeenth Dynasty, serious attempts to oust the Hyksos began. A ruler/warrior by the name of Seqenenre Tao made a mighty effort and was apparently gravely injured. A big axe wound was found on the skull of his mummy and this nasty gash may have been the result of a direct blow from a Hyksos battle weapon.

His successor, Kamose, resumed the struggle, but it would be the next Theban ruler, Ahmose, who would be successful in sacking Avaris, kicking out the Hyksos, and reuniting Egypt. Ahmose was so successful that he took some of the fighting into Palestine, perhaps to pursue any remaining Hyksos support to be found there. Ironically, the Egyptians were aided by new military technology that seems to have been introduced by the Hyksos, including the horse and chariot.

With Ahmose's victory, a new era began in Egypt, and a new dynasty, the Eighteenth (c. 1550–1295 BC), commenced. It would be the age of the warrior pharaoh, and Egypt would exercise its might to the south in Nubia and far to the northeast in Palestine and Syria. Ahmose's successor, Amenhotep I, continued with the reconsolidation efforts begun by his predecessor.

The name Amenhotep (literally, "the god Amun is satisfied") is representative of the New Kingdom. The cult of the god Amun was dominant for much of that period, with huge temples dedicated to him maintained by a large, wealthy priesthood. Amenhotep I initiated major building at the temple of Karnak at Thebes, an activity that was actively continued by many who followed. Also during this time, the god Amun became even more popular in his coalescence with the sun god Re in the form of Amun-Re.

The well-organized Egyptian army would become increasingly capable. Armed with spears, bows and arrows, daggers, maces, axes and sickle-like swords, and defended by shields, they were a serious threat to any opponent. The ruler, himself, was often depicted on temple walls, leading the troops in battle, typically in a moving chariot while drawing a bow. Enemy deaths and booty acquired were well advertised, and if one were to believe all the ancient propaganda, the Egyptians rarely lost a battle. This probably wasn't the case, but during the New Kingdom, they probably experienced more military successes than otherwise.

The pharaoh Tuthmosis I expanded Egypt's dominance into Nubia and Syria during his short reign. Not very much is known about his short-lived successor, Tuthmosis II, but we do know quite a bit about his stepsister/wife. Known as Hatshepsut, she is one of the most fascinating women in all of ancient history.

HATSHEPSUT: THE FEMALE PHARAOH

The male heir to the throne on the death of Tuthmosis II was the very young Tuthmosis III, Hatshepsut's stepson. Apparently, Hatshepsut took advantage of the situation and established herself as co-regent with the young Tuthmosis III, eventually presenting herself as the *de facto* ruler.

Hatshepsut ruled for about 20 years and presided over a period of relative peace and prosperity. Her reign is noted for her great building projects and a notable foreign expedition. Her mortuary temple (known today mostly by its Arabic name, Deir el-Bahri) built on the west bank of Thebes, is truly a marvel. It features three terraces on which are carved some of the highlights of her rule. Her expedition to Punt, a region far south along the Red Sea, is wonderfully depicted with ships being loaded with exotic products. The obese Queen of Punt, too, can be seen in her hefty glory. There is also a depiction of the transport of two obelisks, which were erected at Karnak.

Hatshepsut's reign is somewhat controversial among Egyptologists today. Females generally did not rule in Egypt, and this matter of essentially usurping the throne from its rightful, albeit youthful, owner was a bold act. Hatshepsut's political skills must have been extraordinary. In adapting herself to the role of ruler, she is often depicted wearing the symbolic beard of kingship, yet her feminine features are often not hidden. And in inscriptions, a feminine pronoun is frequently used to describe her activities, thus indicating that she was not a female pretending to be a man, but was actually a woman acting as the ruler of Egypt.

Hatshepsut did not have a male consort while ruler, but it has long been suggested that she had a boyfriend: her architect, Senenmut. Senenmut was sufficiently favored to have one of his two tombs situated in the area of Hatshepsut's mortuary temple.

Hatshepsut died after ruling for about 20 years. (More on her tomb and mummy in Chapter 5.) We do know that Tuthmosis III, Hatshepsut's stepson, was next to come to power, and at least in the latter parts of his more than 30 years as sole ruler, he seems to have engaged in the defacement of his stepmom's monuments. Why? There are theories that argue that it was revenge for his being usurped from the throne, or perhaps Tuthmose III wanted to destroy the memory of a precedent for female rulers in Egypt. Or maybe both ... or neither.

Tuthmosis III was a real warrior, and among his actions were 17 military campaigns in Palestine and Syria, taking his battling far east—all the way to the Euphrates River. During one incident, he laid siege for seven months to the city of Megiddo in Palestine, obtaining a huge amount of booty in the process. A fascinating tale from the time of his reign records the Egyptians' capture of the Palestinian town of Joppa. In this story, 200 soldiers are smuggled into the town in baskets, from which they emerge once inside the city walls. This story is very reminiscent, of course, of the famous Greek tale of the Trojan Horse and the Arabian tale of Ali Baba.

There are many advantages to this kind of empire building, and the Egyptians reaped the rewards. Military adventures abroad resulted in the capture of great resources of all kinds. And those towns and regions that wanted to avoid the harsher side of the Egyptian military regularly paid tribute to them. Rather importantly, expanding Egyptian domination to the south and northeast helped to maintain security for Egypt itself.

The son of Tuthmosis III, Amenhotep II, was considered to be quite a fighter and athlete and followed in his father's footsteps. The athletic abilities of Amenhotep II were legendary and it was claimed that he was able to shoot arrows through thick copper targets from a moving chariot. His successor, Tuthmosis IV, might have been involved in a power struggle for the throne, and his right to be ruler was legitimized in some odd ways. The so-called "Dream Stela," found between the paws of the Great Sphinx at Giza, tells a story of how the sphinx spoke to the future ruler while he slept at its base and promised him the throne of Egypt if he removed the sand that encumbered his body. However it happened, Tuthmosis IV became pharaoh, although his rule was relatively short.

During the following reign, that of Amenhotep III, Egypt was incredibly wealthy, and the cult of Amun-Re was dominant. Although there were military campaigns as necessary, Amenhotep III seems to have been quite the diplomat, making peace (or at least truces) with competitors, including the kingdom of Mitanni. Along with his greatly honored principal wife, Tiye, Amenhotep included two Mitannian princesses and one from Babylonia in his household.

Amenhotep III was a great builder. He constructed a magnificent palace for himself on the Theban west bank at a place now called Malkata. Located well inland, this palace featured an artificial harbor fed by the Nile. Amenhotep III also built a huge mortuary temple for himself fronted by two colossal seated statues which the Greeks called the Colossi of Memnon. Records indicate that after an earthquake in 27 BC, one of the statues emitted a moaning sound every morning, perhaps due to a natural process of heat and air. Later repairs to the statue in the third century AD seem to have curtailed the phenomenon. The Colossi were popular with the ancient Greek and Roman tourists, who left extensive graffiti on the statues' legs which can be read today.

Not much of the rest of the temple survives, it apparently having been quarried away for its stones. Recent excavations, however, have revealed some of its former splendor, including more huge colossal statues that are being re-erected on the site.

THE "HERETIC KING"

What happened after the death of Amenhotep III is one of the most interesting and bizarre episodes in ancient history. The throne of Egypt was left to the great pharaoh's son, a fellow also named Amenhotep. The rule of Amenhotep IV, however, would traumatize Egypt, and the country required a number of years to recover from the damage.

For reasons not completely understood, Amenhotep IV became obsessed with the development of a religious cult centered on the worship of a manifestation of the sun referred to as Aten. The Aten was typically depicted as a solar disk with outstretched hands, and Amenhotep soon changed his name to "Akhenaten" (spirit of the sun-disk), to reflect his devotion to this deity. This, of course, was a major and devastating affront to the status quo of the wealthy priesthood of Amun, especially when Akhenaten cut off the funds, and many of the normally operating temples were shut down.

To top things off, Akhenaten moved the Egyptian political and religious capital to a site in Middle Egypt. This new city, called Akhetaten—"horizon of the sun-disk"—was located at the site known today as Tel el-Amarna (thus the term *Amarna Period*, which is used as a name for this unique time period and cultural phenomenon during the Eighteenth Dynasty). Far away from the normal centers of power, Akhenaten pursued his obsession.

Temples to Aten were built at Akhetaten and elsewhere. Unlike the traditional temples of the time, which contained dark and mysterious inner chambers and cult statues, those dedicated to Aten were open to the sky, allowing the sun-disk to display itself fully. There are plenty of depictions of Akhenaten and his principal wife, Nefertiti, along with their daughters, engaged in worship. It has often been suggested that Akhenaten was practicing some sort of primitive monotheism—that is, a belief in one supreme god. Even though Akhenaten promoted the sun-disk as superior, he was hardly a monotheist, though, as he, himself, was also considered to be divine offspring as the ruler of Egypt.

Apart from the unusual religious and political situation, the Amarna Period was a time of distinct and innovative art. In contrast to the typical stoic and idealized official art forms, Amarna art tends to be lively and more expressionistic. Perhaps the most interesting manifestations of this trend are the artistic depictions of Akhenaten with his family who are often shown with peculiarly shaped heads and pot bellies. Several examples of royal statuary depicting Akhenaten show him with an elongated face, broad hips, and feminine features. Some claim that several of these odd and almost androgynous-looking sculptures actually depict his wife, Nefertiti. The artistic style is, nonetheless, unusual and has led to all kinds of speculation about the physical condition of the Amarna royal family. There has been speculation that Akhenaten might have suffered from some sort of disease or physical abnormality, such as the endocrine disorder known as Froehlich's Syndrome, or perhaps hydrocephaly, or the genetic disease known as Marfan's Syndrome.

There have been some spectacular discoveries at Tel el-Amarna. In 1885, a local villager at Tel el-Amarna stumbled across a large cache of clay tablets bearing texts written in Akkadian cuneiform, the ancient language of Mesopotamia. These texts, known as the Amarna letters, are diplomatic correspondence with Egypt, and provide interesting insights into foreign relations of the time. The famous sculpted bust of Nefertiti was discovered there by a German expedition in 1911. It was brought back to Berlin where it is now on display in the Neues Museum.

As one might easily imagine, Akhenaten made many enemies. He died of unknown causes in the seventeenth year of his reign. A royal cemetery was constructed near Amarna, but there is little left of those burials. It's likely that his body was destroyed soon after it was buried, but at least a couple of scholars have suggested that his remains and those of his family were later removed from Amarna and cached in the New Kingdom royal cemetery at Thebes: the Valley of the Kings.

Akhenaten's queen, Nefertiti, seems to have played a very important role during his reign, perhaps even serving as co-regent. At Akhenaten's death, an obscure individual known as Smenkhkare became the ruler for about two years. Some have suggested that this successor might have actually been Nefertiti. Whoever Smenkhkare was, he was quickly succeeded by a young boy of about 8 years old by the name of Tutankhaten, meaning "living image of the sun-disk." The young pharaoh soon changed his name to Tutankhamun, "living image of the god Amun," thus ushering out the Amarna Period and returning things to some semblance of the way they were before the heretic pharaoh.

Tutankhamun was likely the offspring of Akhenaten, but the identity of his mother is not known for certain. It might have been Nefertiti but possibly Kiya, Akhenaten's second wife. As a very young ruler, he was probably manipulated by those familiar with the way things had been before Akhenaten, and "the boy king" served as a post-Amarna transition figure. Tutankhamun would have likely been a passing character in Egyptian history, had it not been for the discovery of his virtually intact tomb in the Valley of the Kings in 1922. (More on this in Chapter 5.)

Tutankhamun's wife was named Ankhesenamun (formerly, Anksenpa-aten—she changed her name, too.) The king's death at age 18 has been the subject of much speculation. Various theories include murder, poor health, a chariot wreck and even a hippo attack! An older Amarna official by the name of Aye married Tut's widow and took over the throne for a few years, and he was followed by a powerful general named Horemheb. These two rulers began the difficult process of restoring order in Egypt including reopening the old temples and regaining military and diplomatic lost ground. While Akhenaten was preoccupied with his sun cult, Egyptian dominion in territories to the east was being threatened by another great regional power, the Hittites.

Horemheb was actively involved in tearing down the remnants of the Amarna Period and reinstating the cult of Amun. A later formal list of kings reflects official disdain and doesn't mention Akhenaten, Smenkhare, Tutankhamun, nor Aye, but instead skips from Amenhotep III to Horemheb. In his attack on Amarna-era monuments, Horemheb dismantled a temple to Aten at Karnak and used the decorated blocks as filler for a pylon in the great temple complex. Ironically, this served to preserve the blocks through time, much to the delight of modern Egyptologists who have been able to reconstruct portions of Akhenaten's building.

The Amarna Period has attracted a great deal of Egyptological attention and understandably so. It is full of strange and beautiful art, curious individuals, and plenty of mysteries. As a result, there are numerous books and scholarly studies about that intriguing time period. Just a thought, but it seems to me that there are other ancient Egyptian time periods whose histories remain less known and are likewise deserving of intensive investigation; the First and Second Intermediate Periods, for example.

A NEW ERA

Horemheb chose as his successor a close friend, vizier, and military leader who took the throne name of Rameses I. From him, a new dynasty, the Nineteenth Dynasty (*c.* 1295–1186 BC), ensued. Rameses

I ruled for only about a year, and the restoration of Egypt's wealth and power continued under his son, Seti I. Seti was a great builder and warrior who reasserted Egypt's might in Nubia, Palestine, and Syria, battling the Hittites as necessary. Among his restoration projects was the building of a symbolic tomb for the god Osiris at Abydos.

Rameses II continued where his father, Seti, left off, fighting the Hittites and building extensively. He is often referred to as Rameses the Great because of his long and energetic career, although some suggest that his bloated ego was his greatest legacy. Temples and statues commissioned by and dedicated to Rameses II can be found all over Egypt. His cartouche is seemingly everywhere, and he was not above the practice of usurping his predecessors' monuments and adding his own name. Still, he was quite the dynamo. He built a new capital for himself up in the Delta and named it Pi-Rameses and continued to battle the Hittites. Rameses II ruled for about 67 years. He maintained several wives, the most notable being Nefertari (not to be confused with Akhenaten's "Nefertiti"), and was also married to a Hittite princess. He fathered perhaps 40 daughters and approximately 45 sons.

The tomb of Nefertari is considered to be perhaps the most beautifully painted in all of Egypt. Located in a royal Theban cemetery known as the Valley of the Queens, it was discovered in 1904 by the Italian excavator, Ernesto Schiaparelli. After a few decades of tourist visits, the tomb was beginning to deteriorate and was closed. Beginning in the 1980s, a team of conservators from Egypt and the Getty Conservation Institute worked for several years to restore the tomb to its former lovely state. Although their work is finished, visitation is now very restricted in an attempt to save this masterpiece for centuries to come.

One of the most famous battles in ancient history pitted Rameses II against the Hittites at the Syrian site of Kadesh. Rameses barely escaped in what seems to have been ultimately a stalemate. We sure know a lot about the battle because Rameses advertised his own bravery in several major inscriptions. Royal propaganda was not unusual in his time, and Rameses was a master. It reinforced his position as a god-king and probably made his people proud.

Rameses II eventually entered into a peace treaty with the Hittites, which allowed both parties to concentrate on other problems. For the Egyptians, trouble was appearing on the northwest borders as groups of Libyans were beginning to attack.

RAIDERS FROM THE SEA

Rameses II's successor was named Merneptah, and he aggressively fought battles in Palestine and Nubia and against the Libyans. Other groups also began to give Egypt trouble. Referred to as the "Sea Peoples," they seem to have been large, migrating groups of refugees from famine or conflict in the north Mediterranean including, among others, the Philistines who are well known from the Bible. The rich land of Egypt was tempting, and Merneptah had to fight them off in the Delta.

After Merneptah died, there was some odd political maneuvering, but eventually a new dynasty, the Twentieth (c. 1186–1069 BC), was established under Setnakht, whose son, Rameses III, was the last great pharaoh of the New Kingdom. Like his predecessors, he continued to battle it out with the encroaching Libyans and a renewed onslaught of the Sea Peoples. His beautiful and well-preserved temple at Medinet Habu, on the west bank of Thebes, survives as a spectacular monument to his reign.

A conspiracy within the harem of Rameses III resulted in his assassination. Recent CT scans of the king's mummy reveal that his throat was deeply cut. A surviving papyrus document offers a transcript of the culprits' trial. Most if not all of those involved in the murder were killed or committed suicide.

A string of pharaohs, all of them named Rameses, followed Rameses III and Egypt seems to have experienced a sort of cultural, economic and political downhill slide. Very little monumental building took place, and there is evidence of increasing corruption. The power of the priesthood of Amun was growing to such an extent that by the time of the last pharaoh of the New Kingdom, Rameses XI, it was debatable who was really in charge of Egypt.

THIRD INTERMEDIATE PERIOD

It's clear that there was a major change in Egypt's power structure during the reign of Rameses XI. While Rameses ruled from the north, the powerful priesthood of Amun began to assert itself as an authority in the South. One high priest in particular, Herihor, was a prime instigator in the power play. His power base was augmented by his military position as viceroy of Kush. After the death of Rameses XI, it seems as if Egypt's glory days as a mighty unified state were seriously on the decline.

The time known as the Third Intermediate Period (1069–747 BC) can be a confusing historical puzzle. It begins with the Twenty-first Dynasty, when essentially there were two cooperating sets of rulers: a king ruling from Tanis in the Delta and a line of high priests in the south. This odd situation seemed to work out fairly well, with marriage alliances providing bonds between the two sets of rulers.

The last ruler of the Twenty-first Dynasty didn't leave a successor, but a son-in-law named Sheshonq became the first ruler of the Twenty-second Dynasty. This new line is known as the Libyan Dynasty because Sheshonq's family were descendants of Libyans who had settled in the Delta. Their capital was based in Tanis and Sheshonq united Egypt. After a while, the country began to split up into rival power centers. Both the Twenty-third and the Twenty-fourth Dynasties are fairly obscure, and both are actually contemporaneous with the time span of the Twenty-second. The Twenty-third was a rival group of rulers based in the Delta town of Leontopolis, and the Twenty-fourth consists of but two rulers operating out of Sais, another Delta town. Yes, this is a confusing situation and it demonstrates that no one line of rulers controlled all of Egypt. Egypt was once again disunited, as we have seen in the previous "intermediate periods."

The Twenty-fifth Dynasty was ruled by Nubians from their capital at Napata in what is now central Sudan. The Nubians initially only controlled Upper Egypt but eventually ruled over the whole land. In the east, the Assyrians of Mesopotamia were becoming an ever greater threat, and the Nubian rulers had to deal with this. In 671 BC, the Assyrian king Esarhaddon entered Egypt and sacked Memphis. His successor, Ashurbanipal, paid another violent visit to Egypt in 667 BC. Apart from battling the Assyrians, the Twenty-fifth Dynasty was characterized by building projects, especially those dedicated to perpetuating the cult of Amun.

THE LATE PERIOD

The Twenty-sixth Dynasty was established with Egyptian rulers who were selected by the Assyrians for their perceived loyalty. This is the beginning of the "Late Period" (664–332 BC). Reigning from the Delta city of Sais, these rulers employed Greek mercenaries to help secure their power. They also encouraged foreign immigration of Greeks and others, and a vibrant Greek city named Naukratis was established in the Delta. The Twenty-sixth Dynasty was also characterized by a cultural revival, in which the art and other practices of the Old and Middle Kingdoms were emulated. Some of this art is so anachronistically accurate that some Egyptologists are challenged to distinguish the later from the older.

In the greater Near East, the Assyrian Empire was succeeded by that of the Babylonians, who set out to maintain Assyria's former holdings. The Babylonians never made it to Egypt, although they managed to conquer some of Egypt's foreign territories. Egypt's freedom from outside domination, however, would be very short-lived.

Dynasty 27 begins with the invasion of Egypt by the Persian King Cambyses in 525 BC. The Persians, having conquered the Babylonians, became the new superpower in the region. Egypt then became a province of Persia and was ruled by a governor known as a *satrap,* while the Persian king himself ruled from his own capital back at home. The Twenty-seventh Dynasty kings were, in fact, the kings of Persia. An interesting story by Herodotus reports that a large group of Cambyses's Persian soldiers were overwhelmed in a sandstorm and lost in the desert. Modern searches for this "lost army of Cambyses" have not yet located the bodies despite occasional news reporting their imminent discovery.

We know little about the Twenty-eighth, Twenty-ninth, and Thirtieth Dynasties. The Twenty-eighth consisted of a single ruler, a prince of Sais, who declared himself king when the Persian King Darius II died. Taking advantage of temporary Persian weakness, another line (the Twenty-ninth Dynasty), based in the Delta city of Mendes, ruled for a while. The rulers of the Thirtieth Dynasty were temporarily able to rebuff the return of the Persians and initiated another cultural revival, but the Persians returned in force in 343 BC and once again held dominion over Egypt (Dynasty 31).

Meanwhile, elsewhere in the Mediterranean, other civilizations were flourishing and soon turned covetous eyes to the rich bounty of Egypt. During the fifth century BC, Greece was primarily composed of numerous more or less independent city-states, and one of them, Athens, was experiencing its so-called Golden Age, a time when art and architecture, philosophy, literature, and science were flourishing. The Greeks had been successful in routing the powerful Persian forces that sought to subjugate them. But unfortunately, classical Greece would eventually suffer from strife between the city-states themselves, which, along with such distracting factors as the plague, served to weaken the region as a whole.

In the north, the weakening of the city-states was being carefully observed by a large Greek kingdom known as Macedonia. When the opportunity seemed ripe, King Phillip II of Macedonia launched an impressive campaign to conquer his southern brethren. Phillip was assassinated, but his efforts were continued by his young son, Alexander III.

During the next 13 years, Alexander, or "Alexander the Great," as he is regularly referred to, conquered an immense area that would comprise the largest empire in ancient times. Persia was added to Greece as was Asia Minor, Syria/Palestine, and lands extending all the way to the Indus River. Everywhere the conquering Greeks went, they instilled their Greek culture in a process that we might call "Hellenization." Greek religion, thought, and science were passed along and most importantly, the Greek language was instituted as the official means of communication. Numerous vestiges of this process still exist. Old Greek towns, temples, amphitheaters, and other remains of Alexander's conquest can be found throughout his vast empire.

Egypt was conquered in 332 BC, and Alexander was proclaimed pharaoh and welcomed as one who liberated the Egyptians from Persian rule. Alexander contributed to the Egyptians' perception of him as a living god by being crowned in Memphis. More importantly, he established a new city on the site of a small fishing village on the Mediterranean coast. The city came to be named Alexandria, after the great conqueror himself. (The Alexandria in Egypt was not the only city to bear Alexander's name. Several dozen other Alexandrias were established in the ancient world by the conqueror and his admirers.)

Alexander died in Babylon in 323 BC, and it was up to his generals to sort out who would rule which territories. The great empire-builder is said to have been buried in Egypt. A variety of tales speculate about when, where, and how, but the most likely location of his burial seems to be in the city of Alexandria itself. Despite many attempts, neither the tomb nor the body of Alexander has been located.

Within a few years, a general named Ptolemy established a dynasty that would rule Egypt for close to 300 years. These were Greek, not Egyptian, rulers of Egypt yet they retained most of the roles and obligations of their pharaonic predecessors, albeit with a distinctly Hellenistic flavor. All of Ptolemy's male successors bore his name and altogether there would be 15 Greek rulers of Egypt with the name Ptolemy. As a result, this era of Greek rule is often referred to by scholars as the *Ptolemaic Period*.

Ptolemy II was a clever and creative leader and made real efforts to integrate Greek rulership into Egyptian culture, including the Egyptian practice of brother/sister royal marriage. New temples were built to the Egyptian gods, and a religious cult was initiated around a new god—Serapis—a hybrid deity incorporating aspects of both Egyptian gods such as Osiris and those of Greece. Serapis became quite popular and had temples dedicated to him, and had his own priesthood. Much of the history of Ptolemaic Egypt reads like the most contrived of soap operas. There is plenty of family intrigue, betrayals, and worse. In short, there's lots of bad behavior, yet several of the Ptolemies were great rulers and left lasting legacies.

With a Hellenistic ruler in place, large numbers of Greek colonists began to flow into Egypt. Greek farming estates and commercial enterprises began to pop up all over, especially in the broad and agriculturally rich Nile Delta and Fayyum regions. Local Egyptian labor was typically employed. Greeks were generally appointed as government officials in a bureaucracy headquartered in Alexandria.

The sites of many of these towns can still be identified today. They survive in various stages of preservation—from a few mud bricks to large, standing walls far out in the desert. Surprisingly, much of what we know about this time period comes from garbage! During the late nineteenth century, a few enterprising archaeologists discovered that large quantities of Greek documents written on papyrus could be recovered from ancient refuse dumps on the outskirts of these old towns. Dozens of local workmen were hired to plow through the dumps, pulling out bits and pieces of written material by the thousands. The documents cover a wide range of subjects, from personal letters to inventories, contracts, and receipts.

Two Oxford gentlemen, Bernard Grenfell (1869–1926) and Arthur Hunt (1871–1934), were perhaps the most successful of the "papyri hunters," archaeologists who dug in ancient Egyptian town sites in search of documents. The two retrieved a huge number of scraps of Greek manuscripts, and because the old towns were often occupied for centuries, the town dumps also sometimes contained Roman and Christian documents of equal interest. The site of Oxyrynchus in the Fayyum region is especially noted for its quantity and variety of retrieved papyri.

Greek and Roman authors often referred to the writings of others, many of whose works remain unknown but for perhaps their titles. It is considered a significant discovery, therefore, when one of these "lost" works comes to light ... in an ancient Greek garbage dump in Egypt, for example. By the way, the study of (primarily Greek) papyrus documents, typically from Egypt, is known as *papyrology*.

THE CITY OF ALEXANDRIA

Alexandria was one of the great intellectual, cultural and commercial centers of the ancient world. The boundaries and layout of the city were intentionally planned. Among the highlights of the city was an institute or "museum" that played host to professional scholars in a variety of fields. Numerous Greek philosophers, mathematicians, and scientists thrived in the city, including Euclid and Erastosthenes. Attached to the museum was an amazing library that held perhaps more than half a million manuscripts. Legend has it that the library represented an attempt to collect and preserve the accumulated knowledge of the (now) ancient world. One of the projects undertaken at the museum and library was to translate the Hebrew Bible (Old Testament) into Greek. According to an ancient tradition, seventy-two scholars were gathered for the task, and the result is known as the *Septuagint*.

The museum and library no longer exist. Its contents are said to have been burnt, a tragedy of epic proportions for human knowledge. Several individuals have been accused of starting the fire, including Julius Caesar (*c.* 47 BC); Theophilus, the Christian patriarch of Alexandria (391 AD); and the Muslim Caliph Omar, around the time of the Arab conquest of Egypt (642 AD). The fact remains that we really don't know who torched the library, or if it really did perish in a great conflagration as often claimed. In 1990, an international commission met at Aswan and agreed to build another great library at Alexandria. Millions of dollars were contributed to the cause, and a Norwegian firm designed this large and sophisticated new building, the *Bibliotheca Alexandrina*, which opened in 2002.

Another great monument of the Hellenistic rulers was a great lighthouse built on a small island named Pharos, located just off the coast from Alexandria. The lighthouse was commissioned by Ptolemy I, and when completed, it stood at least 380 feet tall and was covered in white marble. During the day, the lighthouse beacon was produced using a mirror to reflect the sun's light; at night, fires were reflected in the mirror to guide the ships. It must have been a magnificent sight, and it no doubt saved many a sailor's life. The lighthouse was in operation for several centuries until it was demolished by a series of earthquakes.

CLEOPATRA

After King Tutankhamun, Cleopatra VII is probably the most recognized name from ancient Egypt. This is perhaps a bit unusual, I suppose, because she wasn't even an Egyptian, and the greatest days of native Egyptian civilization were arguably long over when she lived. Nonetheless, quite a bit of information has survived through the writings of her fellow Greeks, and the dramatic stories about her are full of romantic and political intrigue. Cleopatra presided over the end of Greek rule in Egypt, and some say that her death closed the curtain on what we might consider ancient Egypt.

Cleopatra was apparently quite alluring, very articulate, and well-educated. It has been said that Cleopatra was fluent in several languages, including Egyptian. Apparently she was the only Greek ruler of Egypt actually able to converse in the native tongue. Her story takes place during a time of the rapid expansion of the Roman Empire. Ptolemaic Egypt had made several concessions to the Romans, who eventually acted as their "guardians." During Cleopatra's lifetime, Egypt played a very significant role in the power struggle among the leaders of Rome itself, including such big names as Julius Caesar, Pompey, Mark Antony, and Octavian.

Are you ready for a very much abbreviated version of a soap opera? Cleopatra shared the rule of Egypt with her brother/husband, Ptolemy XIII, with whom she was a political rival. The Roman leader Julius Caesar visited Egypt in 48 BC and met the young queen. After Ptolemy XIII died in battle, Cleopatra married her younger brother (Ptolemy XIV), but she gave birth to Caesar's child. In 44 BC, her Roman boyfriend, Caesar, was murdered by a Senate conspiracy. A new power struggle broke out, this time primarily between the Roman leaders Mark Antony and Octavian.

Mark Antony, too, became romantically involved with Cleopatra, and there were other Romans, including Octavian, who thought that she was actively manipulating him at the expense of the Roman Empire (he was apparently giving her gifts of Roman territory). Rome declared war on Cleopatra in 32 BC and in a great sea battle at Actium off the coast of Greece, Octavian defeated Mark Antony, who was accompanied by the naval forces of Cleopatra. Antony retreated to Egypt with Cleopatra where he killed himself. Octavian arrived in Alexandria in 30 BC and had little interest in playing games with Cleopatra. Egypt was declared a Roman province, and Cleopatra committed suicide (with a poisonous snake, so the story goes, or, according to one Greek author, simply by taking poison). Cleopatra and Mark Antony were said to have been buried together in Alexandria, but their remains have never been found despite vigorous attempts to locate their tomb.

Octavian went on to become Rome's first emperor (later better known as Augustus Caesar), and he considered Egypt his own personal property. Governors were appointed, and Roman law was introduced. Egypt became a significant resource for Rome, especially in terms of grain and tax revenues. Like most of the previous foreign rulers, the emperors of Rome adopted the role of divine ruler. When considering the rule over Egypt by the two great European civilizations, Egyptologists often use the terms *Graeco-Roman Period*, or *Graeco-Roman Egypt*, to refer to the time period during which the Greeks and Romans ruled Egypt, beginning in 332 with the invasion of Alexander the Great through the period of the Roman emperors.

FINAL CHANGES

The Christian religion appeared during the first century AD in neighboring Palestine, which, like Egypt, was under Roman rule. It is not surprising that the new religion appeared quite early in Egypt, where its message was adopted by many. Christianity did have quite a bit of competition with the Egyptian, Greek, and other cults. Egypt, especially Alexandria, was also home to a large Jewish community, including the prominent philosopher Philo of Alexandria. Various Roman emperors were notorious for their brutal treatment of the non-conformist Christians, and many people were martyred, especially in the third century AD. Eventually, Christianity became the official religion of the empire under the Emperor Constantine in the fourth century, and it thrived in Egypt, where it developed as the *Coptic* Church.

Among the contributions of the church in Egypt is the development of the monastic tradition. Egypt was home to hermits, who lived in harsh contemplative isolation, and to devout monastic communities. The Coptic Church, with its own patriarch, hierarchy of priests, churches, and monasteries, still survives in Egypt today, and Copts comprise approximately 10 percent of the Egyptian population. Coptic, the last vestige of the Ancient Egyptian language, is no longer actively spoken, but it remains the liturgical language of the Christian Orthodox Coptic Church of Egypt. Interest in the history, culture, theology, and language of the church remains high and these are the focus of an academic field known as *Coptology*. With its modified Greek alphabet, Coptic didn't have to be deciphered, and the first Coptic grammar in Europe was written in the 1600s. When Champollion and other early Egyptologists began to sound out words in hieroglyphs, Coptic helped them identify the correct meanings.

With the age of the Roman Empire, we have reached the end of our chronology for ancient Egypt, but one more essential event needs to be noted. In the year 570 AD, the prophet Mohammed was born in the city of Mecca in Arabia, and the Islamic religion would follow. The new universalistic faith spread quickly by way of conquering Arab armies, and within a few centuries, its influence was widespread. Egypt was conquered in 642, Islam became the majority religion, and the Arabic language became the status quo. Egypt developed into an important and powerful intellectual and cultural center of the Arab world, and it remains so today.

5

SOME BIG DISCOVERIES

Thousands of years of ancient Egyptian civilization have produced a lot archaeological remains. While much is absolutely interesting and can lend some insights into the bigger picture, there are some discoveries that are exceptional in one way or another. In this chapter, we'll look at several of the most intriguing, if not classic discoveries.

FROM THE OLD KINGDOM

HETEPHERES

In 1925, a photographer with an American archaeological expedition was setting up his tripod near the Great Pyramid when one of its legs slipped, revealing a plastered surface. Upon inspection, it covered a shaft about 100 feet deep, leading to a room sealed with limestone blocks, apparently undisturbed since antiquity. The excavator, George Andrew Reisner (1867–1942), was one of America's greatest Egyptologists. He spent much of his career excavating pyramids and their surrounding temples and adjacent cemeteries. The chamber contained the remains of all sorts of funerary equipment. Much of it had been gilded, but the wood had rotted from underneath leaving bits and pieces of gold foil. This excavation, as you can imagine, required an incredible amount of patience and documentary excellence on the part of the archaeologists involved. When reconstructed, the tomb's contents included some chests, a carrying chair, a bed and a canopy, and two armchairs. A set of four intact canopic jars was found in a sealed niche. It appeared to be the tomb of Hetepheres, the wife of Snefru and the mother of Khufu.

A sealed sarcophagus stood in the chamber, and, in 1927 it was finally opened with much anticipation. It was empty, leaving the Egyptologists with a genuine puzzle. There have been at least a couple of suggested scenarios to explain the empty sarcophagus. One idea suggests that Hetepheres was originally buried south at Dahshur near her husband's pyramids and that her tomb was robbed and her mummy was destroyed. What was left of her burial was then transferred to Giza (Khufu perhaps not being informed that his mother's mummy was missing, thus the empty sarcophagus). Another idea is that this was the original tomb for the queen and that her body was transferred to a small subsidiary pyramid near her son's giant monument. We might never know for sure.

KHUFU'S BOATS

While clearing away material along the south face of the Great Pyramid in 1954, an Egyptian archaeologist, Kamal el-Mallakh (1918–1987), noticed a thin line of mortar running across the bedrock surface. Subsequent investigation revealed a pit carved into the rock covered by 41 giant limestone slabs. Inside this pit was one of the most remarkable discoveries in a land full of remarkable discoveries: a complete, dismantled boat dating to the reign of Khufu, or his immediate successor, Djedefre, *c.* 2560 BC. There were 1,224 pieces of wood, much of it imported cedar, plus ropes and other associated materials. The airtight seal of the covering stone slabs allowed for the incredible preservation of the pit's contents.

It took years to put this veritable jigsaw puzzle back together, but the results are magnificent. The reconstructed boat is 142 feet long and 19 feet across at its widest point. Both its bow and stern are upturned in papyriform fashion. The boat was equipped with six pairs of long oars and a cabin. It is generally believed that the boat played a symbolic role in the solar journey of the deceased ruler, and it's possible that it might have actually been used during Khufu's funerary procession. Today, Khufu's reconstructed ship, often called "the Solar Boat," can be visited in a special museum built directly above the pit in which it was found on the south side of the Great Pyramid.

Another set of stone slabs was found near the first, and, in 1987, a camera was inserted though a small hole in one of the stones to examine its contents. When a camera was inserted to investigate the second covered boat pit on the south side of the Great Pyramid, it quickly became obvious that this pit hadn't remained perfectly sealed as had the first: a beetle was found cavorting about inside. Indeed, another dismantled boat was found within and but in poor condition. A Japanese expedition from Waseda University has taken on the difficult task of investigation. In 2011, they removed the slabs and have begun the long process of preserving the boat which they hope to reconstruct.

PYRAMID OF SEKHEMKHET

Sakkara is a vast and complicated cemetery adjacent to the ancient site of Memphis. It is dramatically dominated by the Step Pyramid of Djoser and its surrounding funerary complex. Very little was known of Djoser's successor, Sekhemkhet, until the discovery of his unfinished pyramid at Sakkara in 1951 by Egyptian archaeologist Zakaria Goneim (1911–1959). The platform of what was likely to be a very large stepped structure was found with a ramp cut into the rock leading down to a blocked doorway. A passageway leading to a large unfinished burial chamber was cleared of loose debris. Some objects found during excavation bore the name of Sekhemkhet, thus attaching an ancient name to this intriguing find. In the center of the chamber stood a beautiful sealed sarcophagus cut from a single block of translucent alabaster. The tomb showed no indication of ancient robbery, but when it was opened in 1954, the sarcophagus was empty. It remains a mystery; perhaps the final resting place of Sekhemkhet is to be found elsewhere.

FROM THE MIDDLE KINGDOM

MEKETRE'S TROVE

In 1920, an expedition from the Metropolitan Museum of Art was working in the Twelfth Dynasty tomb of Meketre on the west bank of Thebes. There they discovered a well-hidden cache of beautiful funerary figures and little diorama-like models. The nicely preserved models included several different kinds of boats, models of a butcher at work, a carpenter shop, a bakery, a brewery, and a granary, along with servants and offering bearers. Meketre, a high steward and royal chancellor, was certainly very well equipped for the Egyptian afterlife!

The tomb was excavated and published by American Egyptologist Herbert Eustis Winlock (1884–1950), one of the most outstanding archaeologists working in Egypt during the twentieth century. Between 1906 and 1931, he investigated a variety of important ancient sites while working for New York's Metropolitan Museum of Art. His excavation of Middle Kingdom sites is especially notable, and he was the author of many excellent archaeological reports and articles.

THE SLAIN SOLDIERS

While excavating on the west bank of Thebes in 1923, Winlock encountered a mass grave of 60 slain warriors. Some of the bodies had been shot with arrows, and others had serious head wounds. He believed that these may have been members of the Theban army of Mentuhotep II, founder of the Middle Kingdom, fighting the enemy forces of the Herakleopolitans. Although this is a satisfying explanation, other scenarios might be possible, and perhaps a re-examination of these warriors will provide more clues.

FROM THE NEW KINGDOM

KING TUT'S VALLEY

As impressive as the pyramids built during the Old and Middle Kingdom were, they failed to protect the remains of the divine rulers that they were built to hold. The great monuments stood out against the skyline for all to see. To robbers, they must have been irresistible, seemingly begging to be violated.

During the New Kingdom, a different strategy was begun. Instead of burying their dead in large structures visible to anyone, an isolated desert valley in southern Egypt was selected in which tombs could be constructed and then easily guarded, in theory at least. Known to us today as the Valley of the Kings, it is the site of some of the most memorable discoveries in all of Egyptian archaeology. There are actually two Valleys of the Kings. The easternmost is the most famous and contains the vast majority of the tombs. The western-most consists of two huge branches and has not been completely explored. It holds just a few known tombs, including those of the rulers Amenhotep III and Aye.

Located in the desert mountains across the Nile from the ancient capital of Thebes, the Valley contains about 30 tombs of New Kingdom rulers carved into the limestone bedrock and about an equal number of smaller tombs belonging to family members or special friends. Most of the royal tombs had walls that were beautifully painted with religious and funerary motifs; a heavy stone sarcophagus in a lower chamber held the mummy. Despite its relatively remote location, the Valley of the Kings ultimately failed to protect most of the mummies of the rulers of Egypt from tomb robbers and others. A virtually intact burial of one king, that of Tutankhamun, was discovered by excavators in 1922, and the Valley of the Kings will be forever linked with his name. More on his tomb later.

In 1827, early British Egyptologist John Gardner Wilkinson (1797–1875) began a numbering system for tombs in the Valley that continues to be used to refer to these tombs today. Egyptologists use the prefix "KV" to designate tombs located in the Valley of the Kings. Thus Tomb 44, which is in the Valley of the Kings, is typically referred to as "KV 44." The system is not perfect. Some tombs in the same numbering scheme aren't found in the Valley itself, and a couple aren't even really tombs. On the other hand, it's quite handy in referring to various tombs, especially those for which we haven't identified an owner. Back in Wilkinson's day, there were 21 known tombs, but by 1922, dozens more had been discovered and Tutankhamun's tomb is designated as KV 62. That remained the case until KV 63 was discovered by an American expedition in 2005, and KV 64 by the Swiss in 2012. (And while we are on the topic of Egyptological nomenclature, it should be noted that tombs in another New Kingdom cemetery, the Valley of the Queens, are often referred to with the designation "QV" plus number, and the many tombs of officials and others in the Theban cemeteries are likewise numbered but prefixed with "TT"—"Theban Tomb.")

Thutmosis I was the first ruler to have a tomb in the Valley. Like several of the earlier Eighteenth Dynasty tombs that would be constructed there, his tomb was cut into a non-obvious place in a limestone cliff. This tomb (KV 20) seems to have been expanded by his daughter, Hatshepsut, and penetrates deep down through the solid rock into a loose layer of crumbly shale that expands and cracks when wet. Today it remains one of the deepest and most treacherous to be found in Egypt and as a result of flooding, the lower portion of the tomb is nearly destroyed. The tomb has been home to thousands of bats, and the air down deep is vile.

As more tombs were constructed, they began to vary in design, a few with cartouche-shaped (oval) burial chambers, and many incorporating a series of corridors and halls. One feature became common: a deep shaft or well, which some say had a symbolic function but could likewise serve very practically as a sump for the waters of flash floods or as an obstacle to robbers. Perhaps surprisingly, there doesn't seem to have been any general plan for the Valley of the Kings; several tombs ran into others during construction.

Interestingly, the builders of the tombs of the later New Kingdom didn't seem to make any attempts to hide the tombs' locations. Some were apparently fitted with cedar doors and their entrance lintels were bedecked with painted red solar disks. Some of these tombs run long and straight into the rock, with no turns. Along with esoteric funerary texts, some tombs display graffiti written in Greek, Latin, and Coptic—evidence of the tombs' later visitors after the Valley was abandoned as a cemetery.

TOURISTS AND DIGGERS

Although the Valley of the Kings had been visited sporadically by tourists and travelers for thousands of years, the first known excavator was Giovanni Belzoni in 1817. Belzoni discovered several major tombs, including those of Rameses I and Seti I. The latter is considered by some to be the most grandly decorated tomb in all of Egypt. Unfortunately, it has since suffered greatly.

Other excavators to follow Belzoni included the Frenchman Victor Loret (1859–1946) and American millionaire Theodore Davis (1837–1915), who both successfully located numerous tombs. The excavating techniques used by the likes of Loret and Davis can be likened to a kind of human bulldozer. Hundreds of local workmen with hoes and baskets were employed to plow the Valley down to the bedrock in search of tomb entrances, and as a result, many were found. For Davis, it was more of a hobby, and he employed several professional archaeologists to supervise the digging.

MAIHERPRI: ROYAL BEST FRIEND?

In 1899, Victor Loret uncovered a very small, undecorated one-room tomb, KV 36, that was absolutely packed with a nearly intact burial of a dark-skinned, apparently Nubian man named Maiherpri who himself was found remarkably well preserved. Robbers had searched for jewelry and made off with linens and such, but much of the tomb's contents remained intact, including a magnificent Book of the Dead. The titles of Maiherpri indicate that he was raised in the royal nursery and was a royal fan-bearer. Such high privileges, and the fact that he was buried in the royal valley, suggest that he was a close companion to the ruler. Some Egyptologists have assumed that the ruler was Amenhotep II, whose tomb (KV 35) lies nearby, but this remains uncertain.

YUYA AND THUYA: ROYAL IN-LAWS

In 1905, James Quibell, working for Theodore Davis, discovered KV 46, the remarkable burial place of Yuya and Thuya, the in-laws of Amenhotep III. Stairs and corridors led to a single large, undecorated chamber. As one might expect, there was evidence of robbery, yet the tomb was remarkably intact. The mummies were found in multiple coffins, and their faces were covered with gilded masks; they are two of the best preserved from ancient Egypt. The tomb contained a huge collection of burial equipment, including the couple's canopic jars, chairs, chests, beds, many *ushabtis*, a chariot, food provisions, and a spectacular funerary papyrus. Before 1922, the tomb was an international sensation, but was quickly forgotten by the public with the discovery of Tutankhamun.

KV 55: A GENUINE MYSTERY TOMB

One of the most controversial tombs in all of Egypt is KV 55. Another excavator for Theodore Davis, Edward Ayrton, found this perplexing tomb in 1907. Its door showed evidence of having been breached and reclosed on at least a couple of occasions. The gilded wall of a large wooden shrine lay across rubble in the entrance corridor, and the tomb's undecorated single room contained more damaged shrine pieces. On the floor was a coffin that contained a much-decayed mummy. Some beautifully carved Amarna-style canopic jars sat in a niche along one wall. The shrine belonged to Queen Tiye, who was both the wife of Amenhotep III and the mother of Akhenaten. Cartouches and an image of the latter were hacked off the shrine's wall.

Whose tomb was this? Some have suggested that it is the cached body of Akhenaten himself, brought from Amarna and stowed in the royal valley. The body, which was initially described as that of a woman, seems to be of a young man in his twenties. This would be too young for Akhenaten unless, as some have suggested, he suffered from an endocrine disorder that interfered with his bodily development. The undecorated walls provide no clues, and even the cartouche on the coffin has been hacked out. Could it be the short-term successor of Akhenaten, Smenkhkare? With such a mix of materials, could this be some sort of burial cache of Amarna-era royal personnel brought south to the Valley from the tombs near Akhetaten?

THE BIGGEST DISCOVERY OF THEM ALL!

In 1912, Theodore Davis gave up digging in the Valley of the Kings. In his own words: "I feel that the Valley ... is now exhausted." A few years later, an English aristocrat, Lord Carnarvon (1866–1923), obtained permission to dig there, and the work was supervised by

Howard Carter, an experienced archaeologist who had spent much of his life in Egypt. Carter (1874–1939) began his career in Egypt as a very talented artist, copying the decorations of tombs and temples for archaeological publications. He eventually became an inspector of antiquities in Egypt and a freelance archaeologist.

After several generally unsuccessful seasons of digging in the Valley, Carnarvon was ready to give up. Carter urged his sponsor to give it one last try, and this persistence paid off. On November 4, 1922, the first of 16 steps was uncovered, leading down to a sealed door. It was the tomb of the obscure late Eighteenth Dynasty pharaoh Tutankhamun.

The plastered and sealed door led to a rubble-filled corridor that ended in another sealed door. What Carter and Carnarvon found was utterly spectacular: a virtually intact royal tomb! Carter's description of his first peek through a small hole in the door is one of the most entrancing moments in all of archaeology:

> At first I could see nothing, the hot air escaping from the chamber causing the candle to flicker, but presently, as my eyes grew accustomed to the light, details of the room within emerged slowly from the mist, strange animals, statues, and gold – everywhere the glint of gold. For the moment . . . I was struck dumb with amazement, and when Lord Carnarvon, unable to stand the suspense any longer, inquired anxiously, 'Can you see anything?' it was all I could do to get out the words, 'Yes, wonderful things.'

The first chamber contained chariots, chests, gilded beds and other furniture, and food provisions, with a side chamber holding even more.

Another sealed door was flanked by two guardian statues. When opened, the chamber beyond was almost completely filled by four nesting golden shrines. Within was a stone sarcophagus containing three nesting coffins, the innermost of solid gold. The mummy inside wore a gold mask, and exquisite jewelry was found in the wrappings and on the mummy itself. Another room attached to the burial chamber contained yet another trove of incredibly preserved objects. It's easy to understand why the world was entranced by the discovery.

It took nearly ten years to empty the tomb of its contents. Most of the material is on display in the Egyptian Museum in Cairo, although the stone sarcophagus with the outermost gilded coffin, and Tut's mummy itself, remain in KV 62 for viewing by visitors.

TUT TRIVIA

The details surrounding the tomb, its contents, and Tutankhamun himself could fill volumes—and they do—but here are a few bits of information that you might find fascinating:

- Carter was smart. He knew where other excavators of the Valley had and hadn't worked and chose his place to dig accordingly.
- There is evidence that the tomb was probably broken into by robbers twice. They obviously didn't get much, which suggests that they were likely caught.
- Tutankhamun's tomb probably was saved from subsequent robbing because the large tomb of Ramesses VI was later built above, and the debris from its construction served to deeply bury KV 62. Recent data also suggests that the tomb was well concealed as the result of flash floods rushing down the valley floor depositing rocks and sediment along the way.
- KV 62 was probably not originally intended as Tut's tomb. Because of his early death, a typical big royal tomb was probably not finished for him, so he was interred in a smaller, or unfinished tomb, probably intended for lesser royalty or special individuals.
- Although Carter wrote a three-volume popular description, he never published a complete scientific report for the tomb and its contents. Reports on individual groups of objects are being written by various scholars, but even nearly a century after the discovery, we are still many years off from having a complete record.
- Because of its fame, KV 62 has been visited by millions of tourists and the tomb has suffered as a result. In 2009, a company named Factum Arte used laser scanners to record in minute detail the tomb's painted burial chamber. As a result, a replica has been constructed next to Howard Carter's old house, a few miles from the Valley of the Kings with the aim of reducing tourist traffic, especially when the original is closed. It opened in 2014.
- The story of the tomb might not be over quite yet. There are clues that suggest that there could be additional chambers attached

to KV 62 which are hidden behind the burial chamber's plastered walls. As of this writing in late 2015, radar studies look promising and further exploration will be required to confirm this exciting possibility.

MORE SURPRISES

Very little archaeological work took place in the Valley of the Kings after the discovery of KV 62. Then, in the late 1970s, activity began to resume. Conservation studies were conducted, tombs were mapped, and the tomb of Ramesses XI was excavated. Eventually, several expeditions were mounted that focused on individual tombs, sometimes with surprising results.

THE LARGEST TOMB EVER

In 1987, as part of an archaeological mapping project in the Valley of the Kings, American Egyptologist Kent Weeks relocated the tomb known as KV 5. The tomb was explored in the early nineteenth century and was found to be poorly preserved and of marginal interest, with its known chambers choked with flood debris. After a few years of carefully removing this sediment, Weeks further explored the tomb by crawling through narrow spaces. The tomb did not end where others had previously thought. In fact, more than a hundred additional rooms have thus far been discovered, making it one of the largest and most complex tombs in Egypt, and certainly in the Valley. The tomb belongs to the numerous sons of Rameses II, whose tomb lies nearby. It will be years before its complete extent is known.

LOST AND FOUND

Although the Valley of the Kings is known for its numerous big royal tombs, most people are unaware that about half of the tombs there are typically small and undecorated. Many such tombs were considered to be boring or of little interest when originally discovered a hundred years ago by explorers on the hunt for big game: large, decorated, and hopefully intact royal tombs.

Beginning in 1989, the author of this book began a project to investigate a series of these tombs. One of these tombs, KV 60, was long-lost but quickly rediscovered on my first day of work (using a broom to sweep across the bedrock searching for clues). Inside, on the floor of the burial chamber, lay what appeared to be a royal female mummy. An investigation by Egyptian scholars has identified the mummy as that of the famous female pharaoh, Hatshepsut.

Another tomb we excavated, KV 21, was deeply buried beneath flood debris, and contained the remains of what are likely two more royal female mummies. Other tombs investigated during our work were found to contain multiple burials, including some dating to the Twenty-second Dynasty after the Valley was no longer used as a royal cemetery. KV 44 was one such tomb, and contained the remains of 13 individuals dating to the Eighteenth Dynasty, including eight infants. We are still examining the evidence of what must be a very interesting story!

The two latest tomb discoveries in the Valley are both fascinating. KV 63 contained what appears to be a cache of mummification and burial materials including seven coffins without occupants and 28 large storage jars containing natron, among other things. The evidence points to a late-Eighteenth Dynasty date. KV 64 is a small undecorated chamber which contained an intact wooden coffin and a funerary stela belonging to a female temple singer named Nehmes-Bastet. The remains of an earlier destroyed Eighteenth Dynasty burial were found, indicating the tomb had been reused.

VILLAGE OF THE ROYAL TOMB-BUILDERS

Building royal tombs required many skilled laborers and the resources to support them and their families. To facilitate the construction of tombs in the Valley of the Kings, a special village was built in the general vicinity to house the workers and their families. This famous village is called today by its Arabic name, Deir el-Medineh, and is one of the most important archaeological sites in all of Egypt. Located against the western cliffs across the river from the ancient capital of Thebes, it was a relatively short walk up and over the cliffs to the royal tombs. The village was apparently begun during the reign of Tuthmosis I, in the early part of the New Kingdom.

When in full force, Deir el-Medineh probably housed about 100 adults, plus children. A wall surrounded much of the settlement, and dozens of houses were located on either side of a central street running north/south. Because they were situated in a somewhat remote location, the workers' village required regular supplies of just about everything, including food and water.

When not working on tombs in the Valley, some of the workers built tombs nearby for themselves and their families. Some of these tombs consisted of a small chapel with a mud-brick pyramid on top. A shaft concealed in the floor of the chapel, or in a courtyard in front, led to underground tomb-chambers, which were sometimes beautifully decorated.

The first major scientific excavations at Deir el-Medineh were conducted by an Italian archaeologist named Ernesto Schiapparelli (1856–1928) during the years 1905, 1906, and 1909. Perhaps the crowning achievement of his work there was the discovery in 1906 of the intact tomb of the architect Kha and his wife, Merit. The tomb contained many things that must have come from their home, including furniture, clothing, chests, and cosmetics—even a wig and hair-care products. There was also quite a bit of food left in the tomb, quite dry but still identifiable.

French Egyptologist Bernard Bruyère (1879–1971) excavated the site over a period of about 30 years, beginning in 1921, and essentially revealed the remains of the village in its surviving entirety. Not only have a large number of houses been excavated in the workmen's village, but thousands of documents have been found, which allows us to learn the details of the daily lives of the occupants of Deir el-Medineh. Many of the workers' names and their relatives, occupations, manner of working, and even personal business and problems were written on papyrus or ostraca.

Because of its great state of preservation and its thorough excavation, Deir el-Medineh has provided scholars with perhaps the best information we have about actual daily life in New Kingdom ancient Egypt. Skeptics might justifiably ask, however, if we should look at the information retrieved from the village as typical of ancient Egyptian life in general; after all, this is a very specialized group of people living in an atypical location. Although this is true, the workers at Deir el-Medineh were people like everyone else, requiring food, clothing, and housing. And apart from the details of their unique work in the Valley of the Kings, the wealth of surviving written material shows that these were people whose concerns and problems were not particularly unusual, but recognizable everywhere in societies today, including our own. Investigations at the village continue still.

MOVING THE MUMMIES

After the Valley of the Kings had ceased to be used for royal burials at the end of the Twentieth Dynasty, most of the royal mummies were collected by priests from their pilfered tombs, rewrapped, and placed in special hiding places. Two such caches of these royal mummies have been found containing most of the great pharaohs of Egypt's New Kingdom, plus some other interesting individuals. One was the tomb of Amenhotep II (KV 35), where that great king was joined by over a dozen other mummies, including Tuthmosis IV, Amenhotep III, Rameses IV–VI, and Seti II.

One of the most famous discoveries of all times in Egypt was a cache of mummies discovered by local villagers around 1878 near the site of Deir el-Bahri in the cliffs on the Nile side of the Valley of the Kings. DB 320, as it is officially designated (or, just call it the Deir el-Bahri royal mummy cache), is a very long tomb at the bottom of a deep shaft very well hidden at the base of a towering limestone precipice. The cache contained over 50 mummies, including many of the New Kingdom's most prominent rulers (Amenhotep I, Tuthmosis I–III, Seti I, and Rameses II), along with coffins and assorted funerary equipment.

Interestingly, some of the coffins and mummies in the Deir el-Bahri royal mummy cache had ancient notes written on them that indicate when the mummies had been rewrapped and moved. A few had been cached more than once before joining their peers in the big collection. And to confuse matters, X-ray studies of the mummies suggest that several of them might have been mislabeled!

The villagers who found the cache secretly looted it, and the quality of objects reaching the antiquities market tipped off government officials that something very special had been found. After some investigation and intrigue, the location of this remarkable mummy hoard was revealed. The cache was cleared out in a period of about two days, and the mummies and their coffins were shipped to Cairo, where many are on display today.

Much of the deep shaft of DB 320 gradually filled up with sand and debris and became inaccessible until 1998 when a German/Russian expedition reopened the site. The tomb, carved into very poor rock, contained assorted small fragments of the famous burials, but the investigation added a lot of details to this extremely important discovery.

Many of the royal mummies are on public display in two rooms in the Egyptian Museum in Cairo. Special nitrogen-filled cases have been provided in the last few years to aid in their preservation and the atmosphere in each room is kept solemn and respectful.

CACHES OF STATUES

Two incredible buried caches of royal sculpture have been found buried in the courtyards of the great temples of Thebes. Beginning in 1903, French Egyptologist Georges Legrain (1865–1917) unearthed over 700 intact and partial stone statues along with many thousands of small bronze figurines, stele, and other objects from a courtyard in the Karnak temple complex. Dozens of the sculptures were of royal individuals representing a couple of thousand years of royal rulers. These items were apparently dumped in a pit there in the Graeco-Roman period in an effort to clear up the clutter from earlier ages.

In 1989, Egyptian archaeologists discovered a similar but smaller cache of buried statues in Luxor Temple. Over two dozen well-preserved stone statues, or fragments thereof, were recovered, mostly dating to the New Kingdom or thereafter. They seemed to have been buried when the Romans were making alterations to the temple.

FROM THE THIRD INTERMEDIATE PERIOD AND BEYOND

TANIS TOMBS

While the public's enchantment with Tutankhamun's tomb has never disappeared, very few people seem aware that other rich royal tombs were later found, and not in the Valley of the Kings. These tombs belonged to some of the rulers of Egypt during the Twenty-first and Twenty-second Dynasties and were discovered at the site of Tanis in 1939 and 1940 by the French Egyptologist Pierre Montet (1885–1966). With the world concentrated on the unfolding events of World War II, these discoveries unfortunately did not receive the attention they certainly deserved.

One burial complex in the form of a series of chambers, contained remains of rulers Takelot II and Orsokon II. Another nearby belonged to Psusennes I and included burials of Shoshenq II, Siamun and Psusennes II. These tombs seemed to have been disturbed to one extent or another in ancient times yet Psusennes himself lay unmolested in a hidden adjacent chamber as did his son, Amenemope. Although these graves were mere small chambers compared to the typical grandiose tombs of the New Kingdom pharaohs, they are equally significant. Many of the dazzling objects found therein, including outstanding examples of artistry in gold, silver and jewelry, are very worthy of admiration. Surprisingly, the stone sarcophagus found in the intact burial of Psusennes I at Tanis originally belonged to the New Kingdom pharaoh Merneptah; the sarcophagus had been removed from the Valley of the Kings and reused.

UNDERWATER ALEXANDRIA

The busy metropolis of Alexandria was a dynamic jewel of the Graeco-Roman period and bits and pieces of it still survive in the modern city which has grown up atop of the old. A good portion of the ancient site, however, has been discovered in a surprising location: underwater and off-shore. Earthquakes and tsunamis caused coastal sections of the city to slide into the sea. French archaeologists who explored the site in the 1990s and beyond encountered stone sphinxes and columns, obelisks and colossal statues. These are not only impressive but extremely interesting, since they show that Alexandria didn't simply look like a "Greek" city. Like previous Egyptian capitals, it included statues brought from earlier cities, such as pieces inscribed for Rameses II and Psamtek II. Plans are being discussed for a new museum to display these finds both on land and underwater. In the latter case, visitors would be able to observe objects as they remain on the seafloor by means of glass tunnels.

6

INFLUENCES AND EFFECTS

You are reading this book, so you no doubt have at least some interest in ancient Egypt. You aren't alone. People have been fascinated by all things Egyptian for a long time, at least as a cultural undercurrent, with occasional widespread outbursts of public enthusiasm, sometimes referred to as *Egyptomania*. The wide reach of Egyptian influence can be found in art, music, literature (including the Bible), film and any number of other expressions. And apart from mainstream scholarship, the unique and sometimes mysterious characteristics of Egypt have generated a unique form of alternative speculation. In this chapter, we'll take a look at some of these influences and ideas.

EGYPTOMANIA!

Although the Greeks were interested in Egyptian art and culture, if anyone should be credited with seriously starting Egyptomania, it would be the Romans. Not only did they collect Egyptian sculptures, obelisks, and other objects when they ruled Egypt, but they began to imitate Egyptian styles themselves, even building a few little pyramids in Italy as tombs. The Roman Emperor Hadrian (ruled 117–138 AD) was very much an Egyptomaniac and in his villa near Rome, he maintained a garden full of Egyptian-inspired statuary and other faux pharaonic features.

With the spread of Christianity and Islam, the perception of ancient Egypt as a pagan land put a bit of a damper on Egyptomania, but it later was revived during the Renaissance and has been going strong ever then. With the Renaissance's renewed and vibrant interest in the arts and the world itself, the wonders of the now-mysterious Egypt once again became attractive. Poking around in the ancient Roman ruins occasionally turned up authentic Egyptian sculptures along with some of the imitations.

And as old Greek and Latin texts were studied and published, knowledge and speculation about the ancient Egyptians increased, including guesses about the true meaning of the hieroglyphs. A couple of the popes—Pius II (1458–1464) and Sixtus V (1585–1590)—got into the act by resurrecting some of the Egyptian obelisks that had been collected by the Romans nearly 1,500 years previously. The notion of Egypt possessing secret knowledge continued for centuries and still persists today. An interesting example is Wolfgang Mozart's 1791 popular opera, *Die Zauberflöte* (*The Magic Flute*), which incorporated mystical Egyptian/Masonic themes, and some of the sets produced for its production emphasized such notions.

As noted in Chapter 1, accurate information about the land of Egypt itself was considerably lacking until the likes of Richard Pococke and Frederik Norden visited and reported on the area in the 1730s. The published descriptions of their trips fueled further interest. Napoleon's expedition, of course, produced a major wave of enthusiasm. Before the publication of the famed *Description,* which published the findings from Napoleon's expedition, one of the expedition members, Baron Dominique-Vivant Denon, wrote his own illustrated account in 1802 that likewise dazzled and inspired artisans and architecture with Egyptian-themed arts ranging from small pieces of jewelry to furniture, to grand and imaginative architecture. Italian explorer Giovanni Belzoni published his *Narratives* (1820) accompanied by color plates, which also generated excitement. Appropriately, his popular exhibition of drawings and antiquities was held in London in a pharaonic-inspired building called the Egyptian Hall.

Scholarly expeditions to Egypt during the nineteenth century offered even more material, with the side benefit of providing inspiration for ideas for artistic designs. The tombs and temples of Egypt were becoming increasingly accessible both by tourists and in print and in publications, such as Prisse d'Avennes' *Atlas de Histoire de l'Art Égyptien* (1878–1879), which served as veritable design handbooks for Egyptomaniacal artists and artisans.

In 1869, the Suez Canal was opened, and the Cairo Opera House was constructed as part of the international celebration. An opera was commissioned which is now one of the most beloved and spectacular ever written and produced, *Aida*. The music was written by the Italian composer, Giuseppe Verdi, with the story line by Auguste Mariette, the French Egyptologist who served as the director of the antiquities service. The opera was first performed in 1871 and was a crescendo of Egyptomania, with carefully designed costumes, props, and grandiose sets. It is often still performed on this grand scale, as it should be.

In the world of literature, Egypt has inspired its fair share over the century. Literary luminaries such as John Milton, Lord Byron, John Keats, Robert Browning, and Alexander Pope all made poetic references to Egypt. There are poems dedicated *To A Pair of Egyptian Slippers* (Sir Edwin Arnold), *To the Obelisk During the Great Frost* (Mathilde Blind), and *To the Nile* (John Keats). Others have been inspired by [On] *Seeing an Egyptian Mummy in Berlin, 1932* (Richard Eberhart), *An Egyptian Tomb* (William Bowles), and *Cleopatra* (numerous poets). Some modern poets have dedicated whole volumes to the theme of ancient Egypt, including John Greening, *The Tutankhamun Essays* (1984), and Clark Coolridge, *At Egypt* (1988).

Percy Bysshe Shelley's *Ozymandias* (1818) is one of the most famous poems in the English language and is an ode to a mammoth fallen statue of Ramesses II (referred to in the poem as "Ozymandias") at his memorial temple in Thebes, as viewed in the early nineteenth century. Here it is:

I met a traveller from an antique land
Who said: Two vast and trunkless legs of stone
Stand in the desert. Near them, on the sand,
Half sunk, a shattered visage lies, whose frown,

And wrinkled lip, and sneer of cold command,
Tell that its sculptor well those passions read
Which yet survive, stamped on these lifeless things,
The hand that mocked them, and the heart that fed;
And on the pedestal these words appear:
"My name is Ozymandias, king of kings:
Look on my works, ye Mighty, and despair!"
Nothing beside remains. Round the decay
Of that colossal wreck, boundless and bare
The lone and level sands stretch far away.

THE TWENTIETH CENTURY

Architectural styles with Egyptian themes continued to be popular in Europe and America during the late nineteenth century and can be found on a variety of structures, including libraries, museums, cemetery monuments, and even prisons. After the turn of the century, Egypt became more popular as a tourist site, and the pyramids, camels, and the romance of the Nile were successful commercial images and were prominently used to sell products ranging from cigarettes to soap and beauty products. The Palmolive company, for example, once advertised its soap with an Egyptian theme and a slogan promoting the "reincarnation of beauty."

The discovery of the tomb of Tutankhamun in 1922 was an utter sensation, as it still is nearly a century later. *Tutmania* was epidemic and spawned all manner of cultural phenomena. There were songs about Egypt and "Old King Tut," Egyptian-inspired clothing styles became the rage, and the once obscure "boy-king" was the trendiest thing in town. The public was now regularly exposed to ancient Egypt, and this popularity has endured.

In the early 1960s, a small number of objects from the tomb went on tour. A larger and spectacular traveling exhibition, *The Treasures of Tutankhamun*, began in 1972, at the British Museum, breaking attendance records and fueling the fire of public enthusiasm for all things Egyptian. Manufacturers exploited the craze to produce hundreds of Egyptian souvenirs and other goods. American comedian Steve Martin had a big hit with his song, "King Tut," which was a satire on the whole phenomenon.

Museum curators learned an important, if not predictable lesson: the public loves ancient Egypt, and any exhibition on the subject will probably do well. Another traveling blockbuster exhibit with objects related to Rameses II visited several museums in the 1980s and was likewise quite successful and in following years, exhibitions containing a limited selection of Tut objects continued to make the rounds.

The monuments of ancient Egypt have inspired some interesting architectural structures over the last few decades. One of the more dramatic examples is the huge glass pyramid erected at the entrance to the Musée du Louvre in Paris, designed by famed architect I. M. Pei. With a completely different function altogether, the Luxor Casino and Hotel in Las Vegas, which opened in 1993, proudly boasts that it is the only 30-story pyramid-shaped hotel and casino in the world. It is decorated with an Egyptian theme and is even graced with a gigantic sphinx.

On a more musical note, the dynamic British duo of Andrew Lloyd Webber and Tim Rice wrote a musical based on the biblical story of Joseph, entitled *Joseph and the Amazing Technicolour Dream Coat* (1968). Much of the story takes place in Egypt, of course, but its modern spin features an Elvis-like pharaoh. For more avant-garde tastes, Philip Glass produced an opera based on Amarna themes, called *Akhenaten* (1984). More recently, a contemporary version of *Aida* has been produced by Elton John and Tim Rice. And who could forget the musical group known as The Bangles, with their big 1986 hit, "Walk Like an Egyptian"?

During the nineteenth century, many books on Egypt were published, including interesting travel narratives and Egyptian histories. The number of these tomes has vastly increased during the past century with both nonfiction and fiction titles selling well. Several prominent late-twentieth-century authors, such as Robin Cook (*Sphinx*, 1979), Allen Drury (*A God Against the Gods*, 1976), and Norman Mailer (*Ancient Evenings*, 1983) have dabbled in ancient Egyptian fiction. *The Egyptologist* (2004) by Arthur Phillips was a best-seller. Mika Waltari's novel *The Egyptian* (1949) was roughly based on the ancient Story of Sinuhe, transposed to the Amarna Period, and was made into a major motion picture. Agatha Christie's mystery, *Death Comes As the End,* is based on a group of authentic

Egyptian letters from the Middle Kingdom. Some recent authors writing ancient Egypt-based series include Lauren Haney, Pauline Gedge, Lynda S. Robinson, Wilbur A. Smith and Chaz Desowl. Egypt is also the subject of many children's books. My favorites are *The World of the Pharaohs* (1960), by Hans Baumann, and *The Golden Pharaoh* (1959), by Karl Bruckner. Dozens more have been published in the decades since these titles were released.

Perhaps the most popular, entertaining, and Egyptologically accurate fiction in recent times are the Amelia Peabody mystery tales, set in Victorian England and colonial Egypt and written by Elizabeth Peters. Peters is a pen name of Egyptologist Barbara Mertz (1927–2013). The several titles in this wonderful series include *The Curse of the Pharaohs*, *Lion in the Valley*, *The Deeds of the Disturber*, *The Mummy Case*, *The Hippopotamus Pool*, *Lord of the Silent*, and *The Golden One*. Another mystery by Mertz (this time using the pen name Barbara Michaels), *Search the Shadows*, also offers fictional Egyptological intrigue.

When movies became popular during the early twentieth century, ancient Egyptian subjects were well represented, even in silent films. Most attention seems to have been directed toward three primary themes: Cleopatra, the Bible, and mummies. The story of Cleopatra, Julius Caesar, and Marc Antony is a screenwriter's dream, with plenty of romance and intrigue. More than two dozen films have been made on the subject. The most famous to date is the 1963 version starring Elizabeth Taylor, Richard Burton, and Rex Harrison. It was one of the most expensive movies ever made, costing perhaps the equivalent of $300 million in today's economy. The film is a long one and was a notorious financial disaster, but it certainly attempted to show the grandeur of Egypt at the very end of its Greek rule.

Several movies have been made about the biblical Exodus. The three most famous are two versions of *The Ten Commandments*, produced by Cecil B. De Mille, and the recent animated film *Prince of Egypt* (1998). De Mille had a penchant for doing things in a big way, which is clear even in his first *Ten Commandments*, a black-and-white silent film released in 1929. A lot of effort was put into building huge sets, including palace façades and an avenue of sphinxes. The 1959 color version, starring Charlton Heston and Yul Brynner, was even more spectacular and involved a cast of many thousands, as well as using well-known Egyptologists as consultants.

In an odd twist of archaeology-meets-art-meets-modern-times, a group of archaeologists set out to locate the remains of the old 1929 set for *The Ten Commandments*, which had been buried in sand at Guadalupe Dunes in California. Using sophisticated equipment to locate things underground, they have found major pieces of the set and other valuable relics of early filmmaking.

Some of the most fun and scary expressions of Egyptomania are the movies featuring animated mummies, and there are many of them. The all-time classic film of this sort is *The Mummy*, starring Boris Karloff, released by Universal Pictures in 1932.

Several more mummy movies followed, including *The Mummy's Hand* (1940), *The Mummy's Tomb* (1942), *The Mummy's Ghost* (1944), *The Mummy's Curse* (1945) and a comedy entitled *Abbott and Costello Meet the Mummy* (1955).

One of the inspirations for Universal's mummies was none other than Rameses III, whose well-preserved mummy has that special look the producers were looking for. Universal Pictures produced a new version of *The Mummy,* which came out in 1999. Its plot vaguely resembles the original, and its special effects are amazing. The film did well and spawned sequels including *The Mummy Returns* (2001). Speaking of mummies, in a curious twist on Egyptomania, a business named *Summum* in Utah offers Egyptian-style mummification, complete with a customized bronze coffin. Needless to say, it's not cheap. They will also mummify your pets.

Ancient Egyptian culture certainly has attracted a large following over the last 2,000 years and continues to do so. One can expect even more books, movies, exhibitions, and television documentaries. If you think you've been bitten by the bug, don't forget to check out Appendix, "Sources for Further Exploration," especially the section on museums with Egyptian collections. They'll help you feed your own personal Egyptomania!

EGYPT AND THE HOLY BOOK

The Bible remains one of the most influential books ever written and Egypt plays an important role in it, garnering hundreds of mentions. Egypt is mentioned in the very first book of the Bible, Genesis, where Noah's son, Ham, is noted as the great ancestor of the Egyptian people and the biblical patriarch, Abraham from Ur, visits Egypt during a time of famine. Abraham's grandson, Jacob, had twelve sons, and he favored one, Joseph, in particular. This, of course, was bound to promote sibling rivalry, and one day his brothers sold him as a slave, and Joseph ended up in Egypt.

Joseph's sparkling personality got him a nice job with an Egyptian official, but when he turned down the naughty advances of his employer's scheming wife, he ended up in jail. There, he was brought to the attention of the ruler of Egypt, due to his ability to interpret dreams as predictions of the future. Joseph was rewarded with a job as one of the highest officials in Egypt.

Meanwhile, there was a dry spell in Palestine, and Joseph's brothers traveled to Egypt to stock up on food. After a few dramatic encounters with his clueless brothers, Joseph revealed himself, and a happy reunion followed. The whole family, including Jacob, immigrated to Egypt. The biblical story of Joseph has interesting parallels in the Egyptian *Tale of the Two Brothers,* in which a man who rejects the advances of his brother's wife is turned upon by the seductress and her angry husband who believes her. But that's where most of the similarity ends.

THE EXODUS

One of the greatest stories in the entire Bible is told in the second biblical book, Exodus. The story begins in Egypt 400 years after Joseph. The descendants of Jacob's twelve sons (whom we can now refer to as the twelve Hebrew tribes, or the Israelites) had been enslaved by the Egyptians, so that a revolt was feared. An order was given to exterminate all newborn Hebrew boys. One mother saved her son by putting him in a waterproof basket, where he was discovered by a bathing Egyptian princess. The boy was given the name Moses and was raised in the royal household. According to Exodus, Moses later killed a brutal Egyptian foreman who was abusing a slave and went into exile. At the age of 80 years old, God contacted him and ordered the fugitive to go back to Egypt to free his people. Moses was understandably reluctant, but with assurances that God would help, he set out with his brother, Aaron, and confronted the pharaoh. There was a new ruler in place since he had left, but the memory of Moses was still alive in Egypt. The pharaoh scoffed at the insistence by Moses that he should set free the Hebrew slaves, and then miracles occurred in the form of ten miserable plagues. The waters of the Nile River were turned to blood, making the water undrinkable and killing all the fish, there were infestations of frogs, gnats, flies, along with livestock disease, boils, hail, locusts, and then three days of darkness. The Book of Exodus makes it clear that God was offering an awesome demonstration of power over the Egyptian gods, to the point of ridicule.

Egypt's Pharaoh was proving very stubborn, and one more miracle would be needed to sway the king to release the Hebrew slaves: the first-born sons of all the Egyptians would die. This final horrible plague had the proper effect. The Hebrews quickly packed up and left, with Pharaoh's permission. (And apart from a lot of valuables, they also took with them a mummy: the bones of Joseph.) The Israelites were miraculously guided in their journey by a cloud during the day and by a pillar of fire at night.

All was going well until the Pharaoh decided to give chase while the Hebrews approached a body of water called the "Sea of Reeds." Trapped between the water and the marauding Egyptian army complete with chariots, God caused the waters to part, allowing the Hebrews to safely cross before crashing down again and drowning the Egyptians. From there, they wandered for forty years in the wilderness during which Moses climbed a mountain, Sinai, and received the laws of God to present to his people. Thereafter, the Hebrews engaged in a campaign of conquest to settle themselves in the promised land of Canaan in the Palestine region.

PHARAOHS OF THE EXODUS

If one looks at the Exodus as an historical narrative, as many do, which rulers were involved? The story involves two pharaohs: one is popularly referred to as "the Pharaoh of the Oppression," and the other is known as "the Pharaoh of the Exodus." The Pharaoh of the Oppression was king when the Book of Exodus begins, and the Pharaoh of the Exodus was the ruler who dealt with Moses and the ten plagues. Egyptologists and biblical scholars have devoted a lot of energy to trying to figure out who these pharaohs might have been, to tie the Exodus firmly into historical chronology.

After years and years of discussion, there is still no consensus, but here are a couple of clues: The Bible mentions that the Hebrew slaves were working on the twin store-cities of Pithom and Pi-Ramses, both of which have been located up in the Nile Delta area of Egypt in the vicinity of where the Hebrews were likely settled. The name Rameses is the big tip-off because there were several kings by that name in the Egyptian Nineteenth and Twentieth Dynasties (c. 1295–1069 BC). As a great builder and a formidable military leader, Rameses II is a favorite candidate for the Pharaoh of the Exodus.

There is but one mention of the Israelite people in Egyptian texts. It is found on a large inscribed stone tablet (known today as "the Israel Stela"), dating to the reign of the successor of Rameses II, Merneptah. Merneptah's stele gives a list of names of cities conquered by the Egyptians in Palestine. Along with these cities is the name Israel, and it is written differently than the other names. Rather than using the special hieroglyph at the end of the word which would indicate that it is the name of a foreign country, the word *Israel* uses the glyphs that indicate a people rather than some sort of settlement. This is fascinating, but it indicates that the Hebrews were already established by that time in the region of Palestine; however, for some, this causes some serious timing problems.

Very interestingly, in the last few years it has been noted that there might also be a depiction of the Israelites on an Egyptian temple. The picture is part of a damaged inscription of Merneptah at the Karnak temple that seems to report the conquests recorded on his stele, and it is accompanied by illustrations. There's a good argument for this being the case, but it's hard to prove. Even so, it's the closest thing to a picture of the ancient Hebrews that we might have.

In an attempt to dismiss the historical reality of the Exodus, critics might point to the lack of Egyptian evidence for the details, but then again, the Egyptians were not known for admitting their mistakes. Would a grandiose pharaoh such as Rameses II brag anywhere that his army was defeated by a ragged group of slaves? Hardly. Even when the Egyptians won a battle, they tended to exaggerate their success in very boastful terms. Even the great Battle of Kadesh, during which Rameses II fought the Hittites, was probably a draw, but this didn't stop Rameses from bragging about his "victory" in several prominent temples.

The miraculous and wonderful story of the Exodus remains precious to Jews today and is commemorated every year in observance of *Pesach*, or *Passover* which celebrates the divine deliverance from Egyptian slavery. Passover is observed for just over a week in the spring, but the most notable event is a meal called a *seder*. This annual dinner, shared among family and friends, ensures that the story will not be forgotten!

THE PROMISED LAND

The Bible tells of Moses receiving the laws of God on Mt. Sinai and eventually leading his people to the edge of the Promised Land—essentially, the geographical territory of Palestine, which today includes the modern state of Israel, the West Bank of the Jordan, and some adjacent regions. The Israelites attacked and conquered much of the area—which was inhabited by Canaanites, Philistines, and a number of other groups—and eventually established a capital at Jerusalem.

It's not the purpose of this book to go into detail about the complex archaeological and historical issues surrounding the Israelites' conquest and settlement of Palestine, but a few additional points can be made. Palestine was in the path of all sorts of marauders and empire-builders, including the Babylonians, the Assyrians, the Persians, the Greeks, the Romans, and, of course, the Egyptians. As has been noted, the Egyptians passed through the area numerous times, subjugating towns, demanding tribute, and fighting battles against their enemies on foreign turf. But it wasn't all mayhem: One of the early Jewish kings, Solomon, was said to have had a pharaoh as a father-in-law in a marriage alliance.

The Bible tells of the attack by an Egyptian pharaoh on the Jewish capital of Jerusalem during which the Temple and the royal palace were looted:

In the fifth year of [the Jewish] King Rehoboam, Shishak king of Egypt came up against Jerusalem; he took away the treasure of the house of the

Lord and treasures of the king's house; he took away everything. He also took away all of the shields of gold which Solomon made.

(II Kings 14:25–26, Revised Standard Version)

"Shishak" is often identified with the Twenty-second Dynasty pharaoh Sheshonq I. Another biblical book (II Chronicles 12:2–3) provides more details, including some military details such as the employment of "twelve hundred chariots and sixty thousand horsemen." And God, through a prophet named Shemaiah, explained to the Jewish rulers why this was allowed to happen to His people: "You abandoned me, so I have abandoned you to the hand of Shishak."

EGYPT BE CURSED!

Elsewhere in the Old Testament, Egypt and other pagan lands are offered dire futures because of their pagan and wicked ways. Here is a small sample, courtesy of the prophet Isaiah (Chapter 19:1, 2, 5, 6):

An oracle concerning Egypt. Behold, the Lord is riding on a swift cloud and comes to Egypt; and the idols of Egypt will tremble at his presence, and the heart of the Egyptians will melt within them. And I will stir up Egyptians against Egyptians, and they will fight, every man against his brother and every man against his neighbor . . . And the waters of the Nile will be dried up, and the river will be parched and dry; and its canals will become foul, and the branches of Egypt's Nile will diminish and dry up, reeds and rushes will rot away.

Given the disintegration of the ancient Egyptian civilization and the environmental changes that have occurred since, one can't help but wonder if some of these things have indeed come to pass!

The Bible notes that the wisdom of the Jewish King Solomon surpassed that of "all the people of the east, and all the wisdom of Egypt" (I Kings 4:30). There are several examples of surviving Egyptian "wisdom texts," and some scholars have pointed about amazing parallels between these and such biblical works as the Book of Proverbs. Are they somehow related? Did one group borrow wise advice from another, or was this sort of information part of a Near Eastern cultural interaction sphere?

JESUS IN EGYPT

Egypt also appears in some of the Christian books of the Bible, the New Testament. The first four books, known as the Gospels, portray the miraculous life and teachings of Jesus of Nazareth. According to the Gospel of Matthew, three wise men from the east set out in the direction of Palestine in search of a special baby. The wise men approached Herod, a Jewish king ruling under the permission and bidding of the Romans, and asked him where they might locate the newborn king of the Jews. This, of course, immediately riled the egotistical and homicidal Herod, who decided to find the baby Jesus and have him killed. He asked the wise men to let him know where the infant would be found. Warned in a dream, they presented their gifts to Jesus and left without informing Herod. Herod, determined to have the baby destroyed, went on a killing rampage of all male children 2 years of age or younger in the vicinity of Bethlehem.

But Jesus was spared after an angel appeared in a dream to Joseph, the husband of Mary, the mother of Jesus, telling him to take his family and escape to Egypt. The details of their travels are not described in the Bible. In Egypt, however, there are rich traditions that trace the path of the Holy Family on their journey. There are lots of interesting stories about the baby performing a variety of miracles, including healing people, calming wild animals, and producing springs of fresh water. On at least a couple of occasions, the legends say, he was able to cause trees to bend over so that their delicious fruit could be picked. Today, churches are located up and down the Nile and elsewhere, built at places where Jesus and his family were thought to have spent time or where miracles occurred.

ALTERNATIVE EGYPTOLOGIES

This book has been written from the standpoint of traditional Egyptology. The information is based on over 200 years of scholarly inquiry. Egyptology generally likes to portray itself as a scholarly, if not a purely scientific, endeavor. It borrows from the best of various disciplines in an attempt to achieve reasonable perspectives about the lives and times of the ancient Egyptians. Egyptologists like to deal with materials that can be measured or reassessed by others—and, if they speculate, they usually (or at least *should*) qualify it with words such as *perhaps, maybe,* or *it seems.* Such words can be very unsatisfying to those who want concrete answers to sometimes difficult questions; however, this is what a careful, scholarly approach demands.

There are others, though, who deal with the past in unusual and sometimes interesting ways, playing by a different set of rules—and ancient Egypt is a veritable magnet for such people. It's worth taking a look at some of the more popular "fringe" ideas, things like ancient astronauts, pyramid theories, ancient Egyptians in the Americas, and mummy curses, in order to gain a perspective as to why they are not generally accepted by mainstream scholars.

For centuries, people have been impressed by the accomplishments of the ancient Egyptians and have put forth many ideas about what it all means, from the stone-cold analytical to the outright silly. While there are a fair number of academic Egyptologists, the numbers of nontraditional Egyptological notions and their promoters are perhaps far greater. Their theories typically are based on ideas that mainstream Egyptologists find to be only superficially credible, at best.

Egyptologists are often annoyed by these sorts of theories and their proponents and followers because their claims typically are outlandishly attractive and often detract from the mainstream—and generally more sober—academic discipline of Egyptology. In fact, mainstream Egyptologists are often painted as the bad guys in all of this, perceived to be too smug to consider what's presented as the hidden "real truth," or they're accused of being part of the great conspiracy to cover it up.

THEY CAME FROM OUTER SPACE

We academic scholars got it all wrong, according to some folks. If we want to know how civilizations were created and how our ancestors accomplished their amazing engineering feats, we need to look to the sky. According to this view, aliens visited our planet in the past and taught the ancient Egyptians sophisticated things like stone carving and pyramid building. Perhaps they are even responsible for the human race itself, having mated with simple-minded hominids. It's a popular notion and an American television series, *Ancient Aliens,* is going on its eighth season as of 2015.

According to Erich von Däniken, the godfather of this sort of speculation, evidence of alien mentors is everywhere. Illustrations and descriptions of these extraterrestrials can be seen in everything from drawings in caves to intricately carved Maya art, to ancient myths and the Bible. And how else can you explain the sophisticated engineering that appears in ancient Egypt and elsewhere? Visits from superior beings, according to von Däniken, solve the mystery of how complex cultures appear seemingly out of nowhere. His best-selling book, *Chariots of the Gods?*, was first published in 1968 and has been followed by many sequels.

It doesn't take a professional archaeologist to find a myriad of holes in such books as *Chariots of the Gods?* A thoughtful reader will soon realize that von Däniken seems to start with a conclusion and finds evidence for it everywhere he looks. One scholar compared it to the psychologist's inkblot test. One person sees a spider, and someone else sees the Statue of Liberty. Von Däniken sees ancient astronauts. It might be argued that many of the theories presented about the past are a reflection of the theorist, and this tell us as much about their philosophy as the idea that they address. In the case of ancient astronauts, for example, the underlying belief seems to be the lack of human ability. There is no reason to believe that people 5,000 or more years ago were any less intelligent than we are today, even though they lacked computers and such. Knowing what we know about the intelligence and mobility of early people, why call on strange and otherworldly forces to account for human achievements?

An interesting and oft-cited example is an inscription in the temple of Seti I at Abydos, which has garnered a lot of attention because it seems to show a jet aircraft or UFO. In reality, the curious depiction is the result of the recarving of a new inscription over an old one. To an Egyptologist who knows hieroglyphs, this is obvious. To those who don't, it appears to be rather extraordinary!

PYRAMIDS OF MYSTERY

The pyramids, especially the Great Pyramid of Khufu at Giza, have attracted an extraordinary amount of attention. Indeed, they are exceedingly impressive and have been a marvel to people for thousands of years. Egyptologists assert that pyramids were the graves of the rulers who were considered to be god-kings and so far, very little has convinced them to believe otherwise. But to some speculators, the pyramids had additional functions or were unrelated to burial practices altogether. The ideas are numerous and include the notions that they channeled energy, that they were factories or machines, or that mystical secrets or calendars are embodied in their measurements or design. Some argue that they are astronomical observatories aligned to constellations, or are located on some sort of energy grids, or were refueling stations for alien spacecraft. Others claim that levitation or other lost powers were used to lift the stone blocks. Some Egyptologists have used the word "pyramidiots" to describe those who have offered such untraditional viewpoints about the pyramids or their builders. Perhaps this is a bit unkind.

It would take volumes to present the points and counterpoints of all the various theories, but, again, there is no need to appeal to extraordinary forces to account for the pyramids. They didn't appear instantaneously out of nowhere, and several hundred years of evolving funerary monuments before the Great Pyramid attest to their indigenous development. Furthermore, experiments have shown that building such monuments was certainly within the capabilities of well-organized and motivated humans.

It seems that the more technological we become, the more difficult it is to believe that ancient people were capable of doing much of anything, lacking all our modern gadgetry. The Egyptians didn't require dump trucks, backhoes, cell-phones, laptops or computer-assisted design programs to build the pyramids. They were masters of the clever and efficient use of simple tools. And if the pyramids aren't convincing to you, consider the amazing medieval cathedrals of Europe which are architectural masterpieces whose builders likewise didn't have access to modern technology.

In the 1970s, there was quite a pyramid fad, and there were all sorts of ideas about the alleged power of that shape. Pyramidal structures oriented to the cardinal directions were said to perform such feats as keeping fruits and flowers fresh and sharpening dull razor blades, along with contributing to the preservation of ancient Egyptian mummies. Some people constructed pyramids over their beds or made special pyramid-shaped solariums in their homes, providing places to experience these mysterious curative and rejuvenating powers. If it really works, then the pyramids must shut themselves down occasionally because scientific experiments have not been able to show any extraordinary effects.

In recent years, some people have argued that the Great Sphinx at Giza was carved between 5000 and 7000 BC, several millennia earlier than Egyptologists generally believe it was created. A promoter of ancient Egyptian mysticism put forth the idea and was backed up by a geologist from an American university. The geologist claimed that the area around the Sphinx was far more eroded than the surrounding monuments known to date to the Old Kingdom (2575–2134 BC).

The Sphinx belongs to an earlier age, so the idea goes, and was created by an early advanced civilization. The head of the Sphinx was probably originally that of a lion, and during the Old Kingdom it was recarved to the likeness of King Khafra, with whose pyramid the monument is traditionally associated. Other geologists are not convinced, and archaeologists point to the fact that there are no related artifacts or other physical evidence of this so-called advanced civilization, just a lot of prehistoric stone tools and such from that era in time.

THE MUMMY'S CURSE

And while we're at it, we might as well talk about the so-called mummy's curse. According to some people, curses were placed on Egyptian tombs long ago, and anyone—tomb raiders and Egyptologists alike—who violates the cursed tombs will die or suffer other misfortunes. The most famous curse story surrounds the tomb of Tutankhamun, discovered in November 1922. It was reported that a tablet or inscription was found stating, "death will come on swift wings" to whoever violated the tomb. In April 1923, Lord Carnarvon, the sponsor of the Tut excavation, died in Cairo, and several visitors to the tomb likewise died in short order.

Let's look at the facts. No written curse was ever found on, or in, Tut's tomb. The story seems to have been the fabrication of at least one bored newspaper reporter posted at the tomb and looking for an angle. After the death of Lord Carnarvon, the newspapers went wild with mysterious stories. At the moment of his death, the lights in

Cairo were said to have gone out, and his beloved dog, Suzy, back in England yelped and keeled over dead. In reality, Lord Carnarvon died of blood poisoning derived from nicking an infected mosquito bite with his shaving razor in the days before effective antibiotics.

But many people associated with Tut's tomb went on to live long lives. Howard Carter, who discovered the tomb and spent ten years working there, died in 1939 of Hodgkin's disease, almost seventeen years after the discovery. Dr. Douglas Derry (1874–1961), who performed the autopsy on the mummy in 1925, lived to a ripe old age. And so did many others involved with the excavation.

The Egyptians did believe in magic, however, and there are actual examples of written curses associated with a few ancient tombs. They essentially threaten death to those who enter the tomb's chapel in an impure state or rob, vandalize, or otherwise violate the tomb. Such curses might serve to scare away a few believers, but in the long run, they were mostly ineffective. Some have suggested that the ancient Egyptians might have intentionally placed poison in some of the tombs to thwart robbers. If so, this strategy was also completely ineffective because the overwhelming majority of high-status Egyptian tombs were robbed. If curses or poisons are to be effective deterrents, they have to work before—or, at least, during—the fact. If someone dies a year later, well, the tomb has already been robbed! And by the way, genuine deadly "booby-traps" in tombs have yet to be found.

There may be some basis in fact for the idea of illness associated with tombs. It's possible that some people may have died from contracting infections from mold, dust, or other material naturally produced in tombs. This author, for instance, became seriously ill on a couple of occasions while sifting fine particles of tomb dust that was mixed with old dried bat guano.

INSCRIPTIONS EVERYWHERE?

Everyone knows the story of Columbus and his 1492 encounter with the "New World." He was the first documented European to visit the Americas, until a single Viking site dating to around 500 years earlier was discovered up north in Newfoundland in 1960. There are those who claim that not only did the Vikings visit

America before Columbus, but so did just about anyone else in the Old World who ever owned a boat, including the Carthaginians, the Phoenicians, the Irish, the Africans, the Romans, the Palestinian Jews, and, of course, the ancient Egyptians. Although these advocates may be sincere in their efforts, their enthusiasm often gets the better of them.

Some individuals have claimed to have found Egyptian inscriptions in North America in such unlikely places as Iowa and Oklahoma. Similarly, there are those who have claimed to have found evidence of an ancient Egyptian presence in Australia and elsewhere. Having reviewed much of the evidence, I remain wholly unconvinced.

The idea of ancient Egyptians traveling far and wide has a certain appeal, but currently is unsubstantiated. Although the possibility (if not good probability) exists for people traversing the oceans to the Americas before Columbus, the Egyptians would be on the bottom of the list of candidates. They just don't seem to have been all that interested in ocean activities, nor is there much evidence of them having traversed very far even into the western Mediterranean, or beyond the Red Sea coast. The fact is, most of the discoveries of Egyptian artifacts or hieroglyphs in the Americas appear to be either very imaginative interpretations or outright hoaxes.

Another interesting controversy involves the alleged finding of traces of nicotine and cocaine in several Egyptian mummies. Were they actually smoking and snorting these things? If they had tobacco and coca, which are both known as New World plants, where did they get it? There are several possible explanations, including the possibility that the residues may have been unintentionally introduced by those who unwrapped the mummies in the nineteenth century, or that the outcome of the tests are a result of a "false positive" from other substances. Or maybe there was a now extinct distribution for these, or similar, plants in the Old World. And there is also the possibility of such items being obtained indirectly through trade. It's an interesting mystery.

BEEN HERE BEFORE

Yes, there are many non-traditional beliefs about ancient Egypt, but one of the most unusual is about reincarnation. Several people have claimed that in a former life they were a citizen of the Nile and that they retain vestiges of old memories. Rarely can such claims be substantiated to scientific specifications. For the most part, if one claims to be a reincarnated priestess in a Hathor temple, I would simply have to believe you or not believe you. A skeptic would at least require that you demonstrate some sort of intimate, verifiable knowledge of your ancient life that could add credibility to your story, including competency in the old language.

I have met a number of people who claim to be reincarnated ancient Egyptians. Most assert that they are royalty or other high-status individuals and I have yet to meet a "reincarnated" farmer, pot-maker, or palace floor-scrubber. There are also duplicate rein-carnated Nefertitis and King Tuts. No wonder I remain skeptical!

Dorothy Eady (1904–1981) is probably the most famous person to have claimed to have once been an ancient Egyptian. Dorothy displayed an unusual attraction to the subject of ancient Egypt as a child, eventually coming to believe that in a previous life she had been a priestess in a temple of the pharaoh Seti I at Abydos. As such, she claimed to have had a clandestine fling with the phar-aoh, and rather than disparage his reputation, she committed suicide. Dorothy believed that Seti himself came back to visit her on numer-ous occasions.

Dorothy had a son with her real-life Egyptian husband, and she named their child Seti, thus the name by which she became well known, Umm Seti, Arabic for "mother of Seti." She worked for the Egyptian antiquities service and settled in Abydos, where she was a true expert on the site. Umm Seti seemed to have detailed knowl-edge of ancient Egypt, but it's unlikely that there was anything authentically original in her stories that she couldn't have picked up in the course of her lifetime. She had many friends and admirers, including professional Egyptologists, and her name is forever linked with Abydos and the pharaoh that she claimed to have loved in ancient times.

Edgar Cayce (1877–1945) was another famous mystic associated with ancient Egypt. He would go into a trance and then give recita-tions about various individuals' former lives. Cayce believed in the existence of an early highly sophisticated civilization called Atlantis, whose citizens fled from destruction as their continental home sank into the ocean. Some, so he claimed, traveled to Egypt where they sparked the civilization that we now know, and they left their library in a "Hall of Records" buried beneath the Sphinx at Giza. I'd be interested in this "Hall of Records" myself if it weren't for the dubious notion of Atlantis and the prophetic credibility of Mr. Cayce. He predicted that Atlantis would rise from the ocean depths in the 1960s. I haven't seen any new continents appear on the map since then, have you?

Examples of "fringe" Egyptology are seemingly endless. Although some of the suggestions are theoretically possible, others don't conform to known laws of nature or to geological or archaeological evidence. Why might some individuals be attracted to this sort of stuff? There are several possible reasons:

- Belief in curious phenomena provides a psychologically satisfying explanation for things that are not readily explainable.
- Calling on outside superior forces reinforces our belief that no one before us could have been as intelligent as we are.
- Some individuals have inexplicable personal experiences that suggest to them that there are mystical realms outside scientific observation.
- Lack of information regarding other possible explanations.
- People have a lack of trust in, or suspicion of, authority.
- It's fun!

But, in short, skeptics who examine unusual phenomena have a saying: "Extraordinary claims require extraordinary proof." It is rarely forthcoming.

The way I look at it, basically two kinds of people are involved in promoting offbeat ideas: true believers and frauds. True believers are those with a sincere belief in a given idea, who usually want to share it with others. Frauds are those who knowingly promote false information to make a profit from the public or to exploit the true believers. Unfortunately, it is very difficult to tell the two groups apart. One should be very careful before calling anyone a fraud, but anyone knowingly taking advantage of others in such a way should be held accountable.

Although I remain unconvinced by most of the untraditional views, I don't condemn those who choose to believe this stuff. They are entitled to their beliefs, and berating them and calling them names (as some Egyptologists do) certainly doesn't help. In fact, it often hardens their opinions and adds fuel to the idea that scientists are closed-minded or conspiratorial. As a rule, an insult greatly lessens the chance that people will listen to and consider traditional perspectives on their subjects.

I have read some of what Egyptologists consider to be fringe literature. Why? I want to be exposed to the range of ideas floating around, and I want to have a polite and informed response when people ask me about such things. Once in a while these people, in their great enthusiasm, also dig up something (usually in a library or museum) or point out something that is genuinely valuable for mainstream investigation.

But if you're going to read the alternative theories, I also encourage you to read the responses to them by archaeologists and other experts. Then think for yourself, and if the odd theory still convinces you, then at least you have considered both sides of the debate. A lot of Egyptologists could benefit from doing the same. Clearly there are many ways of looking at the world, and I hope for at least a degree of respect for others who hold contrary opinions.

As a final word on this subject, I would like to reveal to you the big secret regarding the grand Egyptological conspiracy to suppress a lot of the untraditional perspectives: *There is no big conspiracy!* Sure, there are certain constraints in the academic world that might hinder unfettered speculation, but a well-presented case for one thing or another will invite debate, and many things get sorted out—for better or worse—in the end.

7

EXPLORING EGYPT TODAY

It's wonderful fun to study ancient Egypt, and viewing collections of artifacts in museums is a worthy pastime, but nothing compares to actually visiting Egypt. You might say that Egypt is one of the world's largest outdoor museums. Surviving remnants of the pharaonic age can be found up and down the Nile, along with signs of the subsequent Graeco-Roman, Christian, and Arab civilizations. As of this writing (2015), however, visiting Egypt is not quite as carefree as it once was. The revolution of 2011 resulted in a chaotic security situation from which the country is still trying to recover. As a result, tourism has taken a real beating but the Egyptian government is very serious about attracting and welcoming tourists, and has made great efforts to provide a safe environment for visitors. Check with your country's embassy regarding any security updates they might post. That being said…

GETTING THERE

Egypt isn't a difficult place to get to; a number of major airlines have regular service to Cairo and a few will fly directly to Luxor or other popular cities in the country. Egypt's national airline is called Egypt Air, and it flies from several international airports and also provides air service within Egypt itself. From wherever you arrive, you'll be quickly transported to a lively cultural environment that resembles few elsewhere!

ORGANIZED OR INDEPENDENT?

One of the big decisions to make before visiting Egypt is whether to go on your own or as part of an organized tour group. Both approaches have their advantages and disadvantages. If you go on a tour, the planning is done for you. You'll probably be picked up at the airport, transported to hotels, and taken via buses to a variety of sites. You probably won't get lost, and informed guides will explain what you're seeing. If you don't like traveling with other people or having your life planned, group travel may not appeal to you. Also, you probably won't have many opportunities to interact with many of the wonderful Egyptian people, which is unfortunate. Having said that, a well-organized tour will efficiently take you to the main attractions, and if you fall in love with Egypt, as many people do, you can always come back with a little experience under your belt.

Don't be fooled by Egypt's reputation as a hot country. Egypt has its seasons. It can get quite chilly in Cairo during the winter, when there can be torrential downpours in Alexandria and snow in the Sinai mountains. On the other hand, the climate can certainly live up to its scorching reputation in the summer—especially in the south. To take a hint from archaeologists, most expeditions occur during the months of October through April when it's more climatically conducive to getting the work done.

Many people enjoy the challenge of planning and carrying out their own trip. Fortunately, several good guidebooks are available to help you along. If you choose to go on your own, keep in mind that the national language of Egypt is Arabic. Although you will find that many people involved in the tourist industry can speak at least some English, don't expect that all Egyptians will be able to do so. You will be surrounded by signs in Arabic script, and you might find that you will have to be very resourceful, especially if you leave the beaten track of the usual tourist itinerary. On the other hand, if you're patient and adventurous, you can have a truly marvelous experience.

I am often asked to advise people on whether to visit Egypt as part of a group or solo. Being the independent type, I generally favor the latter option for myself, but I have also participated in some great tours. For a first-timer without a lot of travel experience outside North America or Europe, I suggest the tour—especially for ladies traveling alone or in a small group. Again, you will get a good look at the most famous stuff and will have an opportunity to see if this is a place you might want to revisit.

Some tours allow free time so that you can explore a bit on your own. Tourists on their own in any foreign land can "get into trouble," so to speak, in dozens of ways, and a tour will help you avoid such things. However, having spent a great deal of time in Egypt, I love traveling on my own, and the only tour you'll ever see me on is the one where I've been invited to lecture.

The average first-time visitor to Egypt usually sees Cairo, Luxor, maybe Aswan, and sometimes Alexandria. I'll note some of the main attractions of these places, along with a few other locations. Admission to most of the ancient attractions of Egypt requires the purchase of an admission ticket. This includes most museums, temples, and tombs.

CAIRO

Most tourists interested in ancient Egypt begin their visit in the capital city, Cairo. For the first-timer, it is often a memorable experience. It's a modern, growing, vibrant city and can be very noisy. It might at times appear chaotic, but it is a kind of organized chaos. Tourists can find a wide range of available accommodations, from expensive five-star hotels to fleabag flophouses costing only a few dollars a day. The same goes for restaurants. Most people, if they're not on a tour, get around Cairo in taxis. There are also local buses, which tend to be jam-packed, and a modern subway, which is not so bad. A good guidebook will provide you with the details. One could spend weeks in Cairo examining its many wonders, but here are just a few of the must-see attractions within the city and on its outskirts, for those interested in ancient Egypt.

The Egyptian Museum is one of the most amazing collections of artifacts in the world. Located off Cairo's central square, Midan

Tahrir, it is a very large building packed with exquisite items from Egypt's pharaonic past. Gallery after gallery will take you through the ages, and many of the original objects on display will be immediately recognizable to anyone who has taken a course in art history. There are sculptures in wood and stone, coffins, furniture, jewelry, and objects from ancient daily life, and there are two mummy rooms displaying many of ancient Egypt's deceased royalty.

Some of the highlights, of course, are the treasures from the tomb of Tutankhamun, the gold still gleaming over 3,000 years later. The objects fill a very large gallery. Keep this in mind if you ever visit Tut's tiny tomb in the Valley of the Kings—you'll wonder where they put it all! There is so much in this museum that it's overwhelming; if you have enough time, I recommend a repeat visit. Due to open perhaps in 2018, the new Grand Egyptian Museum should be spectacular. Located near the pyramids at Giza, the Museum will house the best of ancient Egypt. Apart from providing exhibit space, a modern conservation lab will assist in the study and preservation of their collections.

For those who are fascinated with Islamic history and monuments, Cairo has enough to keep you busy for a long time! There are also Christian monuments here and there, especially in a section of the city known as "Old Cairo," and a Coptic Museum. The old Ben Ezra synagogue is in the same neighborhood and is a rare remnant of Jewish life in Egypt. Consult a guidebook for the details.

THE PYRAMIDS AT GIZA

Giza is located southwest of Cairo and across the Nile. Urban sprawl extends all the way to the limestone plateau, where the ancient pyramids sit in somber contrast to the modern development. The quarrying away of the smooth outer casing stones will be immediately apparent, but this does not detract from their impressiveness. A walk around the Great Pyramid will give you a good sense of its size. It's possible to go inside the Great Pyramid (Khufu) as well as those of Khafra and Menkaura, although they're not always all open at the same time.

The Giza plateau consists of more than just the three big pyramids, of course; there are also fields of mastabas and other tombs, some of which are open to tourists. There is also the amazing "solar boat" found sealed in a pit at the base of the Great Pyramid. The boat itself can be seen in a special museum constructed above where it was discovered at the side of the pyramid. And don't forget the Great Sphinx of Khafra.

SAKKARA

South from Giza, on the west side of the Nile, is another vast necropolis, that of Sakkara. Here you'll find the famous Step Pyramid of Djoser, a number of other pyramids, and many mastabas. You can't enter the Djoser pyramid itself, but the pyramids of Unas or Teti, both inscribed with funerary texts, might be accessible. The beautifully decorated Old Kingdom mastabas of Mereruka, Kagemni, and Ptahhotep are other very popular tourist sites. The famous Serapeum, the astounding subterranean cemetery of the sacred Apis bulls, is also one of the many attractions worth visiting. Sakkara also hosts a small modern museum featuring some exceptional objects from the site.

The important ancient capital of Memphis lies close to Sakkara, and you can visit what's left of the remains, which isn't much. But there is an open-air museum near the site with some interesting things to see, including a massive statue of Rameses II. Further south from Sakkara, one can visit the site of Dahshur, home to Snefru's Bent and Red pyramids. The desert setting is dramatic and there are usually few tourists.

MODERN THEBES

If you find Cairo a bit too busy for your tastes, a trip to Luxor, the area of ancient Thebes, might provide a refreshing change of pace. Although it's growing, like all cities in Egypt, Luxor has a relatively small-town atmosphere by Egyptian standards. The main road is a corniche that runs along the Nile, where both cruise boats and sailboats dock, and horse-drawn carriages serve as a transportation choice. As in Cairo, there is a great range of accommodation options and other tourist amenities. The city is found on the east bank of the Nile, but many of its antiquities are found on the west bank. Let's look at both.

Two giant temples are the main ancient attractions on the east bank of the Nile. The Luxor Temple is huge. Even during the day, when its once brightly painted walls appear muddy tan and brown, it is a wonder to behold. And when it is illuminated at night, it can be utterly spectacular!

To the north, the Karnak Temple complex is truly mind-boggling. The accumulated efforts of dozens of pharaohs created this sprawling mass of pylons, pillars, colossal statues, obelisks, and a sacred lake. Wandering through Karnak, you might feel just as dwarfed as if you are at the pyramids, and you will be utterly impressed at the engineering and construction skills of the ancients. Many of the walls and columns are covered with inscribed texts and scenes, which have kept Egyptologists and epigraphers busy for decades.

The west bank of the Nile across from Luxor is one of the largest concentrations of important ancient monuments to be found anywhere in the world. You can reach Luxor by ferry or via a bridge to the south of town. There wouldn't be room in this book to describe the west bank's numerous sites, so I'll list just some of the more famous ones:

- The Colossi of Memnon, two huge seated statues of Amenhotep III, are the primary leftovers of what was once a huge memorial temple to that pharaoh. They almost serve informally as the official greeters to the west bank.
- Memorial (also known as "mortuary" or "funerary" temples. The Medinet Habu temple of Rameses III is impressive, but so are those of Rameses II ("the Ramesseum") and Seti I, likewise found on the west bank. The most spectacular of all is that of Hatshepsut at Deir el-Bahri, with its architectural sophistication and three terraces of decorated reliefs.
- Cemeteries. The west bank includes the royal New Kingdom cemeteries of the Valley of the Kings and the Valley of the Queens. Several tombs in each are usually open to the public. There are also hundreds of private tombs of government officials, priests, and other notables; these are usually grouped under the term "Tombs of the Nobles." There is an immense variety of artistic themes in these tombs, and you can visit some that are well preserved and nicely decorated.

- Deir el-Medineh, the famous workmen's village for the Valley of the Kings. Apart from admiring the layout of this tiny specialized "town," you can visit some of the small private tombs with their colorful paintings.

Before leaving Luxor, don't miss the wonderful Luxor Museum. Although it is quite small compared to its counterpart in Cairo, it features a nicely displayed selection of special objects.

ASWAN

Much quieter and smaller than Cairo or Luxor, Aswan lies to the south and is a real favorite of many people who prefer a slower pace of life, but there is still a lot to see. On an island in the Nile known as "Elephantine," you can see a number of interesting sites, and the excellent new Nubian Museum is well worth a visit. You can visit the prominent ancient quarry that holds the famous "Broken Obelisk," an absolutely immense piece of stone that would have been the largest obelisk ever, had it not cracked.

The giant Aswan Dam and Lake Nasser are south of Aswan. Take a boat to visit the beautiful temple of Philae, which was saved from the flooding waters caused by the damming of the Nile. Even farther south are the massive temples of Abu Simbel, which were also saved from the dam and reconstructed on higher ground. You can reach Abu Simbel by air, land, or water.

ALEXANDRIA

Some people say that the old Greek city of Alexandria has lost its charm. Others say that it is experiencing a rebirth. Either way, reminders of this growing city's once cosmopolitan past remain in its midst. For those interested in the latter days of ancient Egypt, the Graeco-Roman Museum is a great place to visit. And the city's location on the Mediterranean automatically makes it different from any other city along the Nile.

There are several remains of ancient Alexandria to be seen in the midst of the city. "Pompey's Pillar" still stands tall and there an old amphitheater and some tombs. For those interested in the latter days of ancient Egypt, the Graeco-Roman Museum has much to offer. And then there is the new Bibliotheca Alexandrina, the modern resurrected version of its celebrated ancestor.

Egypt certainly has much to offer. I am rather fond of the Fayyum region myself, with its lake, agricultural land, and Graeco-Roman ruins. Nice beaches and spectacular diving can be found along the Red Sea coast. The Sinai Peninsula is also beautiful, and the Western Desert offers several alluring oases for more adventurous tourists. Again, one should consult the latest advisories. Despite the often changing security situation, visitors will find the vast majority of modern Egyptians to be kind and sincerely welcoming.

PURSUING YOUR INTEREST

It seems that not a week goes by that I don't receive some sort of inquiry from an aspiring Egyptologist. Many are young students who have made their minds up that Egyptology is their true love and chosen profession, at least this month. Others are college students who have become hooked on the subject and are seeking guidance on what to do and where to go next. And then there are other adults at various stages of life, some of whom want to fulfill a newly found or lifelong dream.

Yes, Egyptology—and archaeology in general—is a profession that seems almost too good to be true. To the average person, it all sounds like intrigue and adventure. Archaeology certainly has long had that reputation, and our fantasy friend, Indiana Jones, definitely has enhanced it. So what does it really mean to be an Egyptologist and what are the opportunities out there for those aspiring to join the profession?

The fact of the matter is, there aren't many jobs to be had in Egyptology. It's one of those fun fields that sounds great but has fairly dismal employment opportunities. Although Egyptology is a wonderful and interesting subject of significant humanistic worth, it only occasionally produces anything of practical economic value. Egyptologists don't regularly discover cures for diseases or invent new products for improving our comfort or efficiency. So let's ask the basic questions: what does it take to reach a professional level in this field, and how does one get a job?

PROFESSIONAL EGYPTOLOGY

To have much of a chance at all in being employed professionally in Egyptology, an advanced degree—that is, a Ph.D or its equivalent (i.e. a doctorate)—in Egyptology or a related field such as archaeology, is practically a necessity. One needs to be competent in several ancient and modern languages (the scholarly literature of Egyptology is written primarily in English, French, and German). A firm grasp of ancient Egyptian and its hieroglyphic script is mandatory. Students will often begin with Middle Egyptian and then move on to other stages of the language, such as Old and Late Egyptian. Many students also study Demotic and Coptic. Along with the grammar comes the study and translation of lots of texts, and that's where a good deal of the learning takes place. Some students who want to emphasize Egypt's interactions with other cultures in the Near East might choose also to study Akkadian or even Sumerian (languages of Mesopotamia) or Hebrew (a biblical language). Greek is needed if you want to emphasize the Graeco-Roman period. And there is plenty of coursework involving history, art, religion and many other relevant subjects.

If you wish to be an archaeologist and dig in Egypt, one should be aware that the official language of modern Egypt is Arabic, and, as a foreigner, you can't expect everyone to speak your own language. So, for those working there, at least a survival knowledge of Egyptian colloquial Arabic is extremely helpful in going about your business. Learning the written Arabic script will also facilitate the reading of street signs, building and shop names, and even food labels. Although there is a Modern Standard form of Arabic that is widely utilized in official media throughout the Arab world, the spoken forms of the Arabic language vary greatly from region to region. The colloquial forms of Arabic of Morocco, Lebanon, and Saudi Arabia are often quite different from what is spoken in Egypt, with sometimes considerable differences in vocabulary and pronunciation. (And there are even dialects within Egypt itself!) So, if it's Egypt you're interested in, make sure that you study colloquial Egyptian Arabic.

It's sad to say, but there aren't a lot of job openings in the academic world, certainly not enough for those who desire them.

Universities are one of the few places where Egyptologists might find employment in their field, teaching Egyptology to produce more Egyptologists, or as enrichment or specialty courses. Most will probably be required to conduct research as well. In the United States, that typically is in a department of Near Eastern languages and civilizations or perhaps even in Classics, Middle East Studies or Art History.

Another source of employment for Egyptologists is museums, especially those with collections of Egyptian antiquities. Again, not so many jobs are available, but occasionally they have technical or secondary curator jobs that don't require a doctorate. Such work might involve studying the museum's collection, caring for and restoring artifacts, and dealing with the public. Museums can be wonderful places to work. If one doesn't mind staying indoors working with databases and old objects, and if libraries are your thing, then a museum might be for you. If you're artistically inclined, there's work designing new exhibits; if you have a knack for public relations, doing promotional work for the museum might prove fun and challenging. Museums come in all sizes, from massive institutions such as the Metropolitan Museum of Art in New York City or the British Museum in London, to local historical societies in small towns. A few universities even offer courses or degrees in "museology," the study of all aspects of museum work, including general administration, collections management, and exhibitions. One area receiving increasing attention in both museums and archaeological sites is conservation as a response to deterioration of and threats to antiquities.

FIELD WORK

So you want to specialize in Egyptian archaeology and excavate in the Land of the Pharaohs? First of all, it's not all fun and games. Much of archaeology is tedious work. Expedition life can be tough and strenuous, and, depending on where the site is located, it can be brutally hot, muggy, and buggy. Given the necessity of careful recording, the work needs to be done very meticulously and requires a great deal of patience. Depending on the site, living conditions can be absolutely spartan or relatively luxurious. There are things that can make you quite ill if you're exposed to them, and if you have an impatient streak, you might find yourself frustrated beyond imagination when things don't quite happen how and when you would expect them to back at home. Living conditions during some of the author's various archaeological activities in Egypt have ranged from simple tents in an uninhabited part of the desert, to a close and tense group-living situation in a rented house in a very rural village, to a rented apartment, to an air-conditioned hotel with a swimming pool in the Luxor area.

I often hear from wishful volunteers offering their great strength and work ethic. In Egypt, most of the manual labor is conducted by hired and supervised workmen. The actual digging, however, is only the tip of the iceberg. Most analysis is conducted in the field and can involve months of sorting bones, scrutinizing little flakes of stone, drawing maps, entering data into a computer, and numerous other tedious jobs. Once the information is all compiled, it needs to be studied and conclusions must be drawn. This usually involves the preparation of scientific articles, conference papers, and a formal publication presenting the findings of the field work.

AVOCATIONAL EGYPTOLOGISTS

Given the limited employment opportunities, one might argue that it's even better to be an amateur Egyptologist than a professional. That way, you can participate to the extent that you like, without having to deal with the economic uncertainties, and much of the politics. Egyptology is one of those subjects where the "amateur" or avocational participants can often be more enthusiastic than the professionals themselves, and I have met many who are just as well informed. Some are genuine experts on various specific subjects, and others have made significant contributions to the field. Attend an Egyptological conference, and you might find that there are as many, if not more, amateurs in attendance as professionals.

Do you want to go on a dig? There are numerous opportunities for that in various parts of the world, but, unfortunately, not many in Egypt. The Egyptian authorities tend to prefer professionals dealing with their cultural treasures. As far as manual labor is concerned, as previously mentioned, it is traditional to use local workmen, many of whom are skilled professionals and very much appreciate the employment.

One's best bet for participating on a dig in Egypt is as a graduate student or professional in archaeology or Egyptology. It helps if you know or have met the project director because many participants are carefully selected for both ability and compatibility. Here's a suggestion: if you can develop a special skill that is very useful on an archaeological dig, you might become needed and even sought after. Such skills might include photography, surveying, technical drawing, and, as suggested above, artifact conservation. If you're good enough, you might get your expenses paid or even a small salary, which then makes you, in fact, a professional.

If you can settle for some dig action in places other than Egypt, many field schools are offered by universities, and there are volunteer programs that usually accept applicants of all ages and walks of life. Such programs can be found at a number of sites elsewhere in the Middle East, in North America, Europe, and other places in the world. Typically, the volunteers pay their own expenses and are well supervised by professionals or graduate students, and often an educational program is provided, including field trips. Some amateur archaeologists have become sufficiently competent that they are allowed to supervise some of the field work, and sometimes they are promoted to bona fide staff members.

Here are some things one can do to enjoy Egyptology as a nonprofessional. (See the Appendix for some of the details and other resources):

- Read Egyptology and archaeology books. There are lots of them.
- Subscribe to an appropriate magazine, such as *KMT* and *Ancient Egypt*.
- Attend Egyptological lectures and museum exhibitions.
- Keep an eye out for Egyptological, archaeological, or historical programs found on educational television channels.
- Join local or national Egyptological and archaeological societies or museum associations. There are many, especially in the UK.
- Attend annual or special Egyptological conferences.
- Participate in an archaeological field school or volunteer program.
- Surf the Internet for an increasing amount of Egyptological information.

- Offer your abilities to your local Egyptologist or archaeologist as a volunteer assistant. They might say no, but, then again, they might appreciate your help.
- Support your favorite projects with your money, assistance, or good wishes.
- Travel and visit Egypt and Egyptological collections in museums worldwide. There's nothing like seeing the real things!

In terms of the future, there will likely always be a place in our world for Egyptology. We will probably never know all there is to know, and it's unlikely that we will solve all the enduring mysteries of ancient Egypt. There is a wealth of insight still to be gained and from a land of so many amazing things, we can expect the long stream of surprises to continue for a good many years, if not generations, to come. I hope you're as excited as I am to see what turns up next!

APPENDIX

SOURCES FOR FURTHER EXPLORATION

The following is a basic list of English-language resources which should help point those new to Egyptology on their way. Included is a list of books, organizations, museums, and Internet sites that should provide at least a start in pursuing a worthwhile and enjoyable study of ancient Egypt. In being concise of necessity, the selected items which follow are those which I myself recommend, in consultation with several of my wonderfully gifted professional Egyptological colleagues. The listings are limited, ones of preference, and by no means exhaustive. They should be, in fact, regarded as merely a sampling. These recommendations fall within the "mainstream" scholarly approach to Egyptology, so numerous "alternative" histories and metaphysical interpretations of ancient Egypt are not represented. I have listed web-sites throughout the text where relevant, along with a special section emphasizing the Internet sources.

BOOKS

Books, obviously, are an essential resource; they are the basic tools of the scholar. One should be aware that the scholarly or technical literature on the subject is commonly written not only in English, but in German and French, as well. Books and articles in other languages (particularly Italian, Dutch, Spanish and Arabic) are also to be found. Fortunately, though, there are many excellent volumes in English for those with or without facility in foreign languages. Following, listed in categories (alphabetically by author's surname) are recommended books that persons new to the study of ancient Egypt might find useful and enjoyable. Do note that many of the same titles are published in the USA, the UK and elsewhere by publishers with offices in multiple countries. And some have gone through several editions via multiple publishers or may appear in both hardback and paperback versions.

One should be aware, perhaps, of the preponderance of volumes by E.A. Wallis Budge that are regularly found new or used in bookshops. Budge (1857–1934) was an energetic English scholar and museum curator, who authored over 130 works on Egyptian and other Near Eastern subjects. Many of his books with attractive titles have been repeatedly reprinted in recent years, upon entering the public domain. Though a few of the volumes contain information of current value, most are sadly out of date. On the other hand, some other quite prolific modern Egyptological writers, including Joyce Tyldesley, Aidan Dodson, and Salima Ikram, can be considered very competent modern authorities.

INTRODUCTIONS AND REFERENCES

John Baines and Jaromir Malek, *Cultural Atlas of Ancient Egypt*, New York: Checkmark Books, 2000. One of the very best one-volume references. Maps are plentiful, as are concise site descriptions.

Charlotte Booth, *The Nile and Its People: 7000 Years of Egyptian History*, Stroud: The History Press, 2010.

William C. Hayes, *The Scepter of Egypt*, 2 vols., New York: Metropolitan Museum of Art, 1978. A classic survey of ancient Egyptian history and culture, amply illustrated by objects in the Egyptian collection of the Metropolitan Museum of Art. Both volumes can now be downloaded from the MetPublications web-page:

www.metmuseum.org/research/metpublications/The_Scepter_of_Egypt_Vol_1_From_the_Earliest_Times_to_the_End_of_the_Middle_Kingdom

www.metmuseum.org/research/metpublications/The_Scepter_of_Egypt_Vol_2_The_Hyksos_Period_and_the_New_Kingdom_1675_1080_BC

Salima Ikram, *Introduction to Ancient Egypt*, Cambridge: Cambridge University Press, 2009. A solid introductory textbook.

T.G.H. James, *The British Museum Concise Introduction: Ancient Egypt*, London: British Museum, 2005.

Bill Manley, *The Penguin Historical Atlas of Ancient Egypt*, Harmondsworth: Penguin Books, 1997. Great maps and short chapters on a variety of subjects.

Paul Nicholson and Ian Shaw, *The Princeton Dictionary of Ancient Egypt*, Princeton, NJ: Princeton University Press, 2008.

Donald Redford, ed., *The Oxford Encyclopedia of Ancient Egypt*, Oxford: Oxford University Press, 2001. This three-volume encyclopedia is loaded with articles written by experts on a vast variety of subjects. It is very expensive but can be found for consultation in many university libraries.

David Silverman, ed., *Ancient Egypt*, Oxford: Oxford University Press, 2003.

A.J. Spencer, *The British Museum Book of Ancient Egypt*, London: British Museum, 2007. History, religious beliefs, arts and crafts, etc., are nicely summarized in this volume keyed to the Egyptian collection of the British Museum.

Helen Strudwick, *Encyclopedia of Ancient Egypt*, London: Amber, 2006. Colorfully illustrated and organized by theme.

Emily Teeter and Douglas Brewer, *Egypt and the Egyptians*, 2nd edn, Cambridge: Cambridge University Press, 2007.

Toby Wilkinson, *The Thames & Hudson Dictionary of Ancient Egypt*, London: Thames & Hudson, 2005.

Toby Wilkinson, ed., *The Egyptian World*, London: Routledge, 2007. A survey of ancient Egypt presented through articles written by prominent scholars.

TRAVEL AND SITE GUIDES

There are a number of good travel guides that are useful if visiting modern Egypt, a trip that is the dream of many who have fallen in love with that ancient land. Here are a few that serve as detailed and authoritative handbooks to the antiquities sites:

Roger Bagnall and Dominic Rathbone, *Egypt from Alexander to the Copts: An Archaeological and Historical Guide*, London: British Museum, 2004.

Elizabeth Blyth, *Karnak*, London: Routledge, 2006. A detailed examination of the massive temple complex at Luxor.

Neil Hewison, *The Fayoum: History and Guide*, 2nd edn, Cairo: American University in Cairo, 2008. A fascinating region in Egypt not well known to the average tourist.

William Murnane, *The Ancient Egypt Guide*, Northampton, MA: Interlink, 2012. An excellent guide by the late, great Professor Murnane, as revised and updated by Aidan Dodson.

Dan Richardson and Daniel Jacobs, *Rough Guide to Egypt*, 9th edn, London: Rough Guides, 2013. A very practical manual that addresses the needs of visitors at all price ranges.

Donald P. Ryan, *Ancient Egypt on Five Deben a Day*, London: Thames & Hudson, 2010. An entertaining travel guide for visitors to Egypt in 1250 BC. How to get around, sites to see, what to eat, experiencing the culture, etc., and even a list of useful phrases. Also published under the title, *Egypt 1250 BC: A Traveler's Companion*, Cairo: American University in Cairo, 2010.

Bonnie Sampsell, *A Traveler's Guide to the Geology of Egypt*, Cairo: American University in Cairo, 2003. Describes the truly ancient history of the actual land of Egypt and the stones put to good use by its people.

Alberto Siliotti has written a number of nice "*Pocket Guides*" to various places in Egypt as published by the American University in Cairo Press. Titles include: *The Pyramids, Valley of the Kings and Theban Tombs, Aswan, Sinai, Oases, Coptic Egypt* and *Islamic Egypt*.

Nigel Strudwick and Helen Strudwick, *Thebes in Egypt: A Guide to the Tombs and Temples of Ancient Luxor*, Ithaca, NY: Cornell University, 1999. Great coverage of some of the most important and interesting sites from ancient Egypt.

Cassandra Vivien, *The Western Desert of Egypt: An Explorer's Handbook*, 2nd edn, Cairo: American University in Cairo, 2008. A guide to the major oases and the many other wonders to be found out west.

Kent Weeks, *The Illustrated Guide to Luxor: Tombs, Temples, and Museums*, Cairo: American University in Cairo, 2005.

HISTORY

Alan Bowman, *Egypt After the Pharaohs*, Berkeley, CA: University of California, 1996. Describes the period from Alexander the Great to the Arab Conquest.

Aidan Dodson has written a number of very useful volumes that nicely summarize some of the more complicated times in Egyptian history, each published by the American University in Cairo Press: *Amarna Sunset: Nefertiti, Tutankhamun, Ay, Horemheb, and the Egyptian Counter-Reformation*, 2009; *Poisoned Legacy: The Fall of the Nineteenth Egyptian Dynasty*, 2010; *Afterglow of Empire: Egypt from the Fall of the New Kingdom to the Saite Renaissance*, 2012.

Wolfram Grajetzki, *The Middle Kingdom of Ancient Egypt: History, Archaeology and Society*, London: Duckworth, 2006.

Barbara Mertz, *Temples, Tombs and Hieroglyphs: A Popular History of Ancient Egypt*, updated and revised, New York: William Morrow, 2007. An eminently readable and highly recommended classic.

Karol Myśliwiec, *The Twilight of Ancient Egypt: The First Millennium BCE*. (trans. David Lorton), Ithaca, NY: Cornell University, 2000. It wasn't over for Egypt after the New Kingdom!

Ian Shaw, ed., *The Oxford History of Ancient Egypt*, Oxford : Oxford University Press, 2004. A volume that has become a standard reference.

A.J. Spencer, *Early Egypt: The Rise of Civilization in the Nile Valley*, Norman, OK: University of Oklahoma Press, 1995.

Marc Van de Mieroop, *A History of Ancient Egypt*, Chichester: Wiley-Blackwell, 2010.

Robert J. Wenke, *The Ancient Egyptian State: The Origins of Egyptian Culture*, Cambridge: Cambridge University Press, 2009.

Toby Wilkinson, *Genesis of the Pharaohs*, London: Thames & Hudson, 2003. Civilization didn't originate overnight!

Toby Wilkinson, *The Rise and Fall of Ancient Egypt*, New York: Random House, 2011. A somewhat controversial approach that describes a somewhat darker side to ancient Egyptian culture and history.

HISTORICAL CHARACTERS

Darrell Baker, *The Encyclopedia of the Pharaohs*, Greenville, IN: Stacy, 2008. A good reference book on Egypt's rulers through the New Kingdom.

Peter Clayton, *Chronicle of the Pharaohs*, London: Thames & Hudson, 2006. All the pharaohs, dynasty by dynasty.

Aidan Dodson, *Monarchs of the Nile*, revised, Cairo: American University in Cairo, 2015. A nice summary.

Aidan Dodson and Dyan Hilton, *The Complete Royal Families of Ancient Egypt*, London: Thames & Hudson, 2004. Confused about how they all relate? This book can provide some clarity.

Dennis Forbes, *Imperial Lives: Illustrated Biographies of Significant New Kingdom Egyptians, Volume One: The 18th Dynasty Through Thutmose IV*, Weaverville, NC: KMT Communications, 2005.

Kenneth Kitchen, *Pharaoh Triumphant*, Princeton, NJ: Princeton University, 1987. Everything you always wanted to know about Rameses II.

Arielle Kozloff, *Amenhotep III: Egypt's Radiant Pharaoh*, Cambridge: Cambridge University Press, 2012. The life and times of one of Egypt's most prosperous rulers.

Robert Morkot, *The Black Pharaohs: Egypt's Nubian Rulers*, London: Rubicon, 2000.

Stephen Quirke, *Who Were the Pharaohs?* London: British Museum, 2010. Names, titles and cartouches of the pharaohs, covering 3000 years of history.

Donald Redford, *Akhenaten: The Heretic King*, Princeton, NJ: Princeton University Press, 1984. Akhenaten by a man who knows him best.

C.N. Reeves, *Akhenaten: Egypt's False Prophet*, London: Thames & Hudson, 2005. Another great scholar weighs in on perhaps the most controversial pharaoh of them all.

Michael Rice, *Who's Who in Ancient Egypt*, London: Routledge, 1999. Not just the rulers, but a lot of other people as well.

Joyce Tyldesley has authored some wonderful biographies of prominent Egyptian women including: *Hatshepsut: The Female Pharaoh*, London: Viking Penguin, 1998; *Nefertiti: Egypt's Sun Queen*, London: Viking Penguin, 2000; and *Cleopatra: Last Queen of Egypt*, New York: Basic Books, 2008. She has also written another related and useful volume, *The Complete Queens of Egypt: From Early Dynastic Times to the Death of Cleopatra*, Cairo: American University in Cairo, 2006.

Toby Wilkinson, *Lives of the Ancient Egyptians: Pharaohs, Queens, Courtiers and Commoners*, London: Thames & Hudson. 2007. Profiles of a variety of fascinating individuals.

ARCHAEOLOGICAL SITES

Morris Bierbrier, *The Tomb Builders of the Pharaohs*, Cairo: American University in Cairo, 1993. A description of Deir el-Medina, the village inhabited by the workers who constructed the tombs in the Valley of the Kings.

Nancy Jenkins, *The Boat Beneath the Pyramid*, London: Thames & Hudson, 1980. The remarkable story of the discovery and reconstruction of the first boat found entombed at the base of the Great Pyramid of Khufu.

Barry Kemp, *The City of Akhenaten and Nefertiti: Amarna and Its People*, London: Thames & Hudson, 2012. The story of Akhenaten's short-lived capital as explained by its modern excavator.

Mark Lehner, *The Complete Pyramids*, London: Thames & Hudson, 1997. An excellent survey by a foremost expert on the subject.

Lise Manniche, *City of the Dead*, Chicago: University of Chicago Press, 1987. The necropolis of the ancient Theban officials revealed.

Geoffrey T. Martin, *The Hidden Tombs of Memphis*, London: Thames & Hudson, 1992. Discoveries of the New Kingdom tombs at Sakkara.

David O'Connor, *Abydos: Egypt's First Pharaohs and the Cult of Osiris*, London: Thames & Hudson, 2011. A great survey of a complicated and vitally important religious and funerary site.

Donald Redford, *City of the Ram-Man: The Story of Ancient Mendes*, Princeton, NJ: Princeton University Press, 2010. A prominent Egyptologist provides a rare look at an ancient city in the Nile Delta.

C.N. Reeves, *The Complete Tutankhamun*, London: Thames & Hudson, 1995. There are many books about Tut's tomb, but this one is especially recommended.

C.N. Reeves and Richard Wilkinson, *The Complete Valley of the Kings*, London: Thames & Hudson, 1996. An excellent survey of Egypt's New Kingdom royal cemetery.

Ian Shaw, *Exploring Ancient Egypt*, Oxford: Oxford University Press, 2003.

Steven Snape, *The Complete Towns of Ancient Egypt*, London: Thames & Hudson, 2014.

Miroslav Verner, *The Pyramids: The Mystery, Culture, and Science of Egypt's Great Monuments*, New York: Grove, 2002.

HISTORY OF EXPLORATION

John M. Adams, *The Millionaire and the Mummies: Theodore Davis's Gilded Age in the Valley of the Kings*, New York: St. Martin's Press, 2013. A well-crafted biography of an American "robber baron" responsible for some incredible archaeological discoveries.

Leslie Adkins and Roy Adkins, *The Keys of Egypt: The Obsession to Decipher Egyptian Hieroglyphs*, London: HarperCollins, 2000.

Morris Bierbrier, ed., *Who Was Who in Egyptology*, 4th edn, London: Egypt Exploration Society, 2012. An important reference work containing short biographies and bibliographies of persons involved in the exploration and study of ancient Egypt.

Bob Brier, *Egyptomania: Our Three Thousand Year Obsession with the Land of the Pharaohs*, New York: St. Martin's Press, 2013.

Peter Clayton, *The Rediscovery of Ancient Egypt*, London: Thames & Hudson, 1982. The ruins of ancient Egypt, as recorded by artists and writers during the last two centuries.

Margaret Drower, *Flinders Petrie: A Life in Archaeology*, Madison, WI: University of Wisconsin Press, 1995. An excellent biography of William Matthew Flinders Petrie, a truly unique figure who excavated numerous ancient sites in Egypt and revolutionized archaeological method and theory.

Dennis C. Forbes, *Tombs, Treasures, Mummies: Seven Great Discoveries of Egyptian Archaeology*, Weaverville, NC: KMT Communications, 1998. Seven Theban tombs, their occupants and contents comprehensively examined in text and archival photos.

Leslie Greener, *The Discovery of Egypt*, New York: Viking, 1967. Travelers, adventurers and scholars in the land of the pharaohs from Roman times through the nineteenth century.

Ivor Hume, *Belzoni: The Giant Archaeologists Love to Hate*, Charlottesville, VA: University of Virginia Press, 2011. Some may hate him, but they shouldn't!

T.G.H. James, *Howard Carter: The Path to Tutankhamun*, New York: Columbia University Press, 1992. The biography of the remarkable man who found Tut's tomb.

Bill Manley, *The Seventy Great Mysteries of Ancient Egypt*, London: Thames & Hudson, 2003. In reality, there are far more than seventy mysteries, but this book will provide some insights into several.

Stanley Mayes, *The Great Belzoni*, New York: Putnam, 1959. One of the great pioneers of Egyptology was an Italian circus performer. (This classic biography is now available in paperback.)

C.N. Reeves, *Ancient Egypt: The Great Discoveries*, London: Thames & Hudson, 2000. A large selection of amazing discoveries, well illustrated and arranged chronologically in order of their finding.

Donald P. Ryan, *"A Shattered Visage Lies"... Nineteenth Century Poetry Inspired by Ancient Egypt*, Oxford: David Brown Book Co, 2007. Literary musings on themes from mummies to monuments.

Patricia Spencer, *The Egypt Exploration Society: The Early Years*, London: Egypt Exploration Society, 2007. The story of a remarkable organization that continues today.

Jason Thompson, *Wonderful Things: A History of Egyptology: 1: From Antiquity to 1881*, Cairo: American University in Cairo, 2015. A superb history; the first of three intended volumes.

Joyce Tyldesley, *Egypt: How a Lost Civilization Was Rediscovered*, Berkeley, CA: University of California, 2006.

John Wilson, *Signs and Wonders Upon Pharaoh*, Chicago: University of Chicago, 1964. A history of the early days of American Egyptology.

FOR SOME RARE INSIGHTS...

Memoirs of modern archaeologists working in Egypt are quite rare but there are several that offer a real taste of adventure.

Bernard V. Bothmer, *Egypt 1950: My First Visit*, Oxford: Oxbow, 2003. A diary illustrated with many photos, conveying the flavor of his experiences and the times, and his encounter with notable personalities.

I.E.S. Edwards, *From the Pyramids to Tutankhamun: Memoirs of an Egyptologist*, Oxford: Oxbow, 2000. Edwards was a Keeper of Egyptian Antiquities at the British Museum and an expert on pyramids.

Zahi Hawass, *Secrets from the Sands: My Search for Egypt's Past*, New York: Harry Abrams, 2003. The life and times of Egypt's former director of antiquities.

Donald P. Ryan, *Beneath the Sands of Egypt: Adventures of an Unconventional Archaeologist*, New York: William Morrow, 2010. A first-hand account of archaeological exploration including excavations in the Valley of the Kings.

Kent R. Weeks, *The Lost Tomb*, New York: Harper, 1999. The rediscovery of KV 5 in the Valley of the Kings, a truly massive tomb built for the many sons of Rameses II.

DAILY LIFE

Many of the general introductory works listed above discuss the daily living conditions of the ancient Egyptians. The books noted below specifically deal with daily life and various aspects thereof.

James P. Allen, *The Art of Medicine in Ancient Egypt*, New York: Metropolitan Museum of Art, 2005.

Wolfgang Decker, *Sports and Games of Ancient Egypt*, New Haven, CT: Yale University, 1992.

Patrick Houlihan, *The Animal World of the Pharaohs*, London: Thames & Hudson, 1997.

T.G.H. James, *Pharaoh's People*, Chicago: University of Chicago Press, 1994. A discussion of Egyptian society at different levels during the New Kingdom.

Rosalind Janssen and Jac. Janssen, *Growing Up and Getting Old in Ancient Egypt*, London: Golden House, 2007.

Jaromir Malek, *The Cat in Ancient Egypt*, Philadelphia, PA: University of Pennsylvania, 1997.

Lise Manniche, *Music and Musicians in Ancient Egypt*, London: British Museum, 1991.

Barbara Mertz, *Red Land, Black Land: Daily Life in Ancient Egypt*, 2nd edn, New York: William Morrow, 2008.

John Nunn, *Ancient Egyptian Medicine*, Norman, OK: University of Oklahoma, 1996.

Robert Partridge, *Transport in Ancient Egypt*, London: Rubicon, 1996.

William H. Peck, *The Material World of Ancient Egypt*, Cambridge: Cambridge University Press, 2013.

Gay Robins, *Women in Ancient Egypt*, Cambridge, MA: Harvard University Press, 1993.

Gary Shaw, *The Pharaoh: Life at Court and on Campaign*, London: Thames & Hudson, 2012.

Eugen Strouhal, *Life of the Ancient Egyptians*, Cambridge: Cambridge University Press, 1992.

Kasia Szpakowska, *Daily Life in Ancient Egypt*, Chichester: Wiley-Oxford, 2007.

Joyce Tyldesley, *Daughters of Isis: Women of Ancient Egypt*, London: Viking Penguin, 1995.

Joyce Tyldesley, *Judgement of the Pharaohs: Crime and Punishment in Ancient Egypt*, New York: Orion, 2000.

LANGUAGE AND HIEROGLYPHS

James Allen, *Middle Egyptian: An Introduction to the Language and Culture of Hieroglyphs*, 3rd edn, Cambridge: Cambridge University Press, 2014. A modern and highly regarded textbook.

Mark Collier and Bill Manley, *How to Read Egyptian Hieroglyphs*, revised edn, Berkeley, CA: University of California, 2003, A somewhat gentle approach to a complicated subject.

Henry Fischer, *Ancient Egyptian Calligraphy: A Beginner's Guide to Writing Hieroglyphs*, New York: Metropolitan Museum of Art, 1988. Learn how to draw hieroglyphs. If you can't find a hard-copy, it's available on-line from the Metropolitan Museum of Art: www.metmuseum.org/research/metpublications/Ancient_Egyptian_Calligraphy

Alan Gardiner, *Egyptian Grammar*, 3rd edn, Oxford: Griffith Institute, 1978. Both a textbook and a reference grammar. Though not particularly casual reading, beginners might especially find useful the introduction and the essays on royal titles, numbers, etc., and the list of hieroglyphic signs.

Janice Kamrin, *Ancient Egyptian Hieroglyphs: A Practical Guide*, New York: Abrams, 2004. This book will soon have you reading actual ancient inscriptions.

Bill Manley, *Egyptian Hieroglyphs for Complete Beginners*, London: Thames & Hudson, 2012. Another great book to get you started.

Bill Petty has produced a series of handy guides to the ancient language and hieroglyphs for use when examining inscriptions, including a *Hieroglyphic Sign List*, a portable *Hieroglyphic Dictionary*, and a "*Glyphery*." More information is available at: www.museum-tours.com

Nigel Strudwick, *Hieroglyph Detective*, San Francisco: Chronicle, 2010. A nice inscription-based introduction.

One more recommendation: if you decide to get serious about studying hieroglyphs, it's good to have a dictionary. A standard volume used by most students (and professionals) is Raymond Faulkner's *Concise Dictionary of Middle Egyptian*, Oxford: Griffith Institute, 1976.

Also, some might enjoy *The Tale of Peter Rabbit* by Beatrix Potter, translated into ancient Egyptian by J. Nunn and R. Parkinson, London: British Museum, 2005. It's cute, it's fun.

LITERATURE

John L. Foster, *Ancient Egyptian Literature: An Anthology*, Austin, TX: University of Texas Press, 2001. Modern translations of ancient romantic poetry and other fascinating texts.

Miriam Lichtheim, *Ancient Egyptian Literature*, 3 vols., 2nd edn, Berkeley, CA: University of California, 2006. Each of the volumes deals with a chronological period and offers a wide range of texts in translation: Volume I, the Old and Middle Kingdoms; Volume II, the New Kingdom; Volume III, the Late Period.

R.B. Parkinson, *Voices from Ancient Egypt: An Anthology of Middle Kingdom Writings*, Norman, OK: University of Oklahoma,1991. A truly diverse collection of texts from various contexts.

W.K. Simpson *et al.*, eds., *The Literature of Ancient Egypt: An Anthology of Stories, Instructions, Stelae, Autobiographies, and Poetry*, 3rd edn, New Haven, CT: Yale University, 2003. A handy one-volume compilation of some of ancient Egypt's best-known and most important literary works and historical-biographical inscriptions.

Joyce Tyldesley, *The Penguin Book of Myths and Legends of Ancient Egypt*, Harmondsworth: Penguin, 2012. Stories and commentary.

RELIGION AND FUNERARY TOPICS

George Hart, *Egyptian Myths*, Austin, TX: University of Texas Press, 1990.

Sigrid Hodel-Hoenes, *Life and Death in Ancient Egypt: Scenes from Private Tombs in New Kingdom Thebes*, Ithaca, NY: Cornell University, 2000.

Salima Ikram and Aidan Dodson, *The Tomb in Ancient Egypt*, London: Thames & Hudson, 2008. An excellent overview.

Geraldine Pinch, *Magic in Ancient Egypt*, Austin, TX: University of Texas, 1995.

Geraldine Pinch, *Egyptian Mythology: A Guide to the Gods, Goddesses, and Traditions of Ancient Egypt*, Oxford: Oxford University Press, 2004. A particularly excellent presentation, highly recommended.

Stephen Quirke, *Ancient Egyptian Religion*, New York: Dover, 1993.

Stephen Quirke, *Exploring Religion in Ancient Egypt*, Chichester: Wiley-Blackwell, 2015.

Steven Snape, *Ancient Egyptian Tombs: The Culture of Life and Death*, Chichester: Wiley-Blackwell, 2011.

John Taylor, *Death and the Afterlife in Ancient Egypt*, Chicago: University of Chicago Press, 2001.

John Taylor, *Journey through the Afterlife: Ancient Egyptian Book of the Dead*, Cambridge, MA: Harvard University, 2010. A beautifully illustrated survey of the guide to successfully achieving eternity.

Emily Teeter, *Religion and Ritual in Ancient Egypt*, Cambridge: Cambridge University Press, 2011. The why and the how.

Richard H. Wilkinson, *The Complete Temples of Ancient Egypt*, London: Thames & Hudson, 2000.

Richard H. Wilkinson, *The Complete Gods and Goddesses of Ancient Egypt*, London: Thames & Hudson, 2003.

MUMMIES

Bob Brier, *Egyptian Mummies: Unraveling the Secrets of an Ancient Art*, New York: Harper Perennial, 1996. A book by "Mr. Mummy" himself.

François Dunand and Roger Lichtenberg, *Mummies and Death in Egypt*, Ithaca, NY: Cornell University, 2006.

Salima Ikram, *Divine Creatures: Animal Mummies in Ancient Egypt*, Cairo: American University in Cairo, 2015. They didn't mummify only people.

Salima Ikram and Aidan Dodson, *The Mummy in Ancient Egypt*, London: Thames & Hudson, 1998. A well-illustrated and fascinating book.

Robert Partridge, *Faces of Pharaohs: Royal Mummies and Coffins from Ancient Thebes*, London: Rubicon, 1996.

ART AND ARCHITECTURE

Cyril Aldred, *Egyptian Art*, London: Thames & Hudson, 1985.

Carol Andrews, *Ancient Egyptian Jewelry*, New York: Abrams, 1997.

Dieter Arnold, *Encyclopedia of Egyptian Architecture*, Princeton, NJ: Princeton University Press, 2003.

James Curl, *Egyptomania: The Egyptian Revival*, Manchester: Manchester University Press, 1994. The influence of ancient Egyptian art and architecture during recent centuries.

Jaromir Malek, *Egypt: 4,000 Years of Art*, New York: Phaidon, 2003.

Gay Robins, *The Art of Ancient Egypt*, revised, Cambridge, MA: Harvard University Press, 2008.

W.S. Smith, *The Art and Architecture of Ancient Egypt*, revised by W.K. Simpson, New Haven, CT: Yale University Press, 1999.

Richard Wilkinson, *Reading Egyptian Art*, London: Thames & Hudson, 1994.

Richard Wilkinson, *Symbol and Magic in Egyptian Art*, London: Thames & Hudson, 1999.

OF GENERAL INTEREST

Shire Publications in the UK publishes a series of little, inexpensive, and typically well-written volumes on a variety of topics in their *Shire Egyptology* series, including: *Predynastic Egypt, Protodynastic Egypt,*

Rock-cut Tombs, Graeco-Roman Egypt, Textiles, Pottery, Household Animals, Metalworking and Tools, Faience and Glass, Woodworking and Furniture, Medicine, Warfare and Weapons, Coffins, Models and Scenes, Boats and Ships, Scarabs, Shabtis, Gods and Myths, Akhenaten's Egypt, Towns and Cities, Tutankhamun's Egypt, and *Food and Drink.* More information is available on their web-site: www.shirebooks.co.uk

FOR A FUN TIME...

Very enjoyable are the Amelia Peabody mysteries set in Victorian/ Edwardian England and colonial Egypt, authored by Elizabeth Peters. Peters is a pen name of Egyptologist Barbara Mertz (author of *Temples, Tombs and Hieroglyphs* and *Red Land, Black Land,* see above). Another mystery by Mertz (this time using the pen name Barbara Michaels), *Search the Shadows,* also offers Egyptological intrigue in a contemporary setting. There are many fans and even some web-sites, e.g., www.mpmbooks.com. Other popular fiction authors include Agatha Christie, of course, (e.g. *Death on the Nile*), and more recently, Lauren Haney, Paul West and Chaz Desowl. For fans of classic fiction, the great Sir H. Rider Haggard wrote several Egyptian historical novels, including *Cleopatra* and *Queen of the Dawn.*

MAGAZINES

Ancient Egypt magazine is published in the UK and offers six colorful issues a year: ancientegyptmagazine.co.uk

KMT: A Modern Journal of Ancient Egypt had its debut in 1990 and continues to offer an outstanding variety of articles and news for the ancient Egypt enthusiast. A quarterly subscription can be ordered from KMT Communications: www.kmtjournal.com. *KMT* is also available where a wide variety of magazines are sold (the chain bookstores, in particular) and in many museum bookshops.

Other periodicals available on newsstands or by subscription with occasional articles on ancient Egypt include: *Archaeology, Near Eastern Archaeology, Biblical Archaeology Review,* and *Minerva. The American Research Center in Egypt,* the *Egypt Exploration Society* and the *Society for the Study of Egyptian Antiquities* all publish annual scholarly journals and other material. (See below under "Organizations").

MUSEUMS

Short of traveling to Egypt itself, a visit to a museum holding Egyptian antiquities will prove a very fascinating and educational experience. And many museums throughout the world have at least a few Egyptian items in their collections. In an effort to be concise, only a few North American, UK and European museums (and Egypt, of course), generally with large Egyptian collections, are listed alphabetically below. Some of their web-sites offer excellent peeks at their artifacts.

EGYPT

Museums in Egypt
www.sca-egypt.org/eng/MUS_List.htm

NORTH AMERICA

Brooklyn Museum of Art, New York, USA
www.brooklynart.org
Cleveland Museum of Art, Cleveland, USA
www.clevelandart.org
The Metropolitan Museum of Art, New York, USA
www.metmuseum.org
Museum of Archaeology and Anthropology, Philadelphia, USA
www.penn.museum
Museum of Fine Arts, Boston, Boston, USA
www.mfa.org
Oriental Institute Museum, Chicago, USA
oi.uchicago.edu/museum
Royal Ontario Museum, Toronto, Canada
www.rom.on.ca

THE UNITED KINGDOM

Ashmolean Museum of Art and Archaeology, Oxford
www.ashmolean.org/
British Museum, London
www.britishmuseum.org
Fitzwilliam Museum, Cambridge

www.fitzmuseum.cam.ac.uk/
Manchester Museum
www.museum.manchester.ac.uk/
Petrie Museum of Egyptian Archaeology, London, UK
www.ucl.ac.uk/museums/petrie

EUROPE

Ägyptisches Museum, Berlin, Germany
www.egyptian-museum-berlin.com/
Kunsthistorisches Museum, Vienna, Austria
www.khm.at/en/
Musée du Louvre, Paris, France
www.louvre.fr/en/departments/egyptian-antiquities
Museo Egizio, Florence, Italy
www.archeotoscana.beniculturali.it/index.php?it/148/firenze-museo-egizio
Museo Egizio, Torino, Italy
www.museoegizio.orgRijkmuseum van Oudheden, Leiden, the Netherlands
www.rmo.nl/
Vatican Museums, the Vatican City, Rome, Italy
mv.vatican.va/3_EN/pages/MV_Home.html

ORGANIZATIONS

The following organizations cater to a special interest in Egypt. Membership includes news-letters and journals, and attendance at organization events is a great way to gain knowledge and to meet others with a shared interest in things Egyptological.

- The American Research Center in Egypt (ARCE) supports scholarly work dealing with both ancient and modern Egypt. The organization maintains a research facility in Cairo which assists individual scholars and expeditions with their projects. The organization produces a Bulletin and the scholarly journal, *JARCE*. and hosts an annual conference. Contact ARCE at: www.arce. org. Regional ARCE chapters sponsor local lectures and typically invite professional Egyptologists to speak. Presently there are chapters in Orange County, California, Northern California, Arizona, Georgia, Illinois, Louisiana, New England, New York, North Texas, Oregon, Pennsylvania, Northwest, Tennessee and

Washington, D.C. and links to each can be found from the main ARCE web-page.

- The venerable London-based Egypt Exploration Society, begun in 1882, sponsors archaeological exploration in Egypt and publishes the annual *Journal of Egyptian Archaeology*, plus a colorful bulletin, *Egyptian Archaeology*, which appears twice a year. The Society also produces and sells a variety of other excellent scholarly publications. Even though those living outside Great Britain might not be able to attend the EES's regular schedule of lectures and other activities, the Journal, Bulletin and book discounts offered with membership make joining the Society quite worthwhile. For membership information, see their web-site: www.ees.ac.uk. The UK is blessed with numerous other Egyptological societies. A listing can be found here:
- www.egyptology-uk.com/besdirectory.htm
- The Society for the Study of Egyptian Antiquities (SSEA) is a Canadian organization that publishes a newsletter and journal. The SSEA hosts Egyptological lectures and an annual symposium. For more information, visit their web-site: www.thessea.org. The Society maintains chapters in Toronto, Montreal, Vancouver, and Calgary.

FIELDWORK OPPORTUNITIES

As noted in Chapter 7, there are few opportunities for volunteers to be involved in field work in Egypt. Most projects make use of local workforces and specific technical skills are often necessary for one to have any chance of consideration. There are, however, excellent volunteer programs with excavations in other countries of the Middle East and elsewhere.

- The Archaeological Institute of America publishes an annual *Archaeological Fieldwork Opportunities Bulletin* which lists programs around the world. Learn the specifics at: www.archaeological.org/fieldwork/afob
- The Biblical Archaeology Review annually publishes a listing of Middle Eastern field projects accepting volunteers. It usually appears in the January/February issue. See: digs.bib-arch.org

ON-LINE RESOURCES

Egyptological information available on the "Information Highway" continues to grow. As is the case with the Internet in general, quality can range from professionally competent to mediocre and everything in between. Web-sites can also be ephemeral, unpredictably appearing and disappearing. The sites listed below are just a small sample and were active as of late 2015. My best suggestion is to choose some of these good sites and do a little "surfing," especially if they have associated links to other places. And try using your favorite search engine to locate specific topics of interest.

Ancient Egypt Films. You'll be surprised how many have been made.
www.ancientegyptfilmsite.nl
Animal Mummies
www.animalmummies.net
Digital Egyptology. A wonderful educational resource.
www.digitalegypt.ucl.ac.uk/Welcome.html
Digital Karnak. Explore the vast temple complex on this information-packed, high-tech site: dlib.etc.ucla.edu/projects/Karnak
Egyptian Tourism Authority
www.egypt.travel
Egyptology Resources. An excellent site with an abundance of useful links.
www.fitzmuseum.cam.ac.uk/er/index.html
Global Egyptian Museum. A virtual museum illustrating a variety of objects from many collections.
www.globalegyptianmuseum.org
Greg Reeder's Egypt Page. A fast way to connect with scores of Egypt links.
www.egyptology.com/
Donald P. Ryan's Page. Egyptological research in the Valley of the Kings and other topics by the author of this book.
www.community.plu.edu/~ryandp
Supreme Council for Antiquities. The Egyptian government agency with the awesome responsibility of supervising Egypt's ancient monuments.
www.sca-egypt.org
The Egyptologist's Electronic Forum, Discussions and resources for the serious.
www.egyptologyforum.org
The Theban Mapping Project. Loads of information on the Valley of the Kings and the Theban Necropolis.
www.thebanmappingproject.com

The Theban Royal Mummy Project.
www.members.tripod.com/anubis4_2000/mummypages1/intro.htm
Tutankhamun Data Base, Griffith Institute. Notes and photographs from the
    tomb.
www.griffith.ox.ac.uk/tutankhamundiscovery.html
Virtual Reality 3-D Tomb Tours. Take an amazing journey through several
    royal and private Theban tombs.
www.osirisnet.net/3d-tours/e_3d-tours.htm

INDEX